ZEN CONQUESTS

D1522405

ZEN CONQUESTS

Buddhist Transformations
in Contemporary Vietnam

ALEXANDER SOUCY

University of Hawai'i Press

HONOLULU

Library of Congress Cataloging-in-Publication Data

Names: Soucy, Alexander Duncan, author.
Title: Zen conquests : Buddhist transformations in contemporary Vietnam /
   Alexander Soucy.
Description: Honolulu : University of Hawai'i Press, 2022. | Includes
   bibliographical references and index.
Identifiers: LCCN 2021050473 | ISBN 9780824889982 (hardback) | ISBN
   9780824892197 (adobe pdf) | ISBN 9780824892203 (epub) | ISBN
   9780824893149 (kindle edition)
Subjects: LCSH: Thiền Viện Sùng Phúc. | Buddhist
   monasteries—Vietnam. | Zen Buddhism—Vietnam—Customs and practices. |
   Buddhist renewal—Vietnam.
Classification: LCC BQ6339.T465 S68 2022 | DDC
   294.3/65709597—dc23/eng/20220223
LC record available at https://lccn.loc.gov/2021050473

ISBN 9780824893132 (paperback)

Cover photo: Drumming at the opening of the ritual on the ancestor day celebration for
Bodhidharma, 2011. Photo by author.

Contents

||||||||

Acknowledgments

||||||||

A project such as this requires the help of many people and organizations along the way. A very special thanks needs to be extended to the monks of Thiền Viện Sùng Phúc, especially the abbot, Thích Tâm Thuần, and the vice abbot, Thích Tinh Thiền. Thích Tuệ Đạt and Thích Thái Phước were especially helpful and ready to take time from their busy schedules to give me guidance. Thích Khế Định was visiting Sùng Phúc for much of the time that I was there and was very generous with his time. Many lay people extended fellowship while I was there and were always happy to discuss their views with me. Although too numerous to name everyone here, I would like to mention Em Tín An, Em Tâm, Em Ngọc Anh, and Em Thông as being especially helpful. I would like to thank Tu Tam Hoang, who generously sent me copies of English translations of five of Thích Thanh Từ's books, and Nguyễn Đại Đồng for his generous time and as-sistance getting copies of Vietnamese Buddhist journals.

I am very grateful for the support of the Vietnam Academy of Social Science, which assisted me in getting a research visa and helped me make important connections. I wish to particularly thank Dr. Nguyễn Quốc Tuấn, director of the Institute for Religious Studies, for his hospitality and assistance. Much of the research for this book was supported by a grant from the Social Sciences and Humanities Research Council of Canada to look at Buddhism and globalization with my long-time colleagues and friends John Harding and Victor Hori. My institution, Saint Mary's University, also provided me with financial support.

Thanks to Will Flanagan of Saint Mary's University for the diagram of the Sùng Phúc complex. Professor Choi Byong Wuk and Phạm Thị Hường helped me with a few items that were difficult for me to translate when venturing into more poetic and classical forms of Sino-Vietnamese, though any lingering mistakes are entirely my own. There are, of course, many others who assisted me and helped me to understand the development of Thiền in contemporary Vietnam. Without their help, this book would not have been possible. Nonetheless, the ideas presented in this book, while informed by our conversations, cannot be said to be representations of their own ideas and understandings. I deeply appreciate the support and expertise of the people at the University of Hawai'i Press who have helped immensely with the project. These include Stephanie Chun, who worked with me and encouraged me in the long process of completing the initial manuscript and seeing it through the review and revision stages; Cheryl Loe, who saw the book through the production stages; and Richard Feit, whose keen eye and editing skills helped me clean up the text.

Along the way, I have published essays in book chapters and journal articles, pieces of which were borrowed and reworked to be included in this book. These include chapters from Philip Taylor's volume *Modernity and Re-enchantment: Religion in Post-revolutionary Vietnam* (ISEAS, Soucy 2007); Michael Dickhardt and Andrea Lauser's volume *Religion, Place and Modernity: Spatial Articulations in Southeast and East Asia* (Brill, Soucy 2016); Jørn Borup and Marianne Qvortrup Fibiger's volume *Eastspirit: Transnational Spirituality and Religious Circulation in East and West* (Brill Publishing, Soucy 2017a); and the essay "A Reappraisal of Vietnamese Buddhism's Status as 'Ethnic,'" published in the *Journal of Vietnamese Studies* 12, no. 2 (Soucy 2017b).

Finally, this book would not have been possible without the love and support of my family, both here in Canada and in Vietnam. In Vietnam, my mother-in-law, Trịnh Thị Loan, is always quick to introduce me to her Buddhist friends, helpfully collects Buddhist books and magazines for me, and watches over my health and welfare whenever I am there. My father-in-law, Nguyễn Quốc An, unflaggingly gives his support and guidance. My sister-in-law, Nguyễn Lan Hương, is always ready to lend a hand in ways big and small and has been a big resource and help over the years. Here in Canada, my wife, Lan, who provided advice with translations when I needed clarification, and my children, Hugh and Eileen, have been a huge support. To them I offer gratitude and all my love.

Introduction

|||||||||

I saw my first Zen mummy on a clear spring day in 1997. I was just beginning my research on Buddhism in Vietnam, and two young Vietnamese friends had taken me to visit ancient pagodas in the vicinity of Hanoi. In a small display case at Phật Tích Pagoda in Bắc Ninh Province, I had my first glimpse of something I had only known about by hearsay. In the course of my research, interlocuters would occasionally reference the remarkably preserved bodies of Vietnamese Zen masters, their mummified remains a testament to their high spiritual attainment and the purifying effects of intense and prolonged meditation, as evidence that Vietnam, too, has had its share of eminent Zen masters and its own long and storied Zen tradition. I continue to hear about these Zen mummies from time to time, and in 2010, I was given a book (Nguyễn Lân Cường 2009) that documented the restoration of some of these naturally mummified remains, including the one I found myself peering at through a dirty glass display case nearly two decades ago, a pile of broken pieces that may or may not have once belonged to the arms and legs of an adept.[1]

The remains of these Zen mummies bolstered a nationalist sentiment, with people proudly pointing to them as evidence of the high attainments of Vietnamese Buddhists. The implication was that these masters could be claimed to equal those of China. During that first period of my research in northern Vietnam in the late 1990s, however, periodic references to the mummies would prove the closest I would come to finding evidence of Zen Buddhism in Vietnam. This absence of the normal components of the Zen experience—kōan practice, philosophical stress on emptiness, and most potently, silent meditation, which was not practiced by any of the Buddhists I met—was made especially irksome by the prevalence of academic accounts that placed Zen (Thiền in Vietnamese) at the center of the Vietnamese Buddhist narrative. As Cuong Tu Nguyen succinctly puts it:

> There are few recognizable traces of any specifically "Zen Buddhism" in Vietnam. In the still extant bibliographies of Buddhist books in Vietnam, we find more writings on sutras, rituals, vinaya, but almost nothing on Zen in the form of either independent works or commentaries on Chinese Zen classics. There are no Zen monasteries, no sizeable Zen communities (we can even say no Zen community), no recognizable Zen monasticism or practices as in the case of Japan or Korea. (C. T. Nguyen 1997, 98)

In my experience, it was (and still is) quite rare that a Vietnamese Buddhist identified the goal of his or her practice as being soteriological—becoming enlightened or reaching the Pure Land. Instead, they mostly sought to improve the material existence of this life or to ensure a beneficial afterlife for themselves or their deceased family members. The primary practices involved supplicating the buddhas, making offerings, and chanting sutras and *dharanis* (magical phrases, usually in the form of Vietnamese transliteration of the Sanskrit sounds) and reciting the names of buddhas, particularly Amitābha Buddha (A Di Đà Phật) (Malarney 1999; Nguyen and Barber 1998, 135; Soucy 2012).

I also found that there was no clearly articulated school of Buddhism. While the usual form of Buddhism practiced by the Vietnamese is described as Pure Land Buddhism (Tịnh độ), this, too, is inaccurate. Like Zen, sectarian Pure Land Buddhism has a particular goal—rebirth in the Pure Land (Cực lạc)—and specific associated practices (V. *niệm Phật;* Ch. *nianfo*). Like Zen, Pure Land is understood as a discrete school. However, in northern Vietnam, the Buddhism that was most commonly practiced was more ambiguous and "utterly eclectic" (Nguyen and Barber 1998, 134). Pure Land understandings and practices were certainly the most prominent influence, but Buddhism as it was usually practiced in Vietnam lacked the constitutive understanding of itself as Pure Land; while people described themselves as following the Buddha, most never claimed identity with a school, and those who did would do so only when pressed. Furthermore, the primary goal of their practices had more to do with worldly goals—bringing good luck and health to oneself and one's family—than it did to an explicit goal of being reborn in Amitābha's Pure Land. The enormous gap between written accounts of Vietnamese Buddhism's Zen-ness and the reality that I encountered while doing ethnographic research had been a bothersome disconnect since I first started doing research with a Vietnamese Buddhist community in Montreal in the early 1990s.

So it was with a sense of irony that at the end of 2004, I was introduced to Sùng Phúc Thiền Tự (later renamed Thiền Viện Sùng Phúc), a new Zen monastery and meditation center on the outskirts of Hanoi. Sùng Phúc was unlike anything I had encountered in Vietnam. Its large meditation hall teemed with earnest lay Buddhists meditating, while a monk walked up and down their ranks with a long stick used to rouse those who looked drowsy. Many wore the gray robes common to lay Buddhists in southern Vietnam rather than the brown robes of the north. It reminded me more of ethnographic films of Zen monasteries in Japan than anything I had encountered in Vietnam up to that point.

While there were many modernist aspects to the practice at Sùng Phúc, it harkened to the fourteenth-century founder of the Trúc Lâm sect, the king-turned-monk Trần Nhân Tông (1258–1308), the lineage from which the monastery claimed to have descended. In one stroke, rhetoric became reality, and the books on Vietnamese Buddhism that stressed Zen went from imagined to living tradition. I began to suspect that this introduction of Zen Buddhism in northern Vietnam was the result of global forces and changes and not simply an isolated local occurrence. My suspicions were confirmed, if not fully fleshed out, as I came to learn the extent of the organization with which the Zen center was associated and the importance that the Zen narrative has played for the transmission and globalization of Vietnamese Buddhism since the 1960s. I began research immediately, but I did not get a chance to do more extended study until 2011, when I spent three months conducting ethnographic research there. I subsequently returned in 2013, 2015, and 2018 for shorter follow-up trips of around one month each.

As an anthropologist, I lack the necessary skills to critically examine the full history of Zen Buddhism in Vietnam, a task I must leave to others. Instead, my objective in this book is to look at how adherents of this neo-Zen group are turning an imagined tradition into a modernist practice. It is worth noting, however, that evidence for how Zen has emerged in the twentieth and twenty-first centuries is scant, particularly since most Vietnamese writers and writer-practitioners are participants in the discourse of Zen's having been central to the Buddhism in Vietnam all along, and even to the Vietnamese spirit as a whole. Thus, they tend to treat Zen as a form of Buddhism that has consistently been a part of Buddhism in Vietnam, though all evidence suggests that until very recently, a Vietnamese Zen was more fiction than reality. Notable exceptions are the works of J. C. Cleary (1991) and Cuong Tu Nguyen (1995, 1997), who have looked

Meditation in the old meditation hall, 2004

critically at the text that forms the basis of the Zen claim and conclude that it does not, in fact, show Zen to have been especially important other than in a rhetorical sense, even during the supposed golden age of Buddhism in Vietnam in the Lý and Trần dynasties (1009–1440, inclusive). The main goal of this book is to understand not only how this discourse of Zen may have arisen but also the form that it is taking in contemporary Vietnam.

CONTEXTUALIZING A TRANSNATIONAL, GLOBALIZED BUDDHISM

While this book is primarily an ethnography of a particular Zen center in Hanoi, it is part of a larger thrust of enquiry that I have undertaken with John Harding and Victor Hori that hypothesizes that Buddhism is undergoing transformations that are best understood through the paradigm of globalization (Harding, Hori, and Soucy 2020). I contend that it is only through looking at the processes of globalization that Vietnamese Buddhism, both in the context of Vietnam and in the Vietnamese diaspora, can be properly understood. We need to acknowledge the tremendous influence that transnational, pan-Asian, and global flows of migration and communication have had and continue to have on the development of the multiple forms of Buddhism everywhere.

Though usually unstated, it is often assumed that Buddhism came from Asia in a pristine "traditional" form and then, upon arriving in the West, was transformed to suit the Western context and disposition. This model seems to be based on earlier observations, such as Kenneth Ch'en's (1972), of Buddhism's nativization in the various countries as it spread from India through East Asia. The expectation is that a similar process will happen, is in the process of happening, or has happened in the West, particularly in the United States (hence the term "American Buddhism").[2]

The "others" in this narrative of transformation have been ethnic Asian communities in the West, who are often seen as having a less important role in making Buddhism American because they are seen as essentially conservative (e.g., Tworkov 1991), bringing their Buddhisms with them like "baggage" (Nattier 1998). This view shapes much that has been written on Vietnamese diasporic Buddhism (and there has not been much), which tends to treat Vietnamese Buddhism as a cultural and psychological anchor in the resettlement process. The only book-length treatment of Vietnamese Buddhism in the United States sees religion for Vietnamese immigrants as "a strategic tool in greater community acceptability and intra-community identification. At times employed interchangeably with ethnicity (i.e., to be Buddhist is to be Vietnamese)" (Rutledge 1985, 74). Thuan Huynh's essay "Centre for Vietnamese Buddhism: Recreating Home" (2000) emphasizes the cultural importance of a Vietnamese Buddhist institution in Houston, Texas. Similarly, while noting such adaptations as offering language courses to youths, Hien Duc Do writes that the Vietnamese pagoda in this study is "a place where members of that generation can continue to practice their traditions and affirm their values even as they adjust to American circumstances" (H. D. Do 2006, 91–92). Similar to Rutledge, Law notes that "Vietnamese in Britain seem to have used religion as a means to maintain their ethnic identity whilst being acceptable to the host community" (Law 1991, 57). A brief essay by Tuong Quang Luu (2011) describes the development of Vietnamese Buddhism in Australia and speculates that the main challenge will be adapting it to be suitable for subsequent generations because of resistance to change. Dorais sees Buddhism for the Vietnamese in Canada as playing a dual role: "It enables its adepts to connect with a spiritual universe and a world view with which they are familiar, while giving them the opportunity to express an ethnic identity they often perceive as jeopardized by emigration" (2006, 136). My own work has not been immune to relegating Vietnamese Buddhism to being conservative and introducing changes in the Canadian context primarily in response to external forces (Soucy 1996).

It is indisputable that Buddhism has served as a resource in the Vietnamese diaspora for what Tweed (2006) calls "crossing and dwelling," but the problem arises when there is not equal acknowledgment of the significant innovations, not all of which are the result of external imperatives. So for example, by viewing Vietnamese Buddhists as conservative and practicing a "traditional" form of devotional Buddhism based on community, we ignore the appeal that Thích Nhất Hạnh's modernist teachings have for a great number of diasporic Vietnamese. We are forced to see him as an anomaly who is unrepresentative of, and unconnected to, Vietnamese Buddhism, as do Nguyen and Barber (1998, 131). This is a mistake, because Thích Nhất Hạnh was shaped by Vietnamese Buddhism, has a large following of Vietnamese Buddhists and is having an influence on the development of Buddhism in both Vietnam and in the diaspora (see Soucy, forthcoming). The assumption also compels us to ignore the significant modernist elements also present in so-called traditional Vietnamese pagodas in Canada, France, the United States, and elsewhere, for example the significant role that organizational structures have had in diasporic Buddhism.

Another problem in studies on "ethnic" Buddhists (and a bias held by many Western practitioners) is the view that the Buddhism practiced by Asians has been tainted by cultural accretions, which are seen as diluting "true" Buddhism. Thus, forms of Asian Buddhism are frequently viewed as somehow less authentic than the Buddhism practiced by Westerners. The irony is that the Buddhism of white Western groups has been claimed to be simultaneously more innovative and truer to the spirit of Buddhism as originally conveyed by Siddhārtha Gautama, the historical founder of Buddhism (e.g., Coleman 2001, 218), and while this view is disappearing in academic writings, it is still prevalent in Western-convert Buddhist communities (Han 2021). Tweed correctly points out, though, that hybridity has been part of Buddhism from the beginning (2002, 19).

These issues arise out of a misrecognition of how Buddhism has been changing in the modern period. The characteristics exhibited by Western Buddhist practitioners and that are definitive of Western Buddhism actually originated in Asia at the same time that Buddhism was being introduced to the West (Soucy 2010). These changes were catalyzed by the meeting between Buddhism and the West, particularly through Western imperialistic hegemony, colonialism, and Christian missionary pressures. The Buddhists who brought Buddhism to the West—people like Daisetsu Teitarō Suzuki (1870–1966), Anagārika Dharmapala (1864–1933), and later figures like Thích Nhất Hạnh (1926–) and Chögyam Trungpa Rinpoche (1939–1987)—were part of, or influenced by, Buddhist reform movements that took place in Asia in the late nineteenth and early twentieth centuries and then introduced a Buddhism that had already been radically transformed by Western ideas to eager Westerners who "failed to recognize their own reflection in the mirror being held out to them" (Sharf 1993, 39).[3]

Many of the Vietnamese monastics who have established Buddhist organizations in the West also share in this reformist lineage. Most were in some way involved in the Buddhist Struggle movement in South Vietnam during the war, and this movement in turn owes something of its existence to the Buddhist Reform movement of the 1920s to 1950s. Many, for example, were educated in monastic schools set up earlier by the Buddhist reformers. Buddhism that is being practiced by Vietnamese Buddhists in Canada, the United States, Europe, and Australia is therefore not a conservative replica of the standard form of Vietnamese Buddhism. The Buddhism that traveled from Vietnam to the West had its roots in the earlier Reform movement and was altered further to come to terms with imperatives presented by the new context, but it had already been substantially transformed. Cultural nationalism propelled by diasporic nostalgia, along with a focus on community, were new, and together, they fundamentally changed the character of pagodas in the West. The creation of rational organizations, which is one of the most pronounced structural (and structuring) activities of diasporic Vietnamese Buddhism, is also a radical departure from premodern Buddhist organizational practices. More practical changes, like meeting once a week on Sundays to fit in with the Western calendar, should also not be dismissed as simply a matter of scheduling but rather as reflecting a fundamental secularization of time that effectively removes the centrality of supernatural potency from conceptions of time and place (see chapter 3 for more on this topic).

The changes to Buddhism that we see in the West, whether as practiced by Western or Asian diasporic communities of Buddhists, are in fact local examples of the globalization of Buddhism. This process of the globalization of Buddhism has been taking place since at least the mid-nineteenth century, and for most of that time, the transformations have primarily happened not in the West but in Asia. The dichotomy between Western Buddhism and ethnic/traditional Buddhism that continue to vex scholars of Buddhism is therefore a false one.[4] Instead of identifying categories, it is more useful to focus on three forces that are at work, stressing that they are influential currents or pressures and not types of Buddhism (Soucy 2014). The first, which I have called "Buddhist globalism," has been the main mode of transmission of the modernist discourses that were a reaction to Buddhism's encounters with the West, first manifest in reform movements in Asia. Today, the carriers of this modernist discourse are the large international Buddhist organizations, many based in Asia (like Foguang Shan [佛光山], Buddhist Compassion Relief Tzu Chi Foundation [慈濟基金會], and Goenka's Vipassana meditation movement), and most of the groups of Euro-American converts in the West. The second force is the conservative pressure, or force of inertia, that results in the continuation of practices in a "traditional" way (as imagined as this might be), particularly in the Buddhist countries of Asia and in diasporic communities in the West. This force can take the form of resistance to modernist reconstructions of Buddhism or, as is more usually the case, manifests as a persistence of habitual practices while remaining disengaged with the hegemonic discourses propelled by Buddhist globalism (though not necessarily unaffected by them). I have called this force "Buddhist parochialism" because of the inward focus of intention, but it is important that the term not be understood as pejorative in any way. The third force, which can be called "Buddhist localism," compels all individuals and groups to situate themselves in their cultural and political contexts, regardless of whether they are more influenced by the forces of Buddhist globalism or Buddhist parochialism. One of the principal reasons why Western Buddhism has been taken as a single group or object is that despite there being a variety of groups and practices in the West, there are a number of similarities shared by Western-convert Buddhist groups that appear to overshadow the particularities of the diverse Buddhist modes. However, we need to acknowledge that many "new," "modern," or "reform" Buddhist organization and teachers in Asia have more in common with these Western forms than they do with the standard practices in the countries from which they have emerged.

The organization that is the focus of this book, called Trúc Lâm Thiền Tông (The bamboo grove Zen sect) by its founder Thích Thanh Từ, is most heavily influenced by the modernist discourses that Buddhist globalism has made dominant. It is outward looking and transnationally engaged, taking onboard the critiques put forward by the earlier Buddhist reformers of the common practices. It positions itself as being distinct from the more standard, devotional form of Buddhism that can be found throughout Vietnam and in the diaspora that tends to exhibit parochial dispositions. In Vietnam and the diaspora, manifestations of Buddhist parochialism are devotional in nature, do not place a great emphasis on textual orthodoxy, and while nominally paying allegiance to one of a number of associations, tend largely to consist of independent, community-based pagodas.[5]

The rhetorical distinction that Trúc Lâm draws between itself and the regular form of devotional Vietnamese Buddhism is central to the argument that I want to make in this book, that to understand the connections and continuities between Buddhisms in Vietnam and the diaspora that are primarily influenced by parochial dispositions and modernist organizations like Trúc Lâm Zen, we need to look at how globalization has amplified discourses that continue to shape Buddhism in various ways.[6] The Sùng Phúc Trúc Lâm Monastery in Hanoi is one instance of how these forces are manifested, but it is not the only one. Indeed, the same argument I will make here with Trúc Lâm as the example could be made with similarly modernist cases, like Thích Nhất Hạnh's Order of Interbeing or even with more parochial examples like the local Vietnamese pagoda in Hanoi that I wrote about in *The Buddha Side* (Soucy 2012). However, the example of Trúc Lâm is particularly illuminating because of the unique ways in which it incorporates various modernist discourses while self-consciously rooting itself in an imagined Vietnamese tradition. Before diving into the case of Trúc Lâm, however, it is worth looking more closely at the particular hegemonic, global, modernist discourse that has shaped Trúc Lâm Buddhism and given it immense popularity among Vietnamese Buddhists in Vietnam and overseas today.

GLOBAL DISCOURSES OF BUDDHISM

Leaning on the systems theory articulated in the works of Niklus Luhmann, Peter Beyer has argued that in the modern period, which he roughly identifies as beginning in the late Middle Ages and accelerating in the Enlightenment, Western society reorganized itself into self-referential and differentiated "function systems." These function systems, which include the economic system, the political system, the scientific system, and others, although deeply interdependent are perceived as being distinct and governed by their own sets of rules. They are also recursive, in the sense that they have a tendency to "refer only to themselves for the rationale of continuing their own communication" (Beyer 2006, 41). Religion has also been restructured in this way, which is to say that it has been constructed and recognized as a form of social activity that is distinguishable from other non-religious forms, thus creating a differentiation between the religious and the secular.

This way of organizing society and structuring behaviors and institutions has become globally dominant as a system, partly as a result of European expansionism and imperial policies and colonization of Asia, Africa, and the Americas that brought Europeans in contact with other cultures. The movement was accompanied by the aggressive spread of Christianity and the probing and defining strategies of enquiry of the Western academy. However, while the model for the globalized religious system is Christian, the religious system has both shaped and been shaped by the interaction with other forms of religion, rather than being a preformed structure that was imposed on dominated cultures by European hegemony. Roland Robertson argues that globalization is not a process of homogenization or erasure of the local. He stresses instead that contemporary understandings of locality and indigeneity have emerged from encounters, not in isolation, and are therefore also an important product of globalization, a dialogical process that Robertson calls "glocalization" (Robertson 1995). To say that religion as a system has become dominant in global society should not, therefore, be understood as indicative of a homogenization of religions. In fact, Beyer shows that the responses to the globalization of the category of "religion" have been extremely diverse. The Western imposition of the label of religion for Confucianism is a case in point; while assumed in the Western academy to be a religion, the responses in China have been considerably more varied, from attempts to reshape Confucianism as a religion to outright rejection of the label (Beyer 2006, 231–241; Sun 2013).

The differentiated religious system has become globalized in the sense that all groups are compelled to position themselves in relation to the global structure of religion. This can be done by remodeling in such a way that previous beliefs, practices, and institutions take on the particular characteristics of religion as a system or by declaring that such beliefs, practices, and institutions are not religion but spirituality, a practice, a way a life, or other similar designations (Beyer 2006, 8). This points to the fact that the process by which religiosities are restructured as religions is not uniform. Within groups and between individuals, there is considerable variation in responses. The result of the globalization of religion as a system has been that in countries around the world, certain constellations of practices and beliefs have come to be defined as religions, and others have not.

One of the main functions of the structuring of religion as a system is that it differentiates. It does this in three ways. First, it differentiates between what is and is not within the boundaries of a particular religion and maps out the internal landscapes of the religion, defining schools, sects, and so on. In other words, it creates orthodoxies, authorities to define them, and strategies to enforce them. Second, the structuring of religion distinguishes one from another, thereby creating and defining unities within one religion and differences between that religion and others. Third, structuring of religion as a system differentiates religious systems from non-religious (i.e., secular) systems, like the scientific system, the economic system, the political system, and the educational system (Beyer 2006, 15). Particularly useful among Beyer's ideas is the recognition that Buddhism, as a result of globalization, has taken on an identity and structure as a discrete religion with a core unity and an internal landscape of distinct schools, sects, and lineages. The Buddhist religion came to be seen—by some, at least—as having distinct borders, so that certain practices and beliefs were included and others were discounted as non-Buddhist, as cultural accretions, or as superstitions. While this has always been somewhat the case with Buddhism depending on location, this globalized systemization of religion has meant that Buddhism has been restructured in fundamentally new ways. I refer to this discourse as hegemonic because of the ways that its modernist, secularized view aligns with state interests and global neoliberal power structures and exerts pressure for conformity through the media, the academy, and the judicial and political systems.

The response to the global systematization of religion has not been uniform, and the restructuring of Buddhism has not evenly permeated all groups and practitioners. Where it did have the strongest influence was with the urban elite intellectuals—precisely those who were most directly confronted with the hegemonic discourses that were fed by colonialism and exposed to the modernist discourses transmitted by the emerging Buddhist globalism. Buddhist reformers and reform organizations emerged in most Asian Buddhist countries. In symbiosis with Western scholars and interested converts (like the Theosophists and the Buddhist Society in London) and through transnational dialogues with other reformist nodes (in the Appaduraian sense [1996, 31]), Buddhism was reconceptualized and restructured to fit more clearly into the category of religion, and more specifically, as one of the world religions. It was not by coincidence that the movements they brought about became most closely aligned with new forms of restructured and reconstituted nation-states in Asia and exhibited strongly nationalistic tendencies more generally. After all, both the reconstructing of Buddhism and modern states in Asia were part of the same process of social reorganization brought about through colonial encounter and globalization.

THE RESTRUCTURING OF VIETNAMESE BUDDHISM

As elsewhere in Asia, the restructuring of Buddhism in Vietnam was not uniform. The reform movements in Vietnam were centered in the main urban areas of the north, central, and south (Tonkin, Annam, and Cochin-china). Although these disparate reform movements were in communica-tion, they were established as separate societies as a result of French colonial regulation (Woodside 1976, 193). The regional organizations were mainly elite and intellectual in nature. Beyond these elite, urban circles, the reform movements had only limited impact at the time (Marr 1981, 304–306; Woodside 1976, 193). The long-term effect on Buddhism in Viet-nam and among diasporic Buddhist communities, however, has been profound (DeVido 2007, 253; McHale 2004, 144–145), and the populariza-tion of Zen to be described in this book is one manifestation of the re-formers' efforts.

The Buddhist Reform movement (Chấn hưng Phật giáo) started in Vietnam somewhat later than in countries such as Sri Lanka, Japan, and China, with societies being formed in the 1920s. The hegemony of foreign domination and colonial rule led to deep soul-searching by Vietnamese intellectuals and to a consensus that the Vietnamese had been so easily subjugated because of their own deficiencies, whether because of the per-ceived inferiority of their cultural heritage and social forms or because there had been a decline in former strength (Marr 1981, 60). The answers to their dilemma ranged from calls for a return to an imagined glorious (mostly) Confucian past to modernist movements (like Communism), which believed that the way forward was a total abandonment of the past. The response by some Buddhists was to take a closer look at Buddhism and, following the ideas of Chinese Buddhist reformers like Taixu (太虛, 1890–1947), to modernize Buddhism (DeVido 2007, 2009).

Thus, the colonial encounter brought about a restructuring in the way Buddhism was conceived, framing Buddhism in conformity with the Western understanding of what constitutes "religion" as a distinct social system. To be sure, Buddhism existed before the French colonization of Indochina as a set of beliefs, practices, texts, and institutions, but there was no consciousness of Buddhism as a unique and differentiated reli-gion that had a pan-Asian identity and an orthodoxy. Buddhist reformers sought to restructure Buddhism as a religion and reimagined it within the parameters of this category.

The Buddhist Reform movement was as much a lay Buddhist move-ment as it was a monastic one. The influential Chinese reformer Taixu argued that Buddhism's weakness was that it was hidden away in monas-teries and pagodas. Critical of the way monks in the Qing period inter-acted with the laity through the performance of mortuary rituals but little else, he called for Buddhism to be directed toward "human life." The Pure Land should consequently be established on earth rather than attained after death (Birnbaum 2003, 435–436; Jones 2003, 129; Tao Jiang 2002). His idea of humanistic Buddhism (Nhân gian Phật giáo) was widely accepted among reformers in Vietnam and frequently discussed in their journals. The reformers understood this refocusing on the laity as crucial, and as a result, while the leaders were primarily monks, there was heavy involvement by lay Buddhists, who were active in these new societies, especially in publishing journals. These lay members were drawn mainly from the urban petite bourgeoisie, who were most inclined to join organizations and study groups and were most involved and concerned with the process of modernization (DeVido 2007, 276; Marr 1981, 31–32).

Internal Boundaries: Creation of a Buddhist Orthodoxy

The reform process of restructuring Buddhism as a world religion meant the creation of distinct boundaries in ways that were completely new. Perhaps the most profound was what can be called the orthodoxification of Buddhism, which brought about an increased importance to communicate the new ideas. This orthodoxy stressed the achievement of enlightenment through individual effort, so that sutra study, meditation, and ethical practices became more central, while supplication (i.e., making wishes to the buddhas for health, wealth, luck, progeny, and so on) were marginalized as ignorant misunderstandings of Buddhism. The orthodoxy also radically reconstructed Buddhism as an individual activity in the sense that it made each practitioner responsible for his or her own salvation (whether that salvation was defined from a Zen or a Pure Land viewpoint).

The Buddhist Reform movement in Vietnam was particularly concerned with discriminating between Buddhism and what were seen as cultural accretions or superstition (mê tín), following trends that started in Japan and China.[7] So, for example, Nguyễn Khoa Tung wrote in the southern journal Pháp âm (The sound of the Dharma) in 1929, "Now, many virtuous persons [vị đạo đức] in the south want to propagate Buddhism so that everyone can know which religious beliefs are useful, not to venerate Buddhism in a superstitious manner, not to curry favor with the Buddha, make offerings, bow, and pray, [all] for one's personal good fortune. That completely misses the goals of Buddhism" (McHale 2004, 159). In the reformist journals in the three regions of Vietnam, we see the identification of particular practices identified as un-Buddhist and a discouragement—if not open ridicule—of practices that had been deemed outside the boundaries of Buddhism. Burning spirit money was seen as particularly superstitious, wasteful, and contrary to the original Buddhism as taught by the historical Buddha. The northern journal Đuốc tuệ (The torch of wisdom) published an article in two issues by the prominent reformist monk Trí Hải (1906–1979) that argued that the practice of burning spirit money was not only useless (*vô ích*) but was not Buddhist, pointing out that such practices are never mentioned in the Buddhist sutras (Trí-Hải 1937a, 1937b). In the article, he writes:

> I hope that we will have conviction in the Buddha to do the right thing, to be loyal and not give way. If we don't keep our conviction, it won't only hurt us but also our children, friends and kin. We will also create doubt in people who don't follow Buddhism and don't understand Buddhism clearly. It gives them the impression that Buddhism is superstitious. If we don't get rid of all of these mistaken beliefs and practices [*sự nhầm*] then we will surely not be happy and fortunate [*phúc*]; we will waste money, create sin, and degrade Buddhist principles instead of honoring them. (Trí-Hải 1937b, 11–12)

The process of orthodoxification resulted in a deemphasis, and even discouragement, of practices and beliefs that emphasized the infusion of the supernatural in the world of humans. In this, the reform Buddhist discourse mirrored the wider discourse of modernity that was taking place in Vietnamese society.

The creation of an orthodoxy required that people not just practice Buddhism but also comprehend Buddhist teachings. Thiện Tòng, a monk in Saigon (now Ho Chi Minh City), complained in the newspaper *Đông pháp thời báo* (*Indochina Times*) in 1927 that "for the most part Buddhist women in our country honor Buddhism, but few understand what taking refuge means; they recite the buddhas' names [*niệm Phật*] and eat vegetarian food but don't understand why" (Thiện Tòng 2008, 27). This new emphasis on orthodoxy compelled efforts to communicate with the laity in new ways. Previous to the Reform movement, Buddhist communication was primarily accomplished through ritual, and Buddhist doctrine did not deeply penetrate either the Buddhist monastics or the laity. The process of orthodoxification was predicated on the need to communicate to the laity its new ideas. Educating monastics so they could teach and serve as examples of the Buddhist orthodoxy to the laity became important, but it needed to be done in ways different from in the past. Though the lineage pattern in Vietnam was admittedly not particularly strong (C. T. Nguyen 1997, 96), the education of monastics had nonetheless taken place mostly within the confines of individual pagodas. New institutions were required to more thoroughly and systematically ensure a uniform understanding of Buddhism. It therefore became one of the priorities of the Reform movement in Vietnam to set up schools that were institutionalized and rationalized, following the patterns of the Western education system. In northern Vietnam, for example, a school for monks was set up at Quán Sứ Pagoda in Hanoi in 1934, in the year that the Tonkin Buddhist Association was established. A school for nuns was later started in 1942 at nearby Bồ Đề Pagoda (Nguyễn Đại Đồng 2006, 15). Similar monastic schools were established in all regions of Vietnam. Some, like the one at Quán Sứ Pagoda, continued to be centers for monastic learning even after the Communists took over, not surprisingly teaching the modernist Buddhist orthodoxy that closely conformed with state anti-superstition campaigns. In the center and south, these schools went on to teach the monks who formed the core of the Struggle movement in the 1960s, which protested against the war, American involvement, and the puppet presidents backed by the United States (see Topmiller 2002). These eminent monks included Thích Trí Quang, a leader of the Buddhist Struggle movement; Thích Thiên Ân (1925–1980), the first Vietnamese monk to emigrate to the United States; and Thích Nhất Hạnh, who has become a global Buddhist celebrity.

Reformers also expected the laity to have a deeper understanding of the doctrine than ever before. In that sense, the formation of monastic schools and the education of monastics was the foundation for the more important purpose of creating an educated Buddhist laity that conformed to the delineated understanding of Buddhist orthodoxy. Dharma talks became a staple activity at reformist pagodas. However, most important for the communication of Buddhism as a distinct system was the creation and distribution of printed matter, particularly journals, which proliferated during this period along with the publication of books, sutras, and religious tracts (McHale 2004, 153). Vietnamese newspapers began in the early 1920s to run columns about Buddhism, but the first dedicated Buddhist journal, *Pháp âm*, was published in the Mekong Delta city of Mỹ Tho in August 1929. By 1935, well-established journals were being published in southern, central, and northern Vietnam—*Từ bi âm* (The voice of compassion) in Saigon, *Viên âm* (The voice of exposition) in Hue, and *Đuốc tuệ* in Hanoi—with several other journals appearing soon after in other provincial centers (Nguyễn Đại Đồng 2008). These magazines, written in the romanized script (*Quốc ngữ*), tended to be internationally oriented and drew on Chinese reformist writings from figures like Taixu. The journals transliterated sutras into *Quốc ngữ* from Chinese characters, gave explanations of Buddhist teachings and philosophical concepts, and provided stories of the Buddha and the Buddhist saints and buddhas and bodhisattvas of the Mahāyāna pantheon, articles about the Reform movement, news of activities of the societies that published the journals, and updates and announcements of national and even international Buddhist activities.

New rationalized organizational structures were another innovation of the Reform movement. Societies and associations became important vehicles for defining the new orthodoxy, coordinating activities, and communicating through the use of print media. This institutionalization happened throughout the Buddhist world, with organizations such as Dharmapala's Mahabodhi Society in Sri Lanka, Taixu's Buddhist Association of China (中國佛教協會), and a number of other national Buddhist associations. This restructuring into modernist organized forms reflected the ways that Buddhism was also being introduced and organized in the West, the Buddhist Society in London being just one example.[8] In Vietnam, societies were established in the major urban centers to promote the reformation of Buddhism along modernist lines; hence, they were frequently called "study societies" (like the Annam Buddhist Study Society [Hội Phật học Trung kỳ]). While the purpose was the promotion of reformist ideas, in the twentieth century, the formation and maintenance of associations has frequently been a central activity in itself, both nationally and internationally. As we will see later, this modernist proclivity for setting up organizations is one of the features of Trúc Lâm and one of the principal characteristics that differentiates it from the broader diffused and localized Buddhist pattern in Vietnam.

Elite criticism of local practice and the desire to reform Buddhism to recover the core of the Buddha's teachings were part of a larger movement of Buddhist reform that took place throughout Asia from early in the twentieth century. The Western academy's study of Buddhism also played a role in this reformation process:

> Especially fascinating is the way in which the modernist academic study of Buddhism actually helped conjure up in the present the very kind of "rational religion" it claimed to have discovered in the past. For example, the "Buddhist modernism" or "Protestant Buddhism" of Walpola Rahula's enormously influential book *What the Buddha Taught* was created in an accommodating response to Western expectations, and in nearly diametric opposition to Buddhism as it had actually been practiced in Theravāda societies. Likewise, the denatured Zen of Suzuki Daisetsu, Hisamatsu Shin'ichi, and Abe Masao; the Buddhist humanism (*renjian fojiao*) of the contemporary Chinese scholar-monk Yinshun Daoshi; and the "Critical Buddhism" (Hihan Bukkyo) movement in contemporary Japan are all

deeply indebted to modern, largely Western notions of what Buddhism ought to be. (Gimello 2004, 240–241)

In Vietnam, the newly created Buddhist orthodoxies of the reformers have combined with historically and politically grounded discourses on religion, superstition, and nationalism, resulting in unique reinterpretations of what constitutes "real" Vietnamese Buddhism. These discourses were largely ineffective in changing the on-the-ground practices of most Buddhists in Vietnam and did not accurately reflect the ways that people actually experience and practice Buddhism. In recent years, however, these discourses have begun to extend beyond an elite core of urban intellectuals and are influencing the patterns of practice for a much greater number of lay Buddhists, some of whom are beginning to self-consciously place a primacy on meditation and to speak of the Zen school of Buddhism as being foundational for Vietnamese Buddhism.

Buddhism as a World Religion

While the reform movements in Vietnam and elsewhere were concerned with defining Buddhism's borders by creating an orthodoxy, they were also concerned with the borders between Buddhism and other religions. This involved a strong drive to reconstruct Buddhism as one of the world religions, a process in which both Asian Buddhist reformers and Western scholars were involved.[9] The Buddhist delegations to the initial World's Parliament of Religions in 1893 were perhaps the first international assertion of Buddhism's equal footing as a world religion. Anagārika Dharmapala, the delegate from Sri Lanka, and the Japanese delegation presented Buddhism as not just a religion but as the religion most suited to modernity (and therefore implicitly superior to Christianity) (Harding 2008, 124; McMahan 2008, 91–92; Snodgrass 2003, 211–213).[10]

As a world religion, Buddhism was reconceived as a unitary tradition, compelling the emphasis on commonalities and defining a core of the religion.[11] The historical Buddha was reconstructed as the founder and symbolic center of the religion (Snodgrass 2009b, 22). In Vietnam, this new emphasis on the historical Buddha could be seen in several developments. Buddhist journals in the 1920s and 1930s featured serialized and detailed accounts of the life of the Buddha.[12] The Saigon journal *Từ bi âm*, for example, featured a serial biography of Siddhārtha Gautama called *Lược truyện Phật Thích-Ca-Mâu-Ni (Sakya Muni)* (Biographical sketches of Śākyamuni Buddha), which continued for thirty-one issues, ending in April 1933 (*Từ bi âm* 1932–1933). In issue 175 of *Từ bi âm*, Trần-Nguyên-Chấn argues that just as Christianity has Jesus, Confucianism Confucius, and Daoism Laozi, so Buddhism has Śākyamuni as the founder and central figure, and therefore all Buddhists should know his biography (Trần-Nguyên-Chấn 1940, 36). By the 1940s, it became a common practice for Buddhist monks in Vietnam to preface their names with the surname of the Buddha, Thích. The festival to celebrate the Buddha's birthday (Wesak, or Phật Đản in Vietnamese) also began to be celebrated as a public ritual around this time, with the first occurrence in Huế taking place in 1934 (Nguyễn-Khoa-Tân 1934, 61). In 1953, Vietnamese Buddhists followed the lead of the World Fellowship of Buddhists, which met in Tokyo, Japan, in September 1952, in adopting usage of the Buddhist calendar, based on the birth of the Buddha (*Tin tức phật giáo* 1953). They stressed the core teachings of the Buddha, particularly as exemplified by his first sermon to build Buddhism as a single religion. Colonel Henry Steel Olcott's *Buddhist Catechism* (1886) was an early expression of this, and Walpola Rahula's later *What the Buddha Taught* (1959) filled the same role. In Vietnam, the Buddhist journals similarly took pains to write about core teachings and ways of declaring identity as a Buddhist, like reciting the Three Refuges and taking the Five Precepts.[13] This Buddhist unity has been symbolically stressed in other ways, too, such as the international Buddhist flag, which was created in 1885 in Ceylon (Sri Lanka), adopted at the first World Buddhist Congress in 1950, and brought back by the Vietnamese delegate.

For reformers, this reconstruction of Buddhism as an (or the) Asian world religion meant an international outlook and engagement. Buddhist journals in Vietnam, for example, regularly published translated foreign articles, a practice that continues today.[14] This outlook was continued in the 1950s and 1960s, when southern Vietnamese monks were sent to study in Japan, the United States, India, and elsewhere. Thích Thiên Ân, who introduced "Vietnamese Zen" to North America, received his doctorate from Waseda University in Tokyo (on a scholarship from Emperor Bảo Đại's wife). Thích Nhất Hạnh, easily the most internationally recognized Vietnamese Buddhist figure, studied at Princeton. Thích Thiện Nghị, the first Buddhist monk in Canada, studied at Foguang Shan in Taiwan (notably, another major international reformist organization).

Buddhism as a Differentiated Religion

The third distinction brought about by the creation and subsequent globalization of religion as a system has been the distinction between religion and other systems (in essence, distinguishing between the religious and secular). Religion was reconstructed as taking place at certain times, in certain places, and comprising particular activities that could be recognized as religious rather than being thoroughly infused in all aspects of life. By contrast, the premodern worldview, which made no separation between religious and secular activities, saw the natural world as interpenetrated with potent supernatural forces that could be equally beneficent or pernicious.

Secularism has taken a particular form in the West of strictly separating the religious from other spheres of human activity—victory in war became a matter of strategy and logistics rather than divine intervention; success in business became a matter of hard work and wise decisions rather than fate; ill health came to be understood through the science of medicine and was no longer a matter of vindictive or punishing gods, ghosts, and spirits or the imbalance of energies. While the extent of actual disenchantment in the West has been questioned (see Josephson-Storm 2017), it is clearer that these differentiations have been much less consistent in Asia (van der Veer 2014). The enchanted worldview in Vietnam was condemned by reformers as superstitious, and there was substantial effort by the Communist government to squelch beliefs and practices related to belief in supernatural potency, but it was never very successful (Malarney 2002). Today we are seeing a re-enchantment in Vietnam, and in Asia more generally, so that the rational humanist viewpoint may be losing ground (P. Taylor 2007). Practices like fortune-telling and enlisting the support of the supernatural for luck in business (for example, by sponsoring spirit-medium rituals) are losing much of the stigma they had during the more intense period of Communist suppression of religion from the 1950s to late 1980s in northern Vietnam. Today, even state officials can be seen praying at religious sites.[15]

The Buddhist Reform discourses emphasized the complementarity between Buddhism and science. This began in the very earliest phase of the reform movements in Asia but has accelerated and become more sophisticated since its inception in the late nineteenth century (McMahan 2008, 90). The discourse of this globalized Buddhist modernism discursively secularizes Buddhism (McMahan 2020, 45), deemphasizing the supernatural aspects and questioning the appropriateness of supplicating the buddhas and bodhisattvas for favor and particularly for material gain. Instead, this discourse has interpreted Buddhist mythology as metaphor. Modernist Buddhists stress individual endeavor, particularly through the technique of meditation, which is understood in natural rather than supernatural terms. Buddhism becomes a psychology, and meditation is seen as a technique for exploring and reorienting one's emotions and psychological balance. The exemplar of this practice in the discourse is the historical Buddha, and therefore his humanity is emphasized along with his individual enlightenment experience under the bodhi tree, where he realized the truth of things through his own effort rather than through divine revelation. Many Buddhist teachers influenced by this globalized discourse pitch Buddhism as not a religion at all and therefore see it as suitable to be practiced alongside other religions, without contradiction. Particularly among Western converts, Buddhism is frequently described as a practice more than a religion. Thích Nhất Hạnh's teachings on mindfulness are a good example of this argument.

The modernist restructuring of Buddhism has an implicitly contradictory stance in relation to secularism. On the one hand, there has been an attempt to put forward Buddhism as a religion—and specifically, one of the world religions—which necessarily separates it from other function systems and constructs it along the parameters of what is expected of a religion. On the other hand, there has been a strong impulse to construct Buddhism as secular and not as a religion at all. Thích Nhất Hạnh and other teachers in the West are particularly—though not exclusively—prone to this viewpoint. With Trúc Lâm Zen, we see a more nuanced attempt to retain Buddhism as a religion while also removing parochial elements of Vietnamese Buddhism that emphasize reciprocal relationships with the supernatural. Nonetheless, the way Zen is configured by Trúc Lâm strongly reflects the secularist discourse prominent within Buddhist globalism.

The secularist views that had been propagated by the reformers dovetailed with state intentions and elite views, and they are largely those that continue to be promulgated today by the instruments of the state, which in Vietnam include, among others, the media, the academy, and the Buddhist institution.[16] The state favored the reformist view of Buddhism because it reflected the rationalist discourse that distanced religion from superstition and most easily fit with the Marxist secular humanist ideology of the Communist state. In the post-Renovation period, the rise of neoliberal forces have taken over, but largely to the same ends. As Schwenkel and Leshkowich note, neoliberalism has shaped views of individual and familial morality through technologies of self-focus (among other instruments) that hold up a middle-class norm as "proper, acceptable and appropriate" (2012, 396). The disenchanted Buddhism of Zen, which focuses on individual perfection, mental health, and so on, fits nicely within this middle-class view of morality.

However, while the Buddhist institution has been complicit in de-supernaturalizing Buddhism, it has not done so in a concerted way. So, for example, at Quán Sứ Pagoda (the center of the Buddhist institution in the north), there was formerly a ban on offering and burning spirit money, but the signs that forbade it in the late 1990s have been removed, and the practice continues unabated today, despite continued articles in the Buddhist media about its being wasteful, useless, and backward. Moving away from the political center to other pagodas that are driven by a more parochial disposition toward Buddhism, the secularist view had even less penetration. In most Buddhist pagodas around Hanoi, there are shrines dedicated to the pantheon of spirits that are a part of the mother goddess cult, and the vast majority of Buddhists also worship spirits, supplicating both to assist with concerns of everyday existence—success in careers, success writing exams or with business deals, help finding a husband or conceiving a child, wealth, health, and so on.

OUTLINE OF THE CHAPTERS

The Buddhism practiced at Sùng Phúc Monastery represents a radical departure from the Buddhism practiced at local Buddhist pagodas found throughout Hanoi and northern Vietnam and that are shaped primarily by parochial dispositions. The monastery is part of an organization started by Thích Thanh Từ that purports to be the heir of the Trúc Lâm Zen tradition, first established in the fourteenth century by the king-turned-monk Trần Nhân Tông. Constructing his organization and teachings in this way, Thích Thanh Từ created a kind of Buddhism that has important symbolic ties with an imagined Vietnamese Zen tradition while simultaneously drawing heavily on the reformist discourses that have been globalized. The place of Zen in precolonial Vietnam and its development in relation to the Reform movement in the twentieth century will be discussed in chapter 1, which will also explore the contemporary Trúc Lâm Zen organization and its founder.

Chapter 2 will look more explicitly at the context in which Trúc Lâm has manifested itself in Hanoi. The way Sùng Phúc Monastery has been constructed has rendered its organization and its activities as distinct from the regular forms found in pagodas in Vietnam and in community pagodas found throughout the diaspora. The uniqueness of Trúc Lâm can be seen in the space that has been created through its architecture and iconography, which invokes an imagined Vietnamese tradition while also reflecting global Buddhist discourses, and it has an important role in shaping how its adherents practice and understand Buddhism in new ways. The activities at Sùng Phúc also show the dual construction of modernist Buddhism in the form of a Vietnamese tradition, as imagined as it may be. An exploration of the space reveals several themes that will be discussed in the subsequent chapters.

The first of these themes is the secularization of Buddhism, discussed in chapter 3. My earlier book, *The Buddha Side: Gender, Power and Buddhist Practice in Vietnam* (Soucy 2012), illustrated the holistic cosmology of most Buddhist practitioners in Vietnam (particularly northern Vietnam), which sees the buddhas and bodhisattvas as being part of a supernatural landscape that also included spirits, gods and goddesses, ancestors, ghosts, and so on. People understood themselves as being engaged in reciprocal relationships with these forces, and like all relationships, these bring both benefits and obligations. While this view is still present and is today even returning in a process of re-enchantment, there is simultaneously a de-supernaturalization and a secularization taking place under the pressures of the modernist discourses of Buddhist globalism. Trúc Lâm Zen embodies this modernist form of Buddhism that emphasizes individual effort and views supplication to the buddhas as superstition, at least in its prominent discourses. It should be noted that though the self-conscious rhetorical thrust is in the direction of a secular-style Buddhism, there are nonetheless elements that continue to show that a more enchanted worldview does continue to persist.

The globalization of modernist Buddhist discourses, of which Trúc Lâm is one of the foremost Vietnamese manifestations, has a dual and seemingly contradictory orientation. It is at once international in outlook and frequently nationalistic. The nationalistic aspect is prominently displayed by the systematic branding of Trúc Lâm as the only Zen school founded in Vietnam. On the other hand, like all groups influenced by the modernist discourse that are impelled by Buddhist globalism, Trúc Lâm is internationally oriented and is involved in actively establishing itself overseas in North America, Europe, and Australia. Chapter 4 will explore this seeming contradiction by looking at how these two orientations form a part of the way Buddhism is constructed at Sùng Phúc and by the Trúc Lâm Zen organization more generally.

The final theme, the constituency of Zen Buddhism, will be explored in chapters 5, 6, and 7. The Buddhism practiced at local pagodas attracts women almost exclusively (Soucy 2012). Younger women make offerings to the buddhas on the first and fifteenth of the lunar month (*ngày rằm và mồng một*) to request help with careers, relationships, fecundity, health, and so on, while older women become more involved in chanting sutras and making Buddhism a more central part of their identities. The few men who participate often transform themselves into specialists. At Sùng Phúc, old women still make up the majority of practitioners, but there is a much more even demographic spread, and the monastery intentionally includes children and youths, with specific activities, a Sunday school for children, and a youth group for adolescents. Men of all ages are also involved in ways that are uncharacteristic of male participation in other pagodas. These chapters will explore the how and why of this wider engagement.

While it is important to understand the structures and discourses that Sùng Phúc manifests, it is also important to understand what is attracting people to Trúc Lâm and how they understand their engagement with Zen. Exploring their lives, aspirations, and motivations will help us understand how Zen is constructed and lived by practitioners. These final three chapters will explore a representative sample of some of the people who go to Sùng Phúc, to better understand Zen's popularity and for insight into the individual—and sometimes idiosyncratic—ways that its practitioners understand their practice.

As Vietnamese Buddhists become increasingly transnationally linked, the seeds of modernist Buddhism that were planted by reformers early in the twentieth century are now materializing. This book is an attempt to look at how these changes are taking place through a case study of one large Zen center on the outskirts of Hanoi. Its size and prominence indicate that it represents more than just one isolated group, though it is unique in the Buddhist landscape of Hanoi. It is part of a large organization that is based in Vietnam and expanding internationally and so represents a new form of Buddhism influenced by the forces of Buddhist globalism rather than the parochial devotional Buddhist dispositions that can be seen at most pagodas around Hanoi. The emergence of Trúc Lâm Zen in the late twentieth and early twenty-first centuries should be seen in light of modernist discourses that attempt to define Buddhism as a religion with an orthodoxy and distinctions and also as one that must be distinguished from more common views that see the world infused with supernatural forces. By doing this, Trúc Lâm has been very successful in attracting not only the usual old women but also men and young people.

NOTE ON LANGUAGE AND NAMES

There are a few conventions of terminology that I use here that I should clarify. The first and perhaps most obvious is that I use "Zen" throughout this book as a general word to describe the meditation school rather than the Vietnamese designation of "Thiền." This is not intended to indicate in any way that Vietnamese Thiền has any direct connection with the Japanese sect. Instead, the roots of Thiền in Vietnam come from China, but the Chinese term, "Chan," has not been adopted internationally to describe the globalized living practice, instead describing specifically the meditation school in China. Thus, "Chan" is not a suitable gloss for Zen in the Vietnamese context. This is somewhat problematic, since the people I discuss in this book are self-consciously trying to reconstruct a form of practice that is specifically and uniquely rooted in their own history and cultural sensitivities. Nonetheless, most readers will not be familiar with the Vietnamese term, so for the sake of readability, I felt it appropriate to use the most familiar term. Another reason for this is that most English-language academic studies of Vietnamese Buddhism also refer to Vietnamese Thiền as "Zen" (see Cleary 1991; C. T. Nguyen 1995, 1997; Topmiller 2002), as do Vietnamese self-descriptions written in English (see Thích Nhất Hạnh 1968; Thích Thiện Ân 1970, 1971, 1975a), including in English translations of Trúc Lâm's own literature (Thích Thanh Từ 2002b, 2002e).

The second term that may strike some as odd is the use of the word "pagoda" rather than "temple" to translate the Vietnamese word "chùa," the term for a Buddhist temple complex. The primary reason for this is the convention inherited from French scholarship on religion in Vietnam. However, it is also useful, as there are an array of temple types in Vietnam that are used to worship a variety of gods and spirits, so "pagoda" usefully denotes a uniquely Buddhist space. It should be understood as referring to a Buddhist temple complex and not to the multi-tiered towers or stupas that are called "tháp" in Vietnamese.

I have tried to be judicious with the use of the word "tradition" as a descriptor for the common forms of practices and the spaces in which they occur. While a convenient shorthand, the term tends to ascribe a uniformity and immutability that obscure the way that "tradition" exists as discourse rather than as a neutral characterization of any inherent nature. Despite the admitted awkwardness, I instead try to refer to the common Buddhist practices that are guided by parochial tendencies with terms like "standard," "normal," or "regular." When I have retained the use of "tradition" or "traditional," it is usually in the context of something like "imagined tradition" or is used with quotes to denote that it is perceived in that way. Similarly, I use modern/modernist/modernism in a specific way to refer to what is admittedly a loose set of discursive values rather than a singular "thing." Juxtaposing itself with "tradition," "modernist" includes such values as individualism, freedom and equality, capitalism, the development of nation-states, democracy, public education, urbanization, secularism, the inevitability of scientific and technological progress, and unattenuated faith in rationalism. While I recognize that a full definition is not possible and that there are, in fact, multiple modernities, this list is recognizable as being some of the main components in the loose discourse that is recognizable as modernist. Importantly, I never use it vaguely to refer to the contemporary.

Finally, I should note that all translations from books or conversations throughout this work are my own except where stated. All personal names in this book are pseudonyms, with the exception of monastic leaders.

PART 1

CONTEXT

CHAPTER ONE

||||||||

The Rise of Zen in Twentieth-Century Vietnam

While Zen has been frequently described as central to Vietnamese Buddhism (and even to the Vietnamese national character), it has not penetrated very deeply in Vietnam until recently. It appears to have come to prominence starting in the 1960s in South Vietnam, particularly in Saigon. The two key figures credited with introducing a supposed Vietnamese Zen to the West, Thích Nhất Hạnh and Thích Thiên Ân, were originally from central Vietnam, in the Huế region, and were active in Saigon, the capital of South Vietnam, during the period of partition. I have been unable to determine conclusively how these figures became interested in Zen, particularly because their legitimacy as teachers in the West rests on the idea that they are heirs to a Zen lineage and tradition, which leads to what I suspect has been extensive revisionism by their biographers. It is notable that both figures wrote books in English and Vietnamese that illustrate Vietnam's long-standing history of Zen.[1]

Thích Nhất Hạnh has been a famous international Buddhist figure with a large following of both Westerners and ethnic Vietnamese for over half a century. He became known in the West as a peace activist in the 1960s and as a Buddhist teacher in the 1980s but was not widely known in Vietnam until the 2000s. Thích Thanh Từ became prominent inside Vietnam in the 1990s. These monks and a handful of others, Thích Chân Quang prominent among them, have developed a reputation as Zen masters (*Thiền sư*), though there is little evidence that they came from Zen lineages. Nonetheless, it would be a mistake to think that they invented a Zen presence in Vietnam. Instead, Zen has had a long and complicated history in the region.

Why the spirit of the Reform movement had a deeper impact in the south than the north is a matter of the vicissitudes of Vietnamese twentieth-century history. The Reform movement ended abruptly in 1954 in northern Vietnam, when the country was divided between the north and the south and the ruling Communist Party in the north discouraged religious practice. Meanwhile, in South Vietnam, Buddhism continued to be influenced by the ideas of the earlier reformers, and the Reform movement morphed into the Struggle movement, resisting first the anti-Buddhist oppression of the regime of Ngô Đình Diệm and then opposing the war, the American military presence, and the succession of presidents perceived as being puppets of the United States (Lê Cung 2008; Phạm Văn Minh 2002; Schecter 1967; Topmiller 2002). Thus, in the south, Buddhism continued to have a public and political life, whereas in the north, the development of the Reform movement was stifled, and Buddhism, banished from public view, was practiced mostly by small groups of old women (Malarney 1999, 195–196). It was not until the Renovation (Đổi mới) in the late 1980s, when Vietnam liberalized the economy and eased social restrictions, that Buddhism reawakened in northern Vietnam. It took a further decade for Buddhist developments that had taken place in southern Vietnam during the war to affect Buddhism in the north. Consequently, many of my informants—both those who were involved in Trúc Lâm and those who were not—viewed southern Buddhist monks as being more advanced and more knowledgeable than those in the north.

The creation of Sùng Phúc Monastery in Hanoi represents a missionary expansion of a neo-Zen Buddhism from southern Vietnam that had been profoundly influenced by the Reform movement, and the main actors in Trúc Lâm were, and still are, southerners. All the senior monks at Sùng Phúc are from either south or central Vietnam, and the headquarters of Trúc Lâm remains in Đà Lạt, in the central highlands, at a monastery founded by Thích Thanh Từ, fittingly called Trúc Lâm Monastery.

The background of Thích Thanh Từ, the monk who is responsible for this new Trúc Lâm movement, and the development of Zen Buddhism in the twentieth century, are important for understanding how Trúc Lâm has established itself in Hanoi and the form that it takes. This chapter will look at the place of Zen Buddhism in Vietnamese history and the development of Zen in the twentieth century to provide context for the discussion of how Zen is presented at Sùng Phúc Monastery. In doing so, it will explore the local and global aspects of the development of Trúc Lâm as a quintessentially Vietnamese Zen school and will introduce the founder, Thích Thanh Từ.

A HISTORY OF ZEN INVENTION

While Buddhism was introduced to Vietnam perhaps as early as the first century CE (Nguyễn Thanh Xuân 2012, 8), the eleventh to fourteenth centuries are typically seen as the golden age of Buddhism in Vietnam (Thich Minh Chau 1994). There are several sources for this view, but the most important has been the *Thiền uyển tập anh* (Outstanding figures in the Vietnamese Zen community).[2] The *Thiền uyển tập anh* is constructed as a series of biographies of famous Zen monks in Vietnam from the sixth to the thirteenth centuries and follows the literary genre of the "transmission of the lamp" texts in Chinese Chan Buddhism (C. T. Nguyen 1997, 3). Therefore, the main source for the formulation of a Vietnamese Buddhist history by scholars in the twentieth century is a Zen history.

Whether Zen Buddhism was the dominant religious communication during the Trần dynasty and the most common Buddhist practice among lay Buddhists and monks at the time is not clearly known, but it likely was not. J. C. Cleary (1991) and Cuong Tu Nguyen (1995, 1997) both make the point that Buddhism as it was practiced at that time was not limited to Zen, though there seems to have been an elite effort to portray it that way. Nguyen writes:

> The mere fact that the compiler of the *Thiền Uyển* connects Vietnamese Buddhism to Zen does not necessarily mean that Zen was actually a dominant school of Buddhism in Vietnam or that Zen was the main kind of Buddhism that was first introduced to Vietnam. Rather, it reflects both the absence of a sustained, active, lasting scriptural school in Vietnam, and the compiler's own intention to portray Zen as the original and main stream of Vietnamese Buddhism. (1997, 28)

Cuong Tu Nguyen theorizes that it was done this way to give legitimacy to Vietnamese Buddhism by copying elite Chinese forms. Buddhism, and Buddhist monks, were in a privileged position of power in the Vietnamese court at this time, with several of the Trần kings being fervent Buddhists. Cleary further shows that many of the Zen masters were also very influential; Khuông Việt (933–1011) was honored by Emperor Đinh Tiên Hoàng (924–979) with the title Great Teacher Who Brings Order to Vietnam; Lão was frequently visited by Emperor Lý Thái Tổ (974–1028); Cứu Chỉ was invited to the court of Lý Thái Tông (1000–1054) several times, and when he failed to appear, the emperor went to visit him at his pagoda (Cleary 1991, 105). That Buddhism was prominent at the time is certain, but it does not seem that Zen was as important as the *Thiền uyển tập anh* made it out to be. While the *Thiền uyển tập anh* makes a claim for the prominence of Zen lineages in Vietnam, it is, in fact, a revisionist collection of various voices, which was nonetheless taken in twentieth-century Vietnam to be the authoritative text on Vietnamese Buddhist history. Its authority has largely gone unquestioned because it provided a convenient framework to study the history of Vietnamese Buddhism in the absence of other comprehensive descriptions (C. T. Nguyen 1997, 24).

The Vietnamese elite, or at least the chroniclers, appear to have been enamored of Zen Buddhism, but this elite interest likely did not percolate down to everyday practice for the majority of Buddhists; despite Zen's intellectual fascination, it is doubtful that Zen ever held much importance for everyday practitioners or even for so-called elite practitioners. Even the supposed Zen masters were enmeshed in a Buddhist practice that does not resemble the contemporary view of Zen as being radically individualistic and doggedly focused on enlightenment attained through meditation. Instead, famous monks like Vạn Hạnh and Không Lộ were pictured as engaging in all kinds of magical practices, healing, divination, fortune-telling, exorcisms, manipulation of natural forces, and power over animals (Cleary 1991, 109–113). Cleary suggests that the inclusion of so many stories of supernatural powers and uncanny feats were intended to "establish the credentials of Zen masters and draw attention to their Zen lessons" (Cleary 1991, 113). For this reason, Cleary posits, the presumptions that underlie the categories of "great" versus "little" traditions or elite versus popular religion are incorrect, at least in the context of medieval Vietnamese religion (Cleary 1991, 93–94). Following scholars of Chinese religion such as Watson (1985), Weller (1987), and Hansen (1990), Thien Do makes a similar argument about the artificiality of presuming that elites in Vietnam were somehow less "superstitious" than the general population (T. Do 2003, 10).

Cuong Tu Nguyen goes further than Cleary in expressing skepticism that Zen had much of an influence on most Vietnamese lay or monastic Buddhists. Instead, he argues that the *Thiền uyển tập anh* represents a rhetorical expression of Vietnamese elite fascination with all things Chinese and a concern with appearing equal to the Chinese by mimicking their Buddhist literary forms, particularly transmission-of-the-lamp texts that record the lineages of Chan schools from master to chief disciple. Cuong Tu Nguyen writes:

> The fabrication of the Zen schools in Việt Nam only stems from the efforts of the élites eager to bring orthodoxy to Vietnamese Buddhism. If the Chinese Buddhists in general and the Zen sectarians in particular endeavor to justify their orthodoxy by connecting their own school to an Indian

lineage that can presumably be traced back to the historical Śākyamuni himself, the Vietnamese Buddhists do so by connecting their own school of Chinese Buddhism, which they believe to be orthodox. . . . In this case, since for the medieval Vietnamese élites Zen is *the* legitimate school of Buddhism, Buddhism is Zen *tout court*. (C. T. Nguyen 1995, 113)

While Zen may not have existed as important and enduring schools and lineages or even as determining Buddhist practice in Vietnam, it was certainly important for elite discourses at the time the *Thiền uyển tập anh* was composed. This rhetorical importance takes on a new life in the twentieth century, when Trần Văn Giáp's discovery of the text plays a pivotal role in the construction of a Vietnamese Buddhist identity.

Trần Văn Giáp and the Invention of a Vietnamese Zen Tradition

Zen does not appear to have figured prominently in the heyday of the Buddhist Reform movement in the 1930s to 1950s. There are scattered references to some of the key figures and places that are associated with Zen in Vietnam, especially Mount Yên Tử, but by and large, there does not appear to have been much discussion in their publications. For example, in *Từ bi âm* (The voice of compassion), the reform Buddhist magazine from the south, there were two articles titled "Thiền-tông" (The Zen school) that were matched with another article, "Tịnh-độ-tông" (The Pure Land school), which went for two issues (Bích Liên 1932a, 1932b). Most of the articles about Zen in the Buddhist journals (primarily those in the northern journal *Đuốc tuệ* [The torch of wisdom]), were focused on Buddhist history rather than doctrine or practice. For example, issues 3–4 of *Đuốc tuệ* published an article on the history of the three patriarchs of the Trúc Lâm Zen school (Bùi Đức Triệu 1935a, 1935b), though Zen was barely mentioned, and published a history of the Zen lineage in Vietnam based on the *Thiền uyển tập anh*, serialized over forty-one issues between 1936 and 1939 (Đ.N.T. 1936–1939). However, an article on the Pure Land school leads each of the issues and goes on for several issues thereafter. Zen is also mentioned in a few articles, but mostly in passing.[3]

Thus, from the early reform period up to the 1960s, Zen was not particularly important for most Buddhists in terms of practice or interest, but it became crucial for the construction of its identity and sense of history. In this developing sense of identity, the academy and practicing Buddhists worked in concert. The key figure in this development was Trần Văn Giáp (1902–1973), who constructed a history of Vietnamese Buddhism based on the *Thiền uyển tập anh*.[4]

Like Anagārika Dharmapala, D. T. Suzuki, and other Buddhist reformers in Asia, Trần Văn Giáp was a member of the Western-educated
Asian elite.[5] He was born in the province of Hải Hưng in northern Vietnam to a family of Confucian scholars. As an adolescent, he studied at a
Franco-Vietnamese school in Hanoi (Trường Pháp Việt Yên Phụ), among
other schools, and was eventually hired by the École française d'Extrême
Orient to do bookkeeping (Nguyễn Quang Ân 1996, 9). In 1920, he was officially appointed to work in the library of the École française d'Extrême-
Orient. In 1927, the director sent him to France to translate texts and to
work as a teaching assistant. While in Paris, he studied at the Sorbonne,
writing a thesis titled "Le bouddhisme en Annam, des origines au XIIIe
siècle" (Buddhism in Annam from the beginning to the thirteenth century) and based on the *Thiền uyển tập anh,* which he had found by accident in the private collection of a retired Vietnamese scholar just before
leaving to study in France (C. T. Nguyen 1995, 83n3; 1997, 444n23). He later
published it in the *Bulletin de l'École Français d'Extrême Orient* in 1932 under the same title (Trần Văn Giáp 1932).

In translating and presenting the *Thiền uyển tập anh* as the definitive
Vietnamese Buddhist history, Trần Văn Giáp has had a lasting impact on
the scholarly view of the history of Vietnamese Buddhism, but more importantly on the self-understanding of Vietnamese Buddhists' own religion. The result of Trần Văn Giáp's interpretation has been a reimagining
of Zen as a tradition that is central to the Vietnamese Buddhists'
self-understanding:

> Feeling themselves part of this "Zen," this cluster of Zen-derived styles
> and lore, seeking self-understanding in terms of a view of Buddhist his-
> tory that makes Zen the paramount achievement, these would-be adher-
> ents of Zen in Vietnam have understood themselves as part of Zen history
> and by so doing have formed an imagined community. A text like the
> *Thiền Uyển* is a site for this imagined community, where its tone and
> style, the tales of its exemplars, its landmarks and history are set out in
> convincingly coherent fashion—and with great artistry and depth. The
> *Thiền Uyển* can connect its readers to each other and their imagined past,
> letting them imagine themselves as part of Zen, and Zen as the core of the
> transmission of Buddhism in Vietnam. (C. T. Nguyen 1997, 8)

While most accounts of Trần Văn Giáp focus on him as a scholar employed by the l'École française d'Extrême-Orient, and although his writings focus primarily on Hán-Nôm scholarship and historical work on
China, his portrayal of Vietnamese Buddhist history may well have been
influenced by his involvement in Buddhism. Not long after his return to

Vietnam in 1932, he joined the Tonkin Buddhist Association, the northern Vietnamese manifestation of the Buddhist Reform movement. As a writer, he actively contributed to the main reform publication in Hanoi, *Đuốc Tuệ*, and was a member of the editorial staff (Nguyễn Đại Đồng 2008, 53). On November 18, 1935, he made a request of the administrative committee of the Buddhist association to move forward with the construction of a library (*Đuốc tuệ* 1935, 31). He also gave public lectures at Quán Sứ Pagoda.[6] In 1934, *Viên âm*, the main journal from central Vietnam, printed Trần Văn Giáp's paper given at the musée Louis Finot (today the National Museum of Vietnamese History in Hanoi), which outlines the history of Buddhism in Vietnam following the format and content of his seminal essay that was published in *Bulletin de l'École française d'Extrême Orient* two years earlier. The article published in *Viên âm* was entirely in French and outlined the Zen schools that were recorded in the *Thiền uyển tập anh* (Trần Văn Giáp 1934a, 1934b). His close involvement with the Reform movement would indicate that he shared many of their concerns, such as increasing knowledge of Buddhism by lay Buddhists and propagating Buddhist orthodoxy.

The impact that Trần Văn Giáp's work had on Vietnamese scholarship, as well as the formation of a Vietnamese Buddhist identity, is hard to overstate. Virtually every description of Buddhism in Vietnam has been either an expansion or an abridgement of Trần Văn Giáp's work (C. T. Nguyen 1995, 82).[7] The lack of critical and sustained work on Buddhism in Vietnam means that Trần Văn Giáp's portrayal still holds considerable sway (C. T. Nguyen 1997, 24–25).

The Heirs of Buddhist Reform in the South

In the 1960s, Vietnamese Buddhism became truly international as transpacific movements became especially relevant, and it is in this period that we start to see an increase in publications on Zen in Vietnamese.[8] The works of D. T. Suzuki, who spent much of his life teaching Americans about Zen, were translated and became accessible in South Vietnam.[9] His work reaffirmed standard views of Zen as being the essence of the Buddha's teachings (C. T. Nguyen 1997, 343–344n4). Nguyen and Barber, however, additionally note that "some Buddhists . . . used this popularity as an excuse for rejecting traditional rituals" (Nguyen and Barber 1998, 310n18). At this time, Vietnamese also became increasingly aware of the attraction of Zen in the West. The rising fascination in Zen led to an increase in iterations of historical studies of Vietnamese Buddhism, particularly by monks and practitioners, that were based on Trần Văn Giáp's view of Buddhism as Zen. In 1960, the reformist monk Thích Mật Thể published *Việt Nam Phật giáo sử lược* (A brief history of Vietnamese Buddhism), which translated the ideas of Trần Văn Giáp from French into Vietnamese. In 1967, Nguyễn Đăng Thục published *Thiền học Việt Nam* (Vietnamese Zen studies), followed in 1973 by Thích Nhất Hạnh's book *Việt Nam Phật giáo sử luận* (History of Buddhism in Vietnam), written under the pen name Nguyễn Lang.

The coalescing of increased awareness of the global attraction of Zen and the modernist discourses with which it was being presented, along with an increased awareness of the deep roots of Zen in Vietnam (as imagined as they may have been), acted as a catalyst. Suddenly, Zen went from being an elite history constructed through the lens of Zen schools and lineages to a way that Buddhism could be practiced. Two individuals were particularly important in setting this in motion, and for both, their international experiences combined with their reformist educations were essential factors in establishing a Vietnamese Zen practice. Both, notably, did not do this until they emigrated permanently to the West. These two leaders are Thích Thiên Ân and Thích Nhất Hạnh.

Thích Thiên Ân

Thích Thiên Ân was born in central Vietnam in 1925 and entered the monastery as an adolescent. He studied at the Buddhist Training Institute at Báo Quốc Pagoda, which had been set up by the Buddhist reformers. His classmates—Thích Nhất Hạnh, Thích Thiện Minh, Thích Chơn Trí, Thích Minh Châu, and Thích Mãn Giác, among others—were to become notable monks active in the Struggle movement in South Vietnam protesting against the war (Thích Mãn Giác 1984a, 41). A gifted student, Thích Thiên Ân received royal support to study in Japan, eventually earning his doctorate in literature from Waseda University in 1960. When he returned to Vietnam, he intended to start a Buddhist university, but his superiors told him that he was not yet ready, so he went back to study at a Rinzai Zen monastery in Kamakura for another two years (Thích Đồng Bổn 2002). It seems likely that he stayed at Engaku-ji, a reformist pagoda where D. T. Suzuki studied Zen under the Japanese reformer Shaku Sōen.[10]

After briefly returning to Vietnam, Thích Thiên Ân went to Los Angeles in 1966 as an exchange professor to teach linguistics and philosophy at UCLA. His students at the university asked him to teach them meditation, which led to the founding of the International Buddhist Meditation Center (Thích Mãn Giác 1984b, 44–45), where he ordained Western monks and nuns in the Lâm tế (Rinzai) Vietnamese Zen lineage. His most famous work in English, *Buddhism and Zen in Vietnam*, was published in 1975 and should be seen in light of his work to establish a Vietnamese Zen lineage in America.

Thích Thiên Ân was a product of the Buddhist Reform movement. As such, he not only placed Zen in the center of Vietnamese Buddhism but made it the defining feature of the Vietnamese as a people: "Zen comes closest to expressing the Vietnamese character, and as such, their attitude in all walks of life can best be described as a 'Zen outlook'" (Thích Thiên Ân 1975a, 27). In his book on Vietnamese Zen, Thích Thiên Ân singles out Lâm tế as being the most important school for Vietnam (Thích Thiên Ân 1975a, 11). While direct causality cannot be proven, it seems likely that his association with Lâm tế comes from his time in Japan, particularly the two-year period that he spent in the early 1960s in a Japanese Rinzai temple. Nguyen and Barber make a point of emphasizing that Thích Thiên Ân was "trained as a Zen master in the Rinzai tradition of Japanese Buddhism" (Nguyen and Barber 1998, 131). What is clearer is that he did not present himself as a Zen teacher until he moved to the United States. Most of his writings before emigrating focus on Japanese culture, philosophy, and education.[11]

Thích Nhất Hạnh

Without a doubt, the most internationally famous Vietnamese monk today is Thích Nhất Hạnh. He was born in central Vietnam and attended the same reformist school for young monks as Thích Thiên Ân. In 1961, he went to study first at Princeton University and then Columbia, where D. T. Suzuki had been a lecturer from 1951 to 1957. While there, he noted in his journal that Zen would be more effective for reaching an American audience:

> You know Nguyên Hưng, the teachings and organization of Pure Land Buddhism are no different from the teachings of Protestantism, both focus on power of forgiveness. So, this kind of religiosity is not new to the British and the Americans. In addition to their interpretation of the Christian doctrine, there are so many theological seminaries, and so many excellent preachers. Meanwhile, the Pure Land organization here lacks educational and training facilities, and they tend to clumsily imitate [Christian forms], which makes us look incompetent and backwards. In fact, the American people have an independent spirit and don't like to rely on other people. Therefore, it is certain that a teaching like the fourfold teachings [giáo lý tứ lục] of Zen will be very suitable for them. The teachings of Zen are completely based on self-reliance as a way to build, develop and enlighten oneself, while Christianity and Pure Land teachings recognize one's inefficiencies and emphasize the saving power of outside forces. So, Nguyên Hưng, you won't be surprised that Pure Land

Buddhism has not been very successful here. We are also not surprised that Zen philosophy has caught on fire here. Professor [D. T.] Suzuki has struck a chord in this country. When you live in a society that is so frenetic and raucous, of course people crave the cool, fresh calm offered by Zen. If you lived here, Nguyên Hưng, it would be obvious to you. (Thích Nhất Hạnh [1966] 2006, 135–136)[12]

Returning to Vietnam in 1964, Thích Nhất Hạnh wrote, published, and became involved in refugee relief efforts. He founded the School of Youth for Social Services, edited the Buddhist magazine *Hải triều âm* (Sound of the rising tide), the main publication of the Unified Buddhist Church, and established the Lá Bối Publishing House. In 1965, he founded Tiếp Hiện (the Order of Interbeing) as an engaged Buddhist organization. The organization, which has become one of the most internationally successful organizations, includes both lay Buddhists and monastics (King 1996, 323) and both Vietnamese and Western adherents. His writings from this period were primarily about peace rather than Zen, meditation, or the mindfulness practice that later became his hallmark.

It is notable that like Thích Thiên Ân, Thích Nhất Hạnh does not seem to have sustained any concerted interest in Zen in his writings before moving to the West. His first work focusing on Zen, *Nẻo vào Thiền học* (The way into Zen studies), was published in 1971 and translated two years later as *Clefs pour le Zen* and a year after that into English as *Zen Keys*. The first volume of his most famous writing on the history of Vietnamese Buddhism, *Việt Nam Phật giáo sử luận* (History of Buddhism in Vietnam), was published in 1973 under a pen name, based on Trần Văn Giáp's earlier account (Nguyễn Lang [1973] 2000). While in Vietnam, Thích Nhất Hạnh's main concern and innovation was engaged Buddhism. He was known as a poet, a writer, an educator, a relief-work organizer, and a peace activist, but there is no evidence that he was seen in any way as a Zen adept. Yet this is precisely what he is noted for in the West. Indeed, while he still speaks of peace and has undertaken actions like the peaceful protests against the American war in Iraq, the principal activities of the numerous groups in his organization, the Order of Interbeing, are meditation and listening to Dharma talks. He has maintained notoriety for his peace activism, but it is his ideas of meditation and mindfulness that draw large numbers of Western and overseas Vietnamese followers. Thích Nhất Hạnh thus appears to have two personae: the peace activist, which was most apparent during the first part of his life in Vietnam, up to 1966, and the Zen master, which is how he is mainly viewed in the West (Temprano 2012). His version of Zen, however, is not particularly rooted in Vietnamese forms of Buddhism (Nguyen and Barber 1998, 131).

Both Thích Thiên Ân and Thích Nhất Hạnh are exceptional individuals, and both sought to reach out to a Western audience by presenting an interpretation of Vietnamese Buddhism that relied heavily on rhetorical traditions of Zen in Vietnam. Both also came to the West at a time when there was no real diasporic Vietnamese community; their initial audiences were young Western hippies, and only after the war ended in 1975 did their audiences expand to include Vietnamese refugees. The teachings of both men have been distinctly modernist, drawing on many of the same themes that made D. T. Suzuki's writings attractive in America. The Buddhism that they presented to a Western audience was rooted in global imaginaries of Buddhism that had been strongly influenced by Western orientalist interpretations of Buddhism and by the reconstructions of Buddhism by Asian reformers. Zen became attractive because it fit well with the predilections of modernist Buddhism, which Donald Lopez describes as focusing on meditation as modeled by the Buddha. He argues that this focus allows modern Buddhists to ignore the rituals central to Buddhist practice in Asia and provides an experience that is not rooted in sectarian or doctrinal formulations. He writes, "Although found in much of modern Buddhism, this view was put forth most strongly in the case of Zen, moving it outside the larger categories of Buddhism and even religion into a universal sensibility of the sacred in the secular" (Lopez 2002, xxxvii–xxxviii).

The process by which both Thích Thiên Ân and Thích Nhất Hạnh recreated themselves as Zen masters in the West is not entirely clear. From their writings, both held Zen in high esteem, but only after emigrating did they write books about the history of Buddhism in Vietnam following Trần Văn Giáp's model (i.e., portraying the history of Buddhism in Vietnam as a description of Zen lineages). Both were educated overseas—Thích Thiên Ân in Japan at Toyo and Waseda University and Thích Nhất Hạnh at Princeton and Columbia Universities in the United States. It seems likely that both were drawn to Zen because of these experiences. Thích Thiên Ân studied Japanese Rinzai and later met the demand for Zen by his Western students by putting a Vietnamese veneer on his Japanese training. Thích Nhất Hạnh became aware of Western interest in Zen and in D. T. Suzuki and appears to have been influenced by Suzuki's writings.

Thích Thanh Từ

Thích Thanh Từ was part of the same cohort of young monks in Saigon in the 1960s as Thích Nhất Hạnh and Thích Thiên Ân. Starting with a Zen center in Vũng Tàu, not far from Ho Chi Minh City, Thích Thanh Từ took it upon himself to revive Zen in Vietnam, and particularly the Trúc Lâm school.[13] Since that time, his organization has expanded throughout Vietnam and internationally, with major Zen monasteries and smaller centers. Overseas, Trúc Lâm monasteries and Zen centers have been established in Australia, the United States, Canada, and France.[14] Thích Thanh Từ was not prominent during the 1960s and 1970s, when monks such as Thích Thiên Ân and Thích Nhất Hạnh established themselves as proponents of Zen. Perhaps this is because while Thích Thiên Ân and Thích Nhất Hạnh established themselves as Zen masters overseas in the United States and Europe, Thích Thanh Từ never studied overseas and never emigrated, so never gained international prominence.

Thích Thanh Từ was born Trần Hữu Phước on July 24, 1924, in a small village near the city of Cần Thơ, a major urban center in the Mekong Delta. The available biography says that his father was a scholar and that the family followed Cao Đài, a syncretic new religion founded in southern Vietnam in the 1920s. He came from a poor family, but he showed great promise. He was quiet, thoughtful, bookish, and respectful toward his parents. When he was around nine years old, he went with his father to Sân Tiên Pagoda on Ba Thê Mountain for a memorial ritual (*lễ cầu siêu*) for a relative. When Trần Hữu Phước heard the sound of the pagoda bell, he had a religious experience and, according to the official biography, spontaneously composed a poem:

> On such a pleasant place as this mountain,
> Where the talented can find joy and leisure,
> The sound of the wooden fish awakens humans from their dreams;
> The ringing bell is echoing their pains and sufferings! (Tịnh Lạc Am n.d.)[15]

From that time, Trần Hữu Phước felt called to become a monk. On the fifteenth of July 1949, he entered Phật Quang Pagoda and was renamed Thích Thanh Từ.[16] He studied the sutras, Vinaya, and Abhidharma at the monastic school at his home pagoda, and in 1951, he entered middle school. Later that year, he followed his master, Thiện Hoa, to Phước Hậu Pagoda. In 1953, he went to Saigon and began studies at the Buddhist School of Southern Vietnam (Phật Học Đường Nam Việt) at Ấn Quang Pagoda, finishing his advanced studies in 1959.[17] After graduating, Thích Thanh Từ went on to hold several academic positions in Saigon, including teaching at Phật Học Đường Dược Sư (Dược Sư Buddhist school) and Quán viện Phật Học Viện Huệ Nghiêm (Huệ Nghiêm Buddhist college). He also taught at Vạn Hạnh University, the main Buddhist university set up in 1964, a year after the formation of the Giáo hội Phật giáo Việt Nam Thống nhất (Unified Buddhist church of Vietnam). Among the group of founders was Thích Thiên Ân and Thích Nhất Hạnh.

In 1964, he decided that this life was not satisfying and that he had fulfilled his obligations to his master, so he made up his mind to go into seclusion to focus on his spiritual advancement. In 1965, he traveled to Japan and was confronted during his voyage by the more distinct schools of Buddhism and felt that that the Pure Land path was not appropriate for him. He decided instead to follow the path of meditation and to learn more about Zen. He built Pháp Lạc Meditation Center in 1966 on Tương Kỳ Mountain near Vũng Tàu, which began as little more than a grass hut. After two years, he announced, "If I don't thoroughly discern the Way, I won't leave the meditation chamber" (Hoang 2006). After a lengthy period of study, writing, and meditation, he felt that he was ready. In 1971, he offered his first study program to ten students, during which he taught Buddhist sutras and Buddhist history and gave meditation instruction. After three years, he offered a second program at three locations, Linh Quang, Chân Không, and Bát Nhã Monasteries.

Thích Thanh Từ continued to teach and write and to expand his organization. Today there are around eighteen Zen monasteries in Vietnam and ten monasteries or Zen centers in the United States, three in Canada, one in France, and six in Australia.[18] Most followers in the overseas centers seem to be ethnic Vietnamese, though I have interviewed one Canadian of European background at the center in Ontario.[19]

There is not much information to help understand the early impulse of Thích Thanh Từ to embrace Zen and to establish an organization that evokes Trần Nhân Tông by reviving the Trúc Lâm Zen school. Thích Thanh Từ does not appear to have been prominent during the pre-Renovation period, with few mentions of him in Buddhist journals of the time. He contributed translations of an article by Taixu about Buddhist developments over the previous thirty years that was serialized over three issues in the Buddhist magazine *Phật giáo Việt Nam,* at the time edited by Thích Nhất Hạnh, but they are not related to Zen (Thích Thanh Từ 1957–1958). Thích Nhất Hạnh mentions Thích Thanh Từ as being a presence at the Phương Bôi hermitage in the period from 1956 to 1960 in *Nẻo về của ý* (1966) (later translated as *Fragrant Palm Leaves: Journals 1962–1966* [1998a, 17]).[20] I have found references to him in only four issues of the magazine *Tạp chí Phật học từ quảng* (Merciful light journal of Buddhist studies), announcing a Dharma talk and meditation courses (*Tạp chí Phật học từ quảng* 1974, issues 252, 254, 256, 258). Two other issues (*Tạp chí Phật học từ quảng* 1974, issues 260, 261) make an appeal for donations to build a road to the Zen center that he was establishing (Thiền viện Chơn Không). I could find no other mentions of Thích Thanh Từ in writings of the period, when Buddhist activism was prominent in South Vietnam. Although associated with Ấn Quang Pagoda, Thích Thanh Từ does not appear to have been involved as an activist, or at least was not prominent, though Ấn Quang was the center of the Struggle movement in the 1960s. I have not, for example, come across his name in US intelligence records of that time, and he is not described in other English language sources that deal with that period (for example, Schecter [1967] and Topmiller [2002]). Consequently, it is difficult to objectively determine what Thích Thanh Từ was doing in the war period up to around the start of the Renovation in the late 1980s.

Equally hazy is how Thích Thanh Từ began to practice meditation and became interested in Zen. He offers a clue in an essay titled *Phương pháp tu Tịnh độ tông và Thiền tông* (Ways of practice in the Pure Land and Zen schools), in which he describes an event while traveling in 1965 (Thường Chiếu n.d.) that illustrated to him that Vietnamese Buddhism disappointedly lacked the distinct schools and teachings of Buddhism in other countries, and especially in comparison with Japan.[21] He was also ashamed when he encountered Vietnamese traveling to Japan to study Zen, when in his mind, Vietnam had a long history of Zen (Thích Thanh Từ n.d., 11–12).

REVITALIZED TRÚC LÂM

Regardless of how Thích Thanh Từ actually learned about meditation or how he established himself, a few things are clear. First, he does not lay claim to being part of a Zen lineage or to being taught about Zen at his home pagoda; instead, he is forthright about coming to the decision on his own after becoming disenchanted with the usual Buddhist practices. He questioned why his own teachers followed devotional Buddhism, despite the example of the Buddha in meditation, with the sutras and sastras, "all teaching about meditation" (Thích Thanh Từ 1997, 22). He became convinced that Zen is the expression of Buddhism that most closely reflects the original teachings of the Buddha. However, he seems to have been largely self-taught. Second, he was particularly taken with the idea of an indigenous Zen that was based on a strong sense of national pride. This link between Buddhism and nationalism is ubiquitous in the writings of the Vietnamese reformers but also in the reform movements elsewhere in Asia.

It is therefore not surprising that in wanting to reestablish Zen in Vietnam, Thích Thanh Từ gravitated toward Trúc Lâm as the only Vietnamese school of Zen. The symbolic value of Trúc Lâm in Vietnam is such that Thích Thanh Từ is not the only one to evoke it. For example, the Hòa Hảo sect, a Buddhist-based and peasant-oriented new religious movement from the Mekong Delta in the south, evoked Trúc Lâm as part of their identity, with some members claiming descent from it (Woodside 1976, 188). From a nationalist perspective, Trúc Lâm's importance is based on its being founded by a national hero, King Trần Nhân Tông, the third king of the Trần dynasty, who repelled two of the major historical invasions by the Chinese (under Mongolian rule) in the late thirteenth century. The story of Trần Nhân Tông and his founding of Trúc Lâm is symbolically central to Thích Thanh Từ's organization so is worth recounting here.

Buddhism was an influential force in the courts of the Trần dynasty (1225–1400). Trần Thái Tông (1218–1277) became king at the age of eight, with the task of governing being left to a regent. Thus relieved from duty, Trần Thái Tông devoted himself to Buddhist studies. As time passed, Trần Thái Tông was uncomfortable with the ethical contradictions involved with ruling. At the age of twenty, he decided to retire from state affairs and become a monk. He traveled to Mount Yên Tử to practice Zen under the Zen master Phù Vân (dates unknown). On learning of Trần Thái Tông's absence, the prime minister assembled a search party made up of the royal family and members of the imperial court. One story relates that when they found him and tried to persuade him to come back with them, he at first refused but finally succumbed after the search party threatened to kill themselves if he did not return with them. In another version of the story, Trần Thái Tông desperately said to his cabinet, "Where the king lives, the cabinet lives too. We must build a palace next to the pagoda." Master Phù Vân, however, stepped forward and counseled his disciple that the Buddha did not live on Mount Yên Tử but in his heart, so there was no reason for him to stay there. Accepting this, Trần Thái Tông then accepted his responsibility as king and returned to the capital. He went on to become a king noted for his wisdom, combining Buddhist and Confucian teachings, which he felt were complementary.

Under Trần Thái Tông's rule, the first Mongol invasion of 1257 was repelled, although the capital of Thăng Long (present day Hanoi) was temporarily taken by the Mongol forces. Trần Thái Tông wrote several books on Buddhism during his life. While most are lost, several still exist, most notably *Khóa hư lục* (Instructions on emptiness), about which Thích Thanh Từ wrote a commentary (1996). Trần Thái Tông reigned for thirty-two years before passing the throne to his son, Trần Thánh Tông (1240–1290), also a devout Buddhist.

The third king of the Trần dynasty, Trần Nhân Tông, was also a devout Buddhist from his early years. He reluctantly assumed the throne at the age of twenty-one (in 1279) and was apparently an effective king. In 1284, the Mongols once again attempted to invade Đại Việt (present-day Vietnam), this time with a force of two hundred thousand. Knowing of the Mongols' intent, Trần Nhân Tông assembled his court to ask what course of action should be taken. With the court's unanimous vote for military resistance, Trần Nhân Tông put the brilliant general Trần Hưng Đạo (1213–1300) in charge of the defense of the kingdom.[22] The Mongols were defeated after six months of fighting, and only a few thousand Mongols were said to have returned to China alive. The Mongols invaded again in 1287 with a force of half a million and were defeated under Trần Hưng Đạo's leadership for the last time after a four-month campaign. Trần Hưng Đạo himself has become an object of national veneration and worship (see Phạm Quỳnh Phương 2006, 2007, 2009).

In 1299, at the age of forty-one, Trần Nhân Tông passed the throne to his son, and in 1301, he retired to Mount Yên Tử. However, he remained politically active in the roles of Buddhist patriarch and court advisor. In these roles, he sought to build Buddhist culture in the country. Most importantly, he united Vietnamese Buddhism and founded the Trúc Lâm Zen Sect on Mount Yên Tử. Trúc Lâm Zen still has national significance today as the only school of Zen founded in Vietnam rather than being transmitted from China or India. Trần Nhân Tông's two Dharma successors, Pháp Loa (1284–1330) and Huyền Quang (1254–1334), also lived on Mount Yên Tử. Trần Nhân Tông's activities are inscribed into the pilgrim's landscape on Mount Yên Tử, and the famous sites on the way up the mountain are intimately connected with his life and influence.

Pháp Loa, the second patriarch of Trúc Lâm Zen, expanded the Trúc Lâm school, gaining fifteen thousand monks and two hundred monasteries (Thích Minh Châu 1994). However, with the death of the third patriarch, Huyền Quang, the Trúc Lâm school stopped expansion and ceased to exist beyond attempts of some of the disciples of the first three patriarchs to establish scattered groups and periodic but unsuccessful attempts to revive the Trúc Lâm sect. Of these, however, the historical record provides no substantive information beyond a list of names (C. T. Nguyen 1997, 342n). Cuong Tu Nguyen writes that the main importance of the Trúc Lâm school is that it "marked the first serious effort to establish a Zen school in medieval Vietnam" (1997, 20).

The Zen Brand

While Thích Thanh Từ does not claim to be part of a direct lineage transmitting an unbroken Trúc Lâm tradition, he does claim to be reviving it for contemporary Vietnamese. In his words:

> When I established the Zen Monastery, I looked carefully at the history of Vietnamese Buddhism to find the key ideas to fit the current situation in our country; to choose an appropriate anchor for us. We practice, propagate and disseminate the Buddhist Dharma for people to follow. We do this in order to be appropriate for the spirit of our people in the present. When I was deciding what to choose, I immediately turned to Buddhism from the Trần period for its outstanding qualities. It was a time worthy of us emulating in our practice, worthy of spreading, and also for showing our dedication to the nation. We must use all of our ability and virtue to spread it to the people of our country, in order to strengthen our children and our beautiful youths. That is why we picked the Buddhism of Trần as our central anchor. (Thích Thanh Từ 2000a)[23]

He has worked to promote Zen Buddhism in Vietnam by resurrecting a native Vietnamese Zen school and by building an organization and a system of monasteries throughout Vietnam and overseas. His organization is only informal; officially, there is only one Buddhist organization in Vietnam, Giáo hội Phật giáo Việt Nam (the Vietnamese Buddhist association). Nonetheless, Thích Thanh Từ's is a substantial organization that has a clear plan to spread Vietnamese Zen. There is a corporate unity that ties the monasteries together, and monks frequently travel or transfer between them. The organization is also quite systematic in the iconography, symbols, rituals, and practices that mark it as uniquely modern in its approach.

The pervasiveness of references to Zen are such that it could easily be seen as following a marketing strategy of branding, with iconography and symbols systematically evoking Vietnamese Zen as a tradition. The youth group attached to Sùng Phúc, for example, is called the Đoàn Thanh Thiếu Niên Phật Tử Trần Thái Tông (Trần Thái Tông Buddhist youth group), named after the grandfather of the founder of the Trúc Lâm Zen school. There was a two-day youth jamboree held at the end of October in 2011 at Sùng Phúc, and the event was named after the Vietnamese "Zen master" Vạn Hạnh (938–1025). The most common representation of the Buddha at Sùng Phúc has him holding a flower, evoking the famous Flower Sermon during which the Buddha transmitted wisdom directly and without words to his follower Mahākāśyapa by holding up a flower. As the mythical origin of Zen, this image holds special meaning for the Trúc Lâm organization and appears repeatedly in statues and icons throughout its monasteries and centers. The image and murals around Sùng Phúc (explored further in the next chapter) systematically evoke Trần Nhân Tông, the Zen patriarchs, and Trúc Lâm more generally as a form of Buddhism both uniquely Vietnamese and uniquely suited for the contemporary context.

Dress and practice are also standardized. Lay adherents wear gray robes, which is the standard dress for lay Buddhists in southern Vietnam but is distinctive in northern Vietnam, where lay Buddhists usually wear brown robes. The daily schedule and the main liturgy (the Penitence Rite, Sám Hối Sáu Căn) is standardized and published in books like *Các nghi lễ trong thiền viện* (Ceremonies of the Zen monastery) (Thích Tỉnh Thiền 2010) and *Nghi thức sám hối và tụng giới (của Phật tử)* (The rite of contrition and the precepts [for Buddhists]) (Thích Thanh Từ 2009a), available in the bookstore at Sùng Phúc as well as on the internet. It is also available in English, translated and distributed by Tu Tam Hoang, one of Thích Thanh Từ's followers in the United States (Thích Thanh Từ 2002b). The meditation form used at the monastery includes playing a recording that tells meditators what they should be doing, and the instructions are published in a booklet written by Thích Thanh Từ, which features photographs of him in the meditation poses and engaged in the rubbing exercises practiced after the conclusion of meditation (Thích Thanh Từ 2010a).

The systematic presentation of Trúc Lâm serves to highlight some distinct features of the Trúc Lâm brand, giving it authority and legitimacy by first tying it to a Zen lineage, which they describe as reaching back to the Buddha through transmission to China by Bodhidharma and continued by the Zen patriarchs in China. Bodhidharma, the mythical founder who brought Zen to China, is frequently evoked, as are the Chan patriarchs of China and Vietnam. More importantly, the historical Buddha is the central focus as an example of self-cultivation leading to enlightenment and the fountainhead of transmission of the truth expressed in the teachings in Zen. Thích Thanh Từ has written several books about the Zen patriarchs of China and the connection leading from Śākyamuni to the founding of Zen in Vietnam.

Trúc Lâm employs Zen as a brand that is reiterated in a systematic way, suggesting links with neoliberal approaches toward the self. Schwenkel and Leshkowich argue that in the Vietnamese context, "what counts as 'neoliberal' . . . is neither fixed nor wholly uncontested; it remains a partial, unfolding, and contingent project that is more discernible in some cultural and economic domains than others; and yet it appears as a pivotal social force that motivates particular desires, actions, and beliefs" (Schwenkel and Leshkowich 2012, 381). Neoliberal discourses are shaping models for personhood that stress self-regulation and self-cultivation as a moral obligation and as imparting moral value to self-improvement in a way that naturalizes "middle classness" (Schwenkel and Leshkowich 2012, 382, 396). While I will not be directly dealing with the resonances between the strengthening and naturalizing of neoliberal values, it is worth keeping in mind how the attraction to Zen also fits in with the development of post-socialist ways of being.

The emergence of Zen Buddhism in Vietnam since the Renovation is ironic. Cuong Tu Nguyen is correct, I believe, in his assessment that the claim that Zen was the core of Vietnamese Buddhism was largely a case of cultural invention. Now, however, the efforts to reform Buddhism that began in the late nineteenth and early twentieth centuries and was transmitted to the West by Buddhist missionaries and academics have brought the imagined tradition into reality. A major part of this has been the portrayal of Zen as an authentic and pure Buddhism that evokes the core of the Buddha's teachings and practice. The story of Zen as central to Vietnamese Buddhism built slowly through the twentieth century. Trần Văn Giáp's popularization of the *Thiền uyển tập anh* was influential in rediscovering Vietnamese Buddhist history, and it gave Zen in particular a privileged position. The histories written subsequent to Trần Văn Giáp's article were, as Cuong Tu Nguyen points out, largely a repetition of his work and served to reinforce the Zen narrative. At first, this historiography and its privileging of Zen does not appear to have had a wide impact beyond scholarly interest, which had, in turn, been influenced by the nationalist agendas of Buddhist reformers. In Buddhist magazines closely associated with Buddhist reformers, there was little mention of Zen beyond some historical notes, which were also taken largely from Trần Văn Giáp's work.

It appears that an interest in Zen practice became more forceful in the 1960s and took place entirely in the south. Thích Nhất Hạnh first expressed interest in Zen after he studied in the United States. Thích Thiên Ân's appreciation for Zen came after his studies in Japan. Even then, these two leading Zen monks do not seem to have reconstructed themselves as Zen masters until they permanently emigrated to the West. All indications were that this was done to establish themselves in the Western context, where Zen and meditation had caught the fascination of Western converts.

These two figures who are so closely associated with Vietnamese Zen in the twentieth century are, perhaps not by coincidence, both from Huế. The connection with the former imperial capital is not clear, but Huế does not seem in any way to have been a center of Zen. Rather, it seems likely that the close association between the Confucian-educated elite and a Chan aesthetic that meshed with the Nguyễn dynasty court's heavy reliance on Chinese cultural forms for legitimacy (Woodside 1971) had a residual presence in Huế that may have been stronger than in other areas. In any case, as Thích Thiên Ân pointed out early in his writing career, the presence of Zen even in Huế was not well developed (Thích Thiện Ân 1963a, 136).

It would be a fair assertion, based on information available, that the rise in interest in Zen springs partly from the recognition that it had wide currency in the West and in Japan, where it was seen by Buddhist reformers to be uniquely suitable with science and modernity.[24] D. T. Suzuki's writings seem to have had as much of an impression on the development of the new Zen in Vietnam as any historical Vietnamese Buddhist figure who had been identified as a Zen master. Indeed, both Thích Thiên Ân and Thích Nhất Hạnh appear to have been deeply influenced by D. T. Suzuki.

With Thích Thanh Từ and the rise of his distinctly nationalistic Trúc Lâm Zen school, a fully revisionist understanding of Zen in Vietnam as equal to Chan and Japanese Zen took life. In the next chapter, we turn to Sùng Phúc Monastery to see how the Zen missionaries from southern Vietnam have returned Trúc Lâm Zen to the north, where it had been born centuries before. Zen has come to be singled out in Vietnamese Buddhism as particularly valuable for its radical individualism, iconoclasm, and demythologization. Correspondingly, devotionalism, usually identified as Pure Land Buddhism, has been devalued as feudal and superstitious. The reformers of the 1920s and 1930s parsed religion and superstition, but it was largely an elite enterprise, and throughout the twentieth century, few Buddhists in Vietnam took up their discourses or put them into practice. More recent trends, however, show that these modernist discourses are gaining ground with the help of the government's and the media's continual criticism of superstition and by neoliberal attitudes toward the self. These discourses are further popularized by figures such as Thích Thanh Từ and Thích Nhất Hạnh and, aided by information flowing more freely than in the past, through Buddhist publications and the internet.

The reformist interpretation of Buddhism, cleansed of local practices and beliefs, that Thích Thanh Từ is promoting is very much in line with Thích Nhất Hạnh's teachings on mindfulness. Thích Thanh Từ's teachings do not focus on the same themes of ecumenist Buddhism, but the Zen Buddhism that he is teaching has striking similarities with Western forms that demythologize Buddhism and accentuate the individualistic aspects of Zen meditation.

||||||||

CHAPTER TWO

The Sùng Phúc Zen Monastery

I first visited Sùng Phúc in 2004 at the beginning of a six-week trip to Hanoi. The monastery had taken over control of a village pagoda and had built their monastery on the site. At the time of my visit, the main shrine of the original pagoda was still there, along with the lotus pond and several of the outbuildings. The overall impression I had was that Sùng Phúc resembled the norm for pagodas in northern Vietnam except for the simplicity of the main altar, which had only a large central statue of the historical Buddha, Śākyamuni (*thích ca mâu ni*), and a few other statues behind it instead of the usual array of statues of Buddhist saints, buddhas, bodhisattvas, and sometimes non-Buddhist deities. To either side of the central altar were sub-altars dedicated to Kṣitigarbha (Địa Tạng) and Guanyin, or Avalokiteśvara (Quan Âm). This pattern, although unusual in northern Vietnam, is standard in the south. It seemed cleansed of many of the elements that would commonly mark the pagoda as northern Vietnamese. Especially remarkable was the omission of a shrine dedicated to the mother goddesses (*nhà mẫu*) that is present on the premises of almost all pagodas in northern Vietnam and is typically located behind the main sanctum. The shrine shows the syncretic nature of religious practice in northern Vietnam, since it is where the spirit-possession practices (*hầu thánh* or *lên đồng*) associated with Đạo Tứ Phủ (the religion of the four palaces) take place.[1] While many Buddhists in Vietnam explained to me that this cult is not Buddhist, expressing a modernist understanding of differentiated religions, they also noted that it is complementary and essential to the spiritual and material well-being of the Vietnamese (Soucy 2012, chapters 1 and 2).

Toward the back of the complex was an even more radical departure . from regular pagodas: a large, two-storey wooden meditation hall that dominated the grounds. This meditation hall was unique in Vietnam in my experience, more closely resembling meditation halls from the Chan monasteries in China.[2] The first floor held a dining hall, and on the second floor was a large open room surrounded completely by an open balcony. At the far end of the room was a small statue of Śākyamuni, about one foot high, covered by a glass case with a pagoda roof. In front of the Buddha was a small replica of the pillars at the famous stupa in Sanchi, India. Other than this altar, the room was striking in its lack of the ornamentation normally found in Vietnamese Buddhist spaces.

At the time of my visit, the monastery's intention was to acquire more land to expand the complex to accommodate their growing number of practitioners. Indeed, by the time I returned in 2011 for more sustained research, they had accomplished this goal, transforming what I thought was already a large assemblage of buildings (relative to standard pagodas) into something so monumental that it reminded me of a lesser version of the massive Foguang Shan complex in southern Taiwan rather than anything I had seen in Vietnam, even in the south. Buildings that once existed had vanished, replaced by a much grander complex. The meditation hall, which I had once thought large, was dwarfed by the new buildings. In fact, the old meditation hall (which was new in 2004) was relegated by 2011 to a neglected storage space behind the new monumental three-storey building that serves as a dining room on the first floor, a meeting hall combined with the ancestor hall (tổ đường) on the second floor, and the meditation hall (thiền đường) on the third.

From the monastery's beginning, space had been organized to accentuate difference from regular pagodas, but with the new structure, those differences became even more obvious. This chapter will explore how the space and activities at Sùng Phúc present a new kind of Buddhism, rooted in globalized, modernist Buddhist discourses. The space is organized in a way that reflects a fundamentally new view of Buddhism, but it also informs the experiences of the people who go there to practice. The secondary purpose of the chapter is to introduce some of the underlying themes that will be explored further in subsequent chapters, particularly the focus on Trúc Lâm as the Vietnamese Zen, the accentuation of the historical Buddha, the nationalist and internationalist discourses, the intentional ways that it reconstructs Buddhism to attract people of all genders and ages, and the Zen–Pure Land distinction.

HISTORY OF SÙNG PHÚC

Sùng Phúc is located in the small village of Xuân Đỗ Thượng, across the Red River from Hanoi.[3] Xuân Đỗ Thượng was formerly a small village in Bắc Ninh Province but has been amalgamated into Hanoi, Long Biên District. The village pagoda was built in the sixteenth or seventeenth century, but by the 1990s, it had fallen into a decrepit state. There had been no monks in residence there for over twenty years, and the building had been ruined by bombing and neglect. By the 1990s, the villagers, who still cherished the memory of their village pagoda, had rebuilt it in the new climate of the Renovation's religious renewal and the easing of state pressure on religion.[4] Lacking resources, they accepted help from a disciple of Thích Thanh Từ's, along with funds from his organization, to help in its reconstruction.[5]

The monk who took over as the first abbot, Thích Thông Giác, was a former businessman from Bắc Ninh Province who had met Thích Thanh Từ while traveling in southern Vietnam and decided to receive ordination under him. After several years in the south, he sought Thích Thanh Từ's permission to return to the north and assumed abbotship of the small pagoda in Xuân Đỗ Thượng village. Meanwhile, Thích Thanh Từ was building his organization in southern Vietnam, establishing new monasteries and centers to strengthen his revitalized Trúc Lâm Thiền Buddhism.

Thích Thông Giác became abbot of the pagoda and began the long process of renovations in 1998. According to Hân Mẫn and Thông Thiền's account (2010, 586–587), the process was difficult, but unspecified obstacles were overcome with patience and perseverance. At some point during this period, the local pagoda was renamed Sùng Phúc Thiền tự, designating it a Zen temple (*thiền tự*) rather than a pagoda (*chùa*). Unfortunately, just as real progress was being made, Thích Thông Giác fell ill. Thích Thanh Từ sent two monks, Thích Tâm Thuần and Thích Tâm Chánh, to assist Thích Thông Giác and help take care of him until his death on December 5, 2000. According to Hân Mẫn and Thông Thiền's account, the villagers, along with the two monks, petitioned Thích Thanh Từ to be allowed to continue the work that had been started by Thích Thông Giác. Thích Thanh Từ readily agreed.

Major building began in early 2004 with the construction of the meditation hall that I saw at the end of that year. Later came the newer and much bigger buildings and the present form of Sùng Phúc, with construction being completed at the end of 2005. Around the time of the expansion, Sùng Phúc changed its name from Sùng Phúc Thiền tự (崇福禪寺) to

Thiền viện Sùng Phúc (禪院崇福), effectively changing its designations from Zen temple (*tự*) to Zen monastery (*viện*), though in addition to its being a monastery, it is also a hub of lay activity.[6]

PHYSICAL LAYOUT

Henri Lefebvre, in *La production de l'espace* (The production of space), demonstrated that space is not a static container in which activity takes place but is entwined with processes of social production and reproduction, a meaning he captured by the coinage "social space" (Lefebvre 1991). Space can be employed as a tool of hegemonic domination and power but also of resistance to that power. Space is produced, in other words, imbued with discourses of domination, but it is consumed and used in ways that reflect the agency of those who live in, employ, and move in those spaces. Therefore, Lefebvre differentiates between the ways that spaces are perceived, conceived, and lived (Lefebvre 1991, 38–40), or as Kim Knott writes, "These three aspects, of 'spatial practice' (perceived space), 'representations of space' (conceived space) and 'spaces of representation' (lived space), provide useful tools for thinking about how people experience the spaces they inhabit, and use and represent space" (Knott 2008, 1110).

The way religious space is both influenced by and influences the interlocutors with that space reflects what Clifford Geertz pointed to in his still-relevant definition of religion as a cultural system, where religion is "a system of symbols which acts to establish powerful, pervasive and long-lasting moods and motivations in men by formulating conceptions of a general order of existence and clothing these conceptions with such an aura of factuality that the moods and motivations seem uniquely realistic" (Geertz 1966). The constructed space at Sùng Phúc reflects many of the understandings of Buddhism that were put forward by Buddhist reformers that have been globalized as what McMahan calls "Buddhist Modernism" (2008). At the same time, it also has considerable influence on the way practitioners at Sùng Phúc engage in Buddhist practice there and on the general view of Buddhism, which diverges in important ways from the standard Buddhist practice in northern Vietnam, particularly in the secular understanding of Buddhism.

What follows in this section is a description of the perceived and conceived space—how it is intended by those who have the power to create the space and to regulate it—and how it reflects a "general order of existence." It is important to note that the way it is lived is largely beyond the control of the Buddhist institution or by Sùng Phúc and the larger Trúc

Sùng Phúc Monastery from the front entrance, 2011

Lâm organization. Instead, it is the people who inhabit that space who give it meaning—often in ways that are not necessarily intended, as we will explore later in the book. Thus, this chapter is largely a description of the discursive intention of Trúc Lâm as embodied in the space and programming at Sùng Phúc.

The newly constructed buildings at Sùng Phúc are enormous in comparison to the usual size of Buddhist pagodas in northern Vietnam. Even Quán Sứ pagoda, the political center of the only official Buddhist organization in Vietnam, the Vietnamese Buddhist Association, is only a fraction of the size of Sùng Phúc. The meditation hall towers over the surrounding rooftops of the village in which it is located. The central buildings are built of concrete in an architectural style that is more generically Asian than specifically Vietnamese. The eaves on the massive roofs are upturned, but they bear no particular resemblance to the low, one-storey buildings of standard Vietnamese pagodas in the north. The physical layout and features of Sùng Phúc and the statuary and iconography that are displayed in the monastery's spaces are similarly unique and intentionally display a very different vision of Buddhism. When seen in juxtaposition with the parochial forms of Buddhism in northern Vietnam, the differences indicate that a concerted effort has been made to distinguish it from the practices of other Buddhists both in the region and in the Vietnamese Buddhist community nationally and internationally.

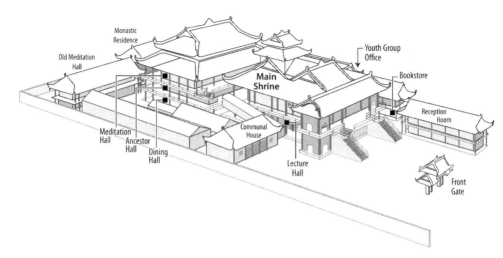

Diagram of Sùng Phúc Monastery, as of 2018

The difference between Sùng Phúc and regular pagodas in Hanoi are evident even from outside the compound, for the front gate also diverges from the norm. Almost all religious sites use Chinese characters for inscriptions, as Chinese characters continue to be seen as having more supernatural potency, cultural prestige, and aesthetic appeal. However, the couplets on the gate at Sùng Phúc are written in *quốc ngữ* (contemporary Vietnamese writing based on the Latin [Roman] alphabet). This substitution of *quốc ngữ* reflects reformist ideas that emerged early in the twentieth century about the importance of internalized meaning over external form. Unsurprisingly, one of the only other pagodas that features *quốc ngữ* on the main gate is Quán Sứ Pagoda, the center of the Buddhist Reform movement in Tonkin (northern Vietnam) in the 1930s (Soucy 2012, 43). David Marr has argued that the adoption of *quốc ngữ* over Chinese characters, or *Chữ Nôm*, a writing system that modifies Chinese characters to represent Vietnamese speech patterns and developed in the twelfth and thirteenth centuries but never widely adopted, was an important aspect of the struggle to modernize Vietnam as part of the overall struggle against French Colonial hegemony (Marr 1971, 183, 214–215; 1981, 33, 137, 150). On the lintel of the gate is written "Đại Giác Môn" (great enlightenment gate). Below that, there is a prominent carved marble inscription, which reads (in translation):

THE VIETNAMESE BUDDHIST ASSOCIATION
SÙNG PHÚC ZEN MONASTERY
XUÂN ĐỖ THƯỢNG PAGODA
ADDRESS: TỔ 10 PHƯỜNG CỰ KHỐI QUẬN LONG BIÊN TP HÀ NỘI

The inscriptions on the four columns comprise two couplets, one pair on the inside and one pair on the outside. The inside couplet reads "Sùng Phúc propagates not one thing / Trúc Lâm teaches a unitary lesson"; the outside couplet reads "Silent eternal illumination [*thường chiếu*] is endless speech / Unchanging true emptiness [*chân không*] takes forms as endless as the sands of the Ganges."[7]

There is a lecture hall (*giảng đường*) on the ground floor of the main hall, which also has an altar holding a statue of the baby Buddha as well as two photographs—the first, in the front and center of the altar, is the founder of Sùng Phúc, Thích Thông Giác; the second is the teacher of Thích Thanh Từ, Thích Thiện Hoa. This hall, therefore, also serves as a sort of ancestor hall for the monastery.[8] Along the upper walls around the room are tiles with images that depict anecdotes from lives of eminent Chan masters of China; one shows a monk hoeing a field. The monastery bookstore sells a book that describes each of the images, and for this one, it described an encounter between Zen Master Trí Nhàn (Zhixian—香嚴智閑 d. -898) and Linh Hựu (Lingyou—潙山靈祐 771–853) in which Linh Hựu asked Trí Nhàn the kōan "What was your face before it was conceived?," which, after time and contemplation, brought about a Zen awakening in Trí Nhàn. The explanation that is given reads, "Zen meditation doesn't come from someone else giving it to you, but requires each person to gain realization on their own" (Tinh Vân [Hsing Yun] 2011, 76), a theme that I often came across in reading Trúc Lâm literature and talking with monastics and devotees at Sùng Phúc.[9] As the name indicates, this room is primarily used for pedagogical rather than ritual purposes, with lines of tables and chairs that can seat perhaps a hundred people. In front and to the left of the altar is a table and chair where the monastic lecturer sits, with his back to the altar, facing the rows of tables and chairs where lay and monastic students sit to listen to the lectures.

What is unusual about the lecture hall is its dual role as a classroom, where monastics and laity gather three afternoons a week to listen to lectures by the more knowledgeable monks staying at Sùng Phúc (many only visiting), but it is also where the ancestor altar for the direct monastic ancestors of Sùng Phúc is located. In regular pagodas in the north, there is always a small room called a *nhà tổ* where the pagoda ancestors are worshiped. While incense is lit daily at the ancestor altar and offerings of fruit and flowers are made, little other ritual activity occurs in this room except on the annual ancestor day (*lễ giỗ tổ*). In many pagodas in the north, the guest reception area, located in front of the ancestor altar, comprises a table and benches or chairs and is where special guests might be served tea. This reflects the traditional house arrangement in which the reception area—the most prestigious and important part of the house—is in front of the ancestor altar. Therefore, the arrangement at Sùng Phúc, where the ancestors are located in the lecture hall, is a significant departure from standard pagoda architecture.

The main shrine (*đại hùng đảo điện*, or "great palace") is in the central place in the compound, and like other physical aspects of Sùng Phúc, it is also significantly different from the main shrines of regular pagodas in northern Vietnam. The main altars of most pagodas in the north are crowded with statues of the Mahāyāna Buddhist pantheon, especially images of the historical Buddha (Thích Ca Mầu Ni Phật), Amitābha Buddha (A Di Đà Phật), Maitreya Buddha (Di Lạc Phật), and bodhisattvas such as Guanyin (Quan Âm) and Kṣitigarbha (Địa Tạng). The shrine room of regular pagodas frequently has figures that are marginal to the Buddhist pantheon, like the ten kings of hell, Dharma guardians, and statues of gods or spirits that are not strictly Buddhist. The main shrine at Sùng Phúc, however, is dedicated almost solely to the historical Buddha, with his large golden statue dominating the center of the main altar. The pose of the statue is also not typical. Instead of the usual statues of the Buddha in meditation, teaching, or pointing down to the ground to get witness, he is portrayed holding up a flower, a pose harkening to the simple gesture that led to his disciple Mahākāśyapa's awakening experience and modeling the importance of direct insight over rational thought, ritual, or scholasticism as a path to enlightenment while also displaying the power of mind-to-mind transmission. It is also taken as rhetorical justification for a religion leading back to Śākyamuni that is silently transmitted and outside the regular Buddhist teachings, thereby providing legitimation to Zen (Welter 2000, 75). To Śākyamuni's right is a white marble statue of Mañjuśrī (Văn Thù Sư Lợi), a bodhisattva representing the embodiment of insight (*prajñā*) (Keown 2004, 172) and personifying meditation, and one of Samantabhadra (Phổ Hiền Bồ Tát), a bodhisattva associated with protecting the Dharma and who is the embodiment of enlightenment (*bodhi*) (Keown 2004, 246).

Main shrine at Sùng Phúc Monastery in 2015

The accent on the historical Buddha is further displayed by bas re-
liefs painted gold and brown around the upper walls that depict important scenes in the standardized hagiography of the Buddha that was
globalized in the nineteenth and twentieth century (Snodgrass 2009b).
Displays of the life of the Buddha are not common in pagodas of the
north, with Quán Sứ Pagoda—the center of the Buddhist Reform movement in the first half of the twentieth century and the current center of
the state-sponsored Buddhist association—being the only other one I
know of. One scene that stands out as not usually present in the standardized portrayals of the life of the Buddha is a scene showing the Buddha's Flower Sermon. At Sùng Phúc, this image of the Buddha delivering
the Flower Sermon is an icon that reoccurs so frequently and in such a
fashion that it takes on symbolic importance as representative of the Zen
school and Trúc Lâm's position within that school. It is also part of their
systematic branding of Trúc Lâm as being both uniquely Vietnamese
and part of the Zen lineage linking back to China, India, and ultimately
to the historical Buddha.

In front of the main shrine, out on the balcony, is a large drum on the
left side (facing the altar) and a large bell on the right side. The inscriptions on the bell reinforce the idea of a sustained Vietnamese Zen tradition. It includes four poems on four sides of the bell by Zen Master Vạn

Hạnh (renowned as a tenth-century Buddhist Zen master), monk ancestor Trần Nhân Tông (the founder of Trúc Lâm), Pháp Loa (the second patriarch of the Trúc Lâm Zen sect), and Zen Master Minh Chánh (a nineteenth-century monk from Ninh Bình Province).[10] The inscription by Trần Nhân Tông reads (in translation):

> Living amid dust and enjoying the way,
> You should let all things take their course.
> When hungry, just eat; when tired, just sleep.
> The treasure is in your house; don't search any more.
> Face the scenes and have no thought; then you don't need to ask for Zen.
> Sơ Tổ Trần Nhân Tông[11]

Taken together, this collection of poems makes a statement about the continuity of the Zen school in Vietnam. It also puts Trúc Lâm firmly at the center of this tradition by including poems from the founder and the second patriarch.

The hall that bears the name ancestor hall is even more unusual. It is situated on the second floor of the building behind the main shrine, in the position where ancestor shrines are located in some pagodas in northern Vietnam (behind the main shrine), including, for example, at Quán Sứ Pagoda. This hall is an expansive space where most activities take place, including meditation sessions, public lectures, and activities for youths. The focal point of the room is another kind of ancestor altar, although it is interpreted in a new way. As mentioned, the photographs of the actual immediate monastic ancestors are located in the lecture hall. The altar in the ancestor hall is instead dedicated to Bodhidharma, the Indian monk who introduced Zen to China, and to the founders of the Trúc Lâm Zen school. Bodhidharma's statue, carved of black stone, assumes the most exalted position, at the top center. At the front of the altar, under Bodhidharma, are three statues in white marble depicting the patriarchs of the Trúc Lâm school. Emperor Trần Nhân Tông (called Trúc Lâm Đầu Đà) is in the central position, while on the other side of him are the second and third patriarchs of Trúc Lâm, Pháp Loa, and Huyền Quang. Together, the three patriarchs are labeled Trúc Lâm Tam Tổ (Three ancestors of Trúc Lâm). Thus, at Sùng Phúc, ancestors are seen as the patriarchs of Zen and of Trúc Lâm, at the expense of the monastic ancestors, who are instead relegated to the lecture hall, which is smaller, darker, lower, and usually closed to visitors. Although there is no lineage continuity between the modern Trúc Lâm and the sect founded by Trần Nhân Tông, and therefore claiming these figures as ancestors is dubious, their central position indicates the central importance of the claim that ties Sùng Phúc to this lineage and brands it as Zen. In fact, the way that this lineage (imagined or otherwise) is systematically thematized at Sùng Phúc often has the feeling of branding that seems to borrow more from the world of marketing than from Buddhism.

The floor above the ancestor hall is called the meditation hall and holds another large statue of the historical Buddha. This statue is in brownish gold and depicts Śākyamuni in the more familiar pose, seated in meditation with hands folded, with a stupa resting in his upward-facing palms. In the background is a bas relief of the bodhi tree under which he reached enlightenment through meditation. In front of the altar is a pedestal on which sits a small wooden statue of Maitreya (Di Lạc) with children. While the statue is large, the most remarkable object in the room is a large glass case in the center of the room that contains a

Ancestor altar at Sùng Phúc, showing Bodhidharma in the back and King Trần Nhân Tông in the front, 2011

collection of small glass stupas, each of which contains a tiny white round fragment. According to the labels glued to the bases of most of the stupas, these fragments are relics of various Buddhist saints and even of the historical Buddha.[12] On the right side of the room is a large model pagoda encrusted with pearls and with more relic-containing stupas around its base.

There are several other major features of the Sùng Phúc compound that distinguish it from regular pagodas. Below the large ancestor hall is an equally large dining hall at which lunch is served daily to all, residents and visitors alike. The monks occupy the central row of tables. On one end of the row is a small altar with a statue of a fat, smiling Maitreya standing with a ball in his right hand; on the other end is a much larger altar in the front and center of the room, dominated by a large white marble statue, also of Maitreya, but this one sitting. Nuns are usually seated at the row of tables to the right of the monks (facing the main altar). Lay women are seated to the right of the nuns, and lay men to the left of the monks.

The reception area (*nhà khách*) is a standard element in all pagodas, though the reception room at Sùng Phúc is notable for the collection of writings, calligraphy, photos, and statues. The main reception table in the center of the room holds a small statue of Maitreya and immediately behind it a bust of Thích Thanh Từ. At the end of a table is a large bookcase, on top of which is a bust of the Buddha and two small statues of Bodhidharma, and on the wall behind is a picture of the Buddha under the bodhi tree with hands forming the mudra (hand gesture) for teaching, with pictures of Mañjuśrī and the bodhisattva Samantabhadra on either side. There are two alcoves on each side of the room, one of which holds the only small statue of Guanyin in the entire monastery. The walls of the room are covered with pictures of some of the Trúc Lâm monasteries, pictures of Thích Thanh Từ, plaques with various Buddhist teachings and aphorisms, and calligraphy. In each of the alcoves on the wall facing the doorway is a large glass bookcase containing pictures of the abbot; the founder of the monastery, Thích Thanh Từ; and other monks, along with many small statues of the Buddha, the Buddhist saints (*la hàn*), and other objects that were likely gifts to the abbot.

In the compound, there is also a bookstore, which is run by a private entrepreneur within the parameters of the monastery's requirements, perhaps an example of Buddhist public-private partnership. The bookstore features books written by Thích Thanh Từ and Thích Thông Phương, a senior monk and author in the Trúc Lâm organization, and also offers a collection of books by other writers, many of which are translations of books written by Western Buddhists and non-Vietnamese Asian Buddhist authorities like the Dalai Lama. There is also an assortment of sutras, children's books, and vegetarian cookbooks. The main theme of the books is Zen. In the center of the room is a large collection of CDs and DVDs for sale, mostly recordings of sermons by Thích Thanh Từ and other prominent monks in the Trúc Lâm organization, though a few are by prominent Vietnamese Zen monks outside the organization, like Thích Nhất Hạnh and Thích Chân Quang. There is also an assortment of Buddhist paraphernalia: gray robes and monastic-style clothing, Buddhist handbags featuring embroidered lotus flowers and swastikas, bowl gongs, bells, wooden fish (a wooden block used to keep time during chanting), an assortment of statues (almost all of which are of either Bodhidharma or the Buddha giving the Flower Sermon), and pictures of Thích Thanh Từ.

Sùng Phúc was intentionally constructed to be fundamentally divergent from the typical pagodas of northern Vietnam. Not only is the monumental multistoried proportions of an architectural style that marks it as substantially different from the usually low, one-floor constructions, but nearly every other aspect of Sùng Phúc is also pointedly unlike other pagodas. Its architecture and iconography are deeply informed by the reformist discourse that stresses differentiations between Buddhism and other religious beliefs and practices that are part of the more holistic understanding that usually shapes people's religiosity in northern Vietnam. There are no tables for putting together plates of offerings and no outdoor furnaces in which to burn spirit money (offerings and spirit money being essential items for the supplication of buddhas and spirits). The shrine features statues of a strictly controlled Buddhist orthodoxy and excludes all non-canonical Buddhist iconography. Instead, it emphasizes the historical Buddha, depicted in the globalized and standardized version of his life. With few exceptions, most statues in the compound are of the Buddha, who is depicted most frequently in the pose indicative of the Flower Sermon. Even the various statues of Maitreya seemed more ornamental than ritualistic.

The other notable aspect is the self-conscious way that the monastery is made into a Zen place. The Flower Sermon icon is repeated throughout, but the prominent statues of Bodhidharma and the three patriarchs of Trúc Lâm also make this claim of being part of the Zen school. The painted tiles of Zen anecdotes in the lecture hall, supported by the book of explanations in the bookstore, do the same. Finally, around the compound, on the walls of several of the buildings are large murals that reiterate this Zen identity: Zen master Wude from tenth-century China, Bodhidharma sitting in a cave, Thích Thanh Từ sitting on a rock (presumably on Mount

Yên Tử, the birthplace of the original Trúc Lâm), a bas relief of Bodhidharma walking on water. These murals also link Trúc Lâm to the Chan lineages of China

The narrative statement is of a continuous line running back through time, from the modern Trúc Lâm organization to the fourteenth-century patriarchs of this Vietnamese school to the patriarchs of Chinese Chan (particularly Bodhidharma) and eventually to the founder of Buddhism, Śākyamuni. This narrative is reinforced in the most commonly performed ritual, the Penitence Rite (Sám Hối Sáu Căn) as constructed by Thích Thanh Từ, where homage is paid to the Trúc Lâm Zen lineage by reciting the names of the buddhas of the past (Phật Tỳ Bà Thi; Skt. Vipaśyin), the present (Thích Ca Mâu Ni; Skt. Śākyamuni), and the future (Phật Di Lặc Tôn; Skt. Maitreya); the chief disciples of the Buddha (Ca Diếp and A Nan Đà; Skt. Kāśyapa and Ānanda); the key patriarchs of Chinese Chan (Bodhidharma, the first patriarch; Hui ke [慧可, 487–593], the second patriarch; and Huineng [慧能, 638–713], the sixth patriarch); the patriarchs of the Trúc Lâm (Trần Nhân Tông, Pháp Loa, and Huyền Quang, collectively known as Trúc Lâm Đầu Đà); and ending with "all of the patriarchs of India, China and Vietnam" (Thích Thanh Từ 2011, 11–12). Missing is any repetition of names of buddhas and bodhisattvas for the purpose of receiving aid or boons of any kind, whether spiritual, soteriological, or material.

The space at Sùng Phúc is clearly influenced by their conception of the Vietnamese Zen tradition. However, it also has the effect of making people realize that they are in a completely different kind of Buddhist space from the norm. It shapes ways of thinking and embodies ways of practice that are novel for Vietnamese Buddhists in Hanoi. The systematic way that these discourses are imparted through the architecture and iconography are reiterated in the rituals and practices of Sùng Phúc and in the sermons and talks that are given and mutually reinforced by its practitioners—all of which are reminiscent of marketing techniques. The result is that it creates a shared sense of a comprehensive identity as being a part of a Buddhist movement that is received as more genuine than those encountered in other pagodas in the north. I will now turn to a description of the activities to show how the branding we have seen in the Sùng Phúc space carries through in the practices.

MAJOR ACTIVITIES

As with the architecture and iconography of Sùng Phúc, the activities there do not conform with those at regular pagodas in northern Vietnam.

This difference is intentional and serves both to draw distinctions with other pagodas and to provide legitimacy to their modernist interpretation of Buddhism. One of these fundamental differences is the regularity with which activities occur at Sùng Phúc. For the most part, they follow a rationalized Western calendar (*dương lịch*) designed around people's work schedules rather than a schedule based on the lunar calendar (*âm lịch*) and the supernatural potency influenced by time and space (a broader discussion of which will come in chapter 3). Activities at Sùng Phúc take place most days, with lectures on some afternoons and the Penitence Rite open to all every evening. That does not mean that everyone takes part in these activities; most people come only to the main activities for laity on the weekend or to the larger full-day program held once a month, but many take advantage of opportunities to be more active. By contrast, most pagodas are sleepy places except during the frenetic activities held on the first and fifteenth of the lunar month, when people go to supplicate the buddhas and spirits, believing that they are more responsive on those days.

Activities at Sùng Phúc can be divided into three types: regular, occasional, and private. Between these various kinds of activities, Sùng Phúc has a constant buzz. Every morning, monks get into cars or hop onto motorcycles and head off to run errands, visiting devotees around Hanoi, going to other pagodas to give Dharma talks, or taking care of other monastery business. The abbot and vice abbot always seem to be on the run, but all monks are busy doing something. The more senior lecturing monks frequently go on trips around northern Vietnam to give lectures at centers or pagodas that have relationships with the Trúc Lâm organization or for groups of lay followers in places that do not have a Zen center but that organize events and invite these monks to come to talk with them. Lào Cai, for example, was one location that was visited on more than one occasion by monks at Sùng Phúc during my stay in 2011, as they were preparing to build a new monastery in Sa Pa at the time.[13] Lay women and men are busy every morning cleaning the monastery, replacing flower arrangements, and sweeping floors. Devotees come by to make donations of food to the monastery and to have a few words with the abbot if they are lucky enough to find him around and available. Visiting monks (mostly from southern Vietnam) pass through Sùng Phúc almost daily, many staying for weeks or months and others coming for only a day or two. Resident monks frequently leave for weeks at a time, visiting Trúc Lâm temples in other parts of Vietnam or abroad, going on pilgrimages to India or Burma, or going to other Trúc Lâm monasteries in Vietnam. There are activities every day of the week for those who wish to attend the evening Penitence Rite and meditation. Throughout the day on most days, there is a trickle of lay Buddhists who come to Sùng Phúc to pay respects to the Buddha in the main shrine or to meditate quietly in the meditation hall. The bookstore is always open. Lunch is free to all every day, and there are usually a couple of dozen lay people eating in the dining room along with the monastics. Novice monks are more or less permanently stationed in the main shrine, the ancestor hall, and the meditation hall to take care of the altars and to ring the bowl gong when people approach the altar to pay respect. Frequent special events punctuate this buzz of regular activity. During the three months I was there in 2011, there were several special festival days and one large youth event.

Regular Activities

The daily schedule follows a regular rhythm, signaled in most cases by the toll of the bell. The schedule is followed by all who are in the monastery, including all monks (whether resident or visiting), nuns (who sleep in a separate building outside the monastery compound), resident lay men (cư sĩ), and volunteers who come in for the day or part of the day. The number of cư sĩ in residence varies, as the period of their residence is not predetermined and can last days or weeks or be permanent. Motivation for these lay men taking up residence at Sùng Phúc varies. Many reside here semipermanently, intending to eventually take monastic vows if they determine that the lifestyle suits them; others are merely on retreat and have no intention of staying permanently. One eighteen-year-old cư sĩ I spoke with, named Sơn, had been there for two weeks and described the schedule as difficult for him, particularly in the first week. He told me that he had to get up every day at 3:00 a.m. and had fifteen minutes to brush his teeth and clean himself before going to meditate with everyone from 3:30 to 5:00. After breakfast, he had to do hard work for the rest of the morning. In the afternoons, he sat in on a lecture that took place three afternoons a week. In the evenings, he attended the Penitence Rite and then meditated with the monks until it was time to go to bed at 10:00 p.m. His description matched well the daily schedule that was posted on a plasticized piece of paper taped to a pillar outside the meditation hall:

Daily Schedule

Morning

3:15 wake up (3 sets of 3 tolls of the bell)
3:30 meditation
5:00 finish meditation (1 toll of the bell)
6:15 breakfast (3 hits on the board)
7:30 work/labor (3 tolls of the bell)
11:00 finish work (1 toll of the bell)
11:30 lunch (3 hits of board)
12:30 rest (3 tolls of the bell)

Afternoon

13:30 wake up (1 set of 3 tolls of the bell)
14:00 study (3 tolls of the bell)
17:00 sound the Great Bell
18:45 Penitence Rite (3 tolls of bell)
20:00 meditation
21:00 end meditation (1 toll of the bell)
22:00 rest (3 tolls of the bell)

This schedule provided only a very rough guide. Many monks had other responsibilities that took them outside the monastery for the day or for multiple days. The main religious events in the daily schedule were the meditation periods in the mornings and evenings and the Penitence Rite in the evening. The meditation period is attended only by the residents of the monastery. The evening Penitence Rite is more open but is still usually attended by only a few lay Buddhists who have the time and commitment. However, lay devotees are encouraged to chant it daily at home.

I had the opportunity to attend the ritual at Sùng Phúc. When I arrived at the monastery around 6:00 p.m., some young lay Buddhists were hanging around the bookstore, the main space in the monastery where people gather to talk, after having returned from an excursion to a nearby handicraft village famous for its pottery (Bát Tràng). They were chatting and laughing with a large monk who was visiting from southern Vietnam. There were a few old women meditating in the center of the floor of the main shrine. In the ancestor hall, a couple of women in their sixties were chatting while another woman sat in front of the altar meditating. Other lay Buddhists, mostly old women, eventually arrived. A novice nun whom I had interviewed a few weeks before came over to say hello as she folded and put on the ceremonial yellow cloth over the shoulder of her gray everyday robe. As the time to start approached, the lay people all went inside while the monastics congregated out in front of the ancestor hall.

At 6:35, a monk began striking the large drum at the front of the main shrine, sending a deep thumping rhythm resounding through the temple complex and out over the surrounding village. The ritual began with a formal procession of monks entering the ancestor hall on the right and nuns on the left, forming two lines in front and perpendicular to the altar. They stood facing inward while the lay women lined up behind the nuns, and lay men and *cư sĩ* lined up behind the monks. They stayed standing facing the center with the palms of their hands pressed together while a particularly melodic chant was broadcast over the loudspeaker, like a Buddhist call to prayer. When the chanting ended, everyone bowed to the altar with the statues of Bodhidharma and the founders of Trúc Lâm, turned back inward, and bowed to each other. Then they filed out around the balcony on the outside of the main shrine, with men and women walking around opposite sides of the building and then meeting up and entering through the front door of the shrine.

In the main shrine, they performed the penitence liturgy, one of the only liturgies chanted by lay Buddhists following Trúc Lâm Zen (most lay followers have it memorized).[14] The rite began with the lead monk chanting and offering incense to the Buddha. Then everyone shifted places so that they were lined up facing the altar, with the monks positioned in the front, still on the right of the center, and the nuns to the left, with lay women lined up behind the nuns and the lay men behind the monks. At this point, I took a count: ten monks, twenty-seven nuns, nine lay men (all resident *cư sĩ*), and thirty-one lay women. Because there were more women than men, some of the lay women lined up behind the men to even out the sides.

Following the incense offering, everyone chanted the Prajñāpāramitā (Heart) Sutra (Tâm Kinh Trí Tuệ Cứu Cánh Rộng Lớn), a popular but esoteric sutra that is especially important in the Zen school. Then everyone paid homage to the Buddhist ancestors (lễ Phật tổ) of Trúc Lâm and Zen. The preliminaries done, the Repentance of the Six Sense Organs (Sám Hối Sáu Căn) was chanted. As the name suggests, the purpose of this is to recognize and correct offenses related to the six senses: karma of the eyes, ears, nose, tongue, body (with subcategories of killing, stealing, and adultery), and consciousness (with subcategories of greed, anger, and ignorance). The

ceremony ended with reciting the Three Refuges and the Five Precepts
(Tam Quy, Ngũ Giới), during which practitioners make twelve vows: to keep
the mind always awakened in stillness, to terminate the untamed mind, to
destroy any doubt, to assure that the moon of concentration is always complete, to acknowledge that all mental objects are non-arising and unceasing,
to detach from the net of affection, to contemplate and practice the virtues
of Ten Earth Bodhisattvas, to thoroughly understand the Dharma to become liberated from the three deva realms, to tame the agitated mind, to
control the mind, to open the mind to listen and understand the Buddha's
teachings, and to admire the Zen patriarchs (Thích Thanh Từ 2002b, 60).
The ritual ended with the transfer of merit:

> As our mind thinks of Sages
> We sincerely prostrate to the World honored One
> We vow to progress on the steps of Ten Earths
> And our true Bodhi mind would never regress.
> (Thích Thanh Từ 2002b, 60)

The lead monk chanted a short memorial for the dead and read out the
names of the recently deceased. There was then a procession back to
the ancestor hall, where everyone bowed to the altar and then turned to
the center and bowed to each other before leaving in procession. When it
was concluded, people trickled out into the night, getting on motorcycles
to go home or walking to the nearby bus stop.

In addition to the daily Penitence Rite, lectures are held in the lecture
hall three times every week, on Tuesdays, Wednesdays, and Thursdays.
The lectures are always given by a monk who is qualified to teach (called
a *giảng sư*). There are six resident monks at Sùng Phúc who are qualified
to give lectures, including the abbot, Thích Tâm Thuần, and the vice abbot, Thích Tỉnh Thiền. During the three months of my primary research
there, lectures were generally given by the vice abbot, by a senior monk
named Thích Tuệ Đạt, or by a visiting monk named Thích Khế Định.[15]
The people who attended were mostly lay Buddhist women, although
there were always around ten lay men who attended as well. I was told
that the lectures, although open to all, were part of a program for lay devotees and that they were given a certificate after completing the course.
While it is primarily lay practitioners who attend these lectures, there are
always a couple of rows of nuns and a few younger monks who come to
listen as well.

Weekends are when Sùng Phúc is the busiest. Every week, there is a
half-day program on Saturday in which lay practitioners come to perform

the Penitence Rite, to meditate, and to listen to Dharma talks. The meditation session starts with rites in which the lay Buddhists prostrate to the
Buddha, the Dharma, and the sangha.[16] Everyone then sits in the lotus position while a recording that gives instructions on posture, breath techniques, and breath awareness is played (these same instructions are
included in a booklet sold at the bookstore called *Phương pháp Tọa Thiền*
[The meditation method], written by Thích Thanh Từ [2010a]). A monk
chants a short verse and ends by chanting the name of the Buddha, which
is repeated by the lay Buddhists. Everyone then falls into silent meditation
for around forty-five minutes while a monk patrols holding a large stick,
which he uses to correct posture and tap on the shoulders of practitioners
who are drifting off to sleep.[17] When the meditation is finished, the recorded voice resumes, going over rubbing and stretching techniques to
bring practitioners out of their meditative state. At the end, the practitioners recite the Heart Sutra and then a verse intended to transfer the merit
of their meditation to all Buddhists and all living beings and to strengthen
Buddhism, and end by reciting the Three Refuges.[18] The Dharma talks
deal with fundamental themes common to all Buddhists, such as the Four
Noble Truths, and make frequent references to Zen and to historical figures of Vietnamese Buddhism, and especially the Trúc Lâm school.

On the last Saturday of every month (according to the Western, not
lunar, calendar), there is an all-day program for lay Buddhists. This day is
a much bigger event that draws a crowd of over a thousand lay Buddhists
who pack the main shrine, the ancestor hall, and the meditation hall and
flow out onto the balconies. They start by performing the Penitence Rite
and follow with one hour of meditation, using the same procedures for
both as described above. After the morning meditation session, a lecture
is given that lasts about an hour. A vegetarian meal is served at noon and
eaten in the Zen style, with the diners eating in silence and one mouthful
at a time, focusing on their actions as they eat. In the afternoon, there is
another meditation session and a second lecture.

Occasional Activities

While the regular schedule at Sùng Phúc is a busy one, with the daily rituals, lectures, and weekly programs, during my stay there the monastery
also regularly hosted special events that drew large crowds. The atmo-
sphere of these events was akin to a festival. Buddhist flags were set out
on the roads leading to the monastery, and vendors lined up their Buddhist wares on sheets outside the gate. Special guests were invited, particularly prominent Zen monks from other Trúc Lâm monasteries in the
north, like Trúc Lâm Yên Tử Monastery, the monastery established at the

birthplace of the Trúc Lâm Zen sect and the head monastery in the north. Young men in white shirts and red ties and young women dressed in gray *áo dài* acted as ushers and gave performances on stages constructed for the events. The young women wore golden sashes over their *áo dài*, proclaiming their membership in the youth group.[19] Elaborate vegetarian banquets were prepared by armies of lay volunteers, monks and nuns were served in long rows of tables in the dining room, and lay Buddhists joined them on the sides, in the lecture hall, and in the courtyard of the village communal house that is on the grounds of the monastery. All this carnivalesque activity served to heighten emotion and attachment to the Trúc Lâm monastery.[20]

During the three months in 2011 when I did my main research at Sùng Phúc, several of these major events took place. The first was the casting of a large temple bell that was then given to a new Trúc Lâm monastery in Tam Đảo, a former hill station of the French about an hour and a half north of Hanoi. Another was the ancestor day (*lễ giỗ tổ*) of Bodhidharma, an all-day event that attracted around eight hundred participants and included a Dharma talk by Thích Khế Định, a recitation of Bodhidharma's biography, an ancestor ritual for him (*cúng tổ*), and a group meditation session.

Another major event during the time I was there took place at the massive Trúc Lâm Monastery complex that has been built at Mount Yên Tử. The site of this monastery is important because it is the place where Trần Nhân Tông retired to become a monk and where he founded the Trúc Lâm Zen sect. The event celebrated the ancestor day of Trần Nhân Tông and took place over two days. On the morning of the first day, some two thousand lay Buddhists took a vow to assiduously pursue the bodhisattva path of compassion, vowing that although they were committed to the path of enlightenment that would last multiple lifetimes, they would forgo their own enlightenment to help other living beings. On the second day was the celebration of the ancestor day for Trần Nhân Tông.

Sùng Phúc organized twenty or thirty buses to take devotees to Trúc Lâm Monastery. Almost all the monks from Sùng Phúc had driven there a few days before the event to help with preparations. From the number of people there, I suspect that most of the lay members of Sùng Phúc were in attendance; certainly all the key members of the youth group were there.

I joined a bus of mostly old women from the neighborhood where I was living. We gathered on a sidewalk by a major road at 3:30 a.m. and waited for the bus (which was late). There was much commotion among the lay women—"Did you remember to call so-and-so?" "Where is X? She should be here by now." "Are we picking Z up on the way?" "Where is that bus? Did you tell them the right place?" One woman ran off and bought a bag of the little crusty baguettes (*bánh mì*) that are a vestige of French colonial rule and shared them with her fellow pilgrims. The women were mostly dressed in gray tunics and pants. Finally underway, one woman collected 100,000 VND (about $5 US at the time) from each person to pay for the bus, while another distributed photocopies of a sermon she had transcribed by hand from a YouTube video of a notable monk from southern Vietnam named Thích Minh Thành. The woman sitting beside me commented, "She is doing it because she thinks it was interesting and would also get a little merit for doing it. She doesn't understand, though, that others here are at a much higher level, and it doesn't help them." Several women in the front of the bus sang (not chanted) the name of Amitābha over and over. The bus had around sixty people, only three of whom were men.

The rest of the day proceeded in a similarly pious way. Almost everyone took the bodhisattva vow. Later in the day, a group of lay women sponsored a ceremony to release birds. Sadly, a number had died in each of the packed cages while waiting to be released. I asked a monk about it, and he explained that although some birds had died, it was still a meritorious action because the intention was right. The whole day was a blending of festivalesque exuberance and earnest piety.

Personal Activities

Finally, there are rituals that are specific for families and individuals that, while they are a part of the ritual life of the monastery, involve only a few individual devotees of Sùng Phúc. In some ways, though, these more individually oriented rituals are more consequential, as the two main ones, the Memorial Rite (Lễ Cầu Siêu) and wedding ritual, are important opportunities to present Trúc Lâm Zen to people who are not necessarily followers. The Buddhism that they introduce is not the standard but instead shows a rational and individual form that is presented as suitable for contemporary urban life.

Mortuary rituals have long been the mainstay of Buddhist ritual function throughout Asia, so it is no surprise that Sùng Phúc deals with death. However, Sùng Phúc's approach to death and associated rituals differs from Buddhist mortuary practices elsewhere. One monk told me that monks visit followers on their deathbeds to instruct them and to ease their passing, although I was not able to witness this. What I did see on several occasions was the ritual held thirty-five or forty-nine days after death, which was notable not for the frequency with which it was held at Sùng Phúc but because of its differences from the way that it was performed at regular pagodas.

Ritual on the thirty-fifth day after death, in a regular pagoda (2004) (left) and at Sùng Phúc (2011) (right)

The performances of mortuary rituals at regular pagodas are heavily ritualistic, involving ritual costumes, with the officiating monastic often wearing a hat and holding a scepter that mimics that worn by the bodhisattva of hell, Kṣitigarbha, special ritual implements, intricate dances, and mudras. At Sùng Phúc, the process was remarkably devoid of the pageantry of these rituals as they are performed elsewhere. The mortuary ritual at Sùng Phúc began in the main shrine, where the monks chanted and bowed to the altar, while two men, usually the sons of the deceased, faced the altar holding the dead person's incense bowl and photograph. Following this, the monastics and family members went in procession to the ancestor hall. There, the monastics paid respect to the altar of the Trúc Lâm ancestors and Bodhidharma, and then all but one left. The family and the one monk went to a small table at the end of the hall, where the image and incense bowl were placed. The monk and the family then chanted and bowed, but they were not ritualistic, without the regular costumes, complicated choreography, mudras, and magical incantations. The ceremony ended with the monk giving a lengthy Dharma talk.

Even more striking than the altered mortuary rituals held at Sùng Phúc was another innovation that I have not seen in any other pagodas: the Buddhist wedding. For all the couples with whom I spoke, the Buddhist wedding was an adjunct to their traditional wedding rather than a replacement for it.[21] This is not surprising, since the traditional wedding is more a family event than a religious one and only becomes religious when respects are paid to ancestors, when the groom goes to pick up his bride and take her to her new home, and when the bride arrives "home" (the home of her new husband's parents, though they may live separately afterward). The wedding ceremony at Sùng Phúc consists of chanting, making vows, and exchanging rings. Like the memorial service, it also affords an opportunity for the monks to teach about the Dharma, particularly as it relates to the lives, responsibilities, and moral practices of lay Buddhists in marriage.

Taken together, these activities, whether regular, occasional, or individual, represent a noteworthy departure from the activities at typical pagodas in northern Vietnam. They say much about how Buddhism is being interpreted and transmitted by the Trúc Lâm organization. Trúc Lâm Buddhism is notable for its ritual impoverishment and its orthodox portrayal of the supernatural, which is heavily rationalized and stripped of elements that could be called—and indeed have been labeled—superstition. As mentioned, the choreography and costumes are missing from the memorial service. There are no external ritual specialists, called *thầy cúng*, who are usually brought in to perform parts of mortuary rituals. These exclusions reflect the reformist efforts to restructure Buddhism as a religion by creating distinctions between what is and is not Buddhist. The incorporation of wedding ceremonies into the ritual repertoire shows how religion is structured as being a conscious choice to believe, in the way described by Charles Taylor (2007), and to follow a path that affects one's entire life. This global understanding of religion is modeled on a Christian, Western form, but as Roland Robertson demonstrated, globalization is inevitably tied to processes of localization (Robertson 1995). As a final point, the wedding ceremony introduces the idea that Buddhism is not merely for the dead, a charge to which the reformers were reacting. Instead, Buddhism is restructured as focused on the living, as a religion for one's whole life.

KEY FEATURES

Having described the activities and setting at Sùng Phúc, I will now turn to how they relate to major themes that show the localization of global modernist Buddhist discourses. While I will deal with these issues more extensively in coming chapters, it is worth surveying here the key departures of Sùng Phúc from the regular sort of Buddhism practiced in pagodas in the north. These divergences are evident in the layout, iconography, and activities of Sùng Phúc.

Evoking History for Legitimacy

Several elements in the architecture of Sùng Phúc stress its identity with the Trúc Lâm Zen school. Perhaps most obvious is the ancestor hall. In most pagodas in the north, these altars (*bàn thờ tổ*) hold statues and images of former monastics who had been resident at the pagoda, indicating the line of masters. However, at Sùng Phúc, the altar is significantly different, instead dedicated to Bodhidharma and the fourteenth-century Vietnamese founders of Trúc Lâm. Other elements also stress this attachment with Trúc Lâm and seek to give legitimacy to the organization through association with Chinese Zen and with the Trúc Lâm sect founded by Trần Nhân Tông particularly (details about this association will be explored in the next chapter).

Transregional and Transnational Buddhism

The orientation of Trúc Lâm is outwardly focused, marking it as distinct from local forms of Buddhism that have a parochial disposition. By this I mean that it is not grounded in a locally focused religious habitus and does not perform the functions of a local pagoda. It is not concerned with serving local community interests but rather with building its own broader community from across Hanoi and linking with Trúc Lâm centers located throughout Vietnam, internationally, and on the internet. Thus, unlike regular pagodas that are central to a real community, Sùng Phúc ties its practitioners to an imagined community (Anderson 1983) that is outward rather than inward looking.

Trúc Lâm Buddhism and the way it is practiced at Sùng Phúc is international in scope and draws on an internationalist and ecumenical understanding of Buddhism. Its members, and especially its monastics, are highly mobile, frequently traveling not only within Vietnam but also internationally to visit pilgrimage sites, give public lectures, and have conversations with Buddhists from other countries. This pan-Vietnamese—and even international—type of Buddhism, with its lack of grounding in the local culture of northern Vietnam, is not surprising, given that all the senior monks at Sùng Phúc (and in the Trúc Lâm organization) are from either southern or central Vietnam. The fact that the leaders are not northern is seen as a positive thing by many devotees, who generally perceive monks from the south as being better trained, having a much better understanding of Buddhist doctrine than Buddhist monks in the north, and to some extent as being more virtuous. As such, Sùng Phúc represents a local node of a global organization that is pursuing an expansionist, missionary agenda.

The reason that the present-day Trúc Lâm organization was founded in the south and has only relatively recently moved north is related to the different historical trajectories that Buddhism in Vietnam took. When the country was partitioned in 1954, the Communists took control of the north, and the American-sponsored regime took over the south. The Buddhist Reform movement that took place throughout Vietnam from the 1920s to the 1940s was able to continue in the south during the war period from the mid-1950s to the mid-1970s. In the north, by contrast, religious practice was discouraged after 1954 until the Renovation period in the late 1980s, when restrictions on religious practices were eased. Buddhism, while officially sanctioned, in practice became calcified, and the transformations that began in the first half of the twentieth century largely ceased in the face of state disapproval. In the south, however, the main figures and centers of the Reform movement became the trainers and training grounds for young monks who then went on to embrace political protest as a legitimate activity for Buddhist practice, giving birth to "engaged Buddhism" in the process.[22] Buddhist activism and internationalism, including the publication of several Buddhist magazines that had a reformist and internationalist vision, continued right up to reunification in 1975.[23] Meanwhile, in the north, there was little activity, and under state control and supervision, the Buddhist institution did very little to educate monks or lay practitioners, and Buddhism stagnated. For example, all publication of Buddhist magazines ceased from 1954 to 1991, when the magazine *Tạp chí Nghiên cứu Phật học* was first published out of Quán Sứ Pagoda in Hanoi (Nguyễn Đại Đồng 2008, 201). For this reason, it is not at all surprising that many Buddhists—and particularly the ones at Sùng Phúc—feel that Buddhist monks from southern Vietnam are superior to ones from the north. The result, however, is that Sùng Phúc is not oriented toward fulfilling a local, northern Vietnamese religious role or toward conforming to local modes of religious expectation.

Emphasis on the Historical Buddha

In concert with the internationalist vision, there was an attempt by reform movements to accentuate the commonalities of different kinds of Buddhism. By and large, this has led to an accentuation of the philosophical basics of Buddhism (especially as encoded in the Four Noble Truths), a stress on practice, particularly meditation and moralistic practices (especially as encoded in the Noble Eightfold Path and the Five Precepts), and in key symbols of Buddhism (especially as encoded in the Three Refuges [Skt. *triratna*, literally, "three jewels"]), the Buddha, the Dharma, and the sangha). Foremost of the changes in discourse about a unified Buddhist religion was repositioning the historicized Buddha at the center of the religion and a corresponding de-emphasis on the Mahāyāna Buddhist pantheon.

Thus, at Sùng Phúc, we see that the main shrine is dedicated entirely to the historical Buddha. The main statues portray the Buddha in the gesture of the Flower Sermon (linking the unifying Buddha with the Zen identity of Trúc Lâm). Along the top of the walls surrounding the room are large panels portraying key events from the life of the Buddha. The only iconography not directly related to the historical Buddha are the statues of Mañjuśrī and Samantabhadra on either side of the main statue in a manner typical of many parts of Mahāyāna Asia. Likewise, the centrality of the historical Buddha in the meditation hall, along with the large collection of supposed Buddha relics that dominates the center of the room, emphatically assert his centrality to the discursive structure of the place.

This centrality of the Buddha is reinforced through practice as well. The repetitive utterance of "Mô Phật!" as a form of greeting, rather than the Pure Land Buddhist greeting of "A Di Đà Phật!" that is the norm in regular Buddhist pagodas, engrains this centrality.[24] Likewise, when people are gathered in a formal setting, they always evoke the historical Buddha with "Nam Mô Phật Bổn Sư Thích Ca Mâu Ni" before the speaker begins. Similarly, the Buddha's name is chanted before lectures, before and after lunch, and at the beginning and end of the Penitence Rite.

In these ways, the historical Buddha is accentuated at Sùng Phúc and in the Trúc Lâm organization as a whole, while the other buddhas and bodhisattvas are pushed to the margin. The placing of Siddhārtha Gautama at the center of the religion as a human founder rather than a divine being is a feature of the prominent discourse of Buddhist globalism. It has its roots in the pan-Asian Buddhist reform movements that took place at the beginning of the twentieth century and has been adopted by Western Buddhists. It serves the dual purpose of humanizing and secularizing Buddhism, while also providing a commonly recognized unifying symbol.

Total Life Practice and Focus on Youth

Another important aspect of Trúc Lâm Buddhism as it is enacted at Sùng Phúc is that it is viewed as a total life commitment. Regular Buddhists rarely do more than participate on the first and fifteenth of the lunar month by making offerings. More committed lay Buddhists may chant sutras four times a month, and some may attend lectures. However, this level of commitment is usually undertaken by a group of committed old women. More often, commitment may take the form of eating vegetarian several days a month, with the number of days increasing with the devotee's level of commitment (or desire to be seen as being devout), or it may manifest in increased donations. At Sùng Phúc, there is a much higher demand made of practitioners. Most lay devotees at Sùng Phúc with whom I spoke tried to go every weekend, and a number tried to go in the evenings as well. Those who could not tried to recite the penitence liturgy and meditate daily at home if they could not get to Sùng Phúc and would watch and listen to recordings of Dharma talks. Many retired people attended lectures held during the week. Therefore, the overall level of commitment was much higher, with the expectation being that devotees made Buddhism a central part of their life. The level of commitment was not always welcomed by unsympathetic family members; one older man whose wife was involved at Sùng Phúc lamented to me about the amount of time she spent on Sùng Phúc–related activities. He said that regular Buddhism was fine because it expected people to do things only a couple of times a month, but Sùng Phúc wanted followers to be doing things all the time, and he felt this was excessive.

Related to this expectation that Buddhism was not relegated to specific times but should be central and formative of one's entire life as a moral guide and life practice is the considerable energy put into youth activities at Sùng Phúc. At most pagodas, one cannot help but notice that virtually all participants other than monastics are older and retired, the reason for which I have written about at length elsewhere (see Soucy 2012). At Sùng Phúc, by noticeable contrast, people of all ages, and not just elders, are fully involved. While the regular Saturday program is attended by adults of all ages, Sùng Phúc has developed a range of activities that are intended to make Buddhism relevant and attractive to young people. This includes a regular Sunday program for youths and the extended program at the end of the month, but also special events like the youth jamboree that I described (youth activities will be discussed further in chapter 7). The weddings that are uniquely held at Sùng Phúc also involve Buddhism in more than just death rituals, making it an integral part in the lifecycle rites of young people. Finally, the Sunday school serves to teach the very basics of Buddhism to children, educating them in such things as the Five Precepts, the Four Noble Truths, and the standardized hagiography of the historical Buddha. Taken as a whole, it is notable that Sùng Phúc's portrayal of Buddhism is that it should be fully integrated into a person's life rather than a segmented aspect, and it is thought to be a life practice rather than a practice merely adopted as one gets older and retires.

The Zen–Pure Land Distinction

Trúc Lâm Zen is influenced by the perspective of the earlier reformers, reinforced by the globalized modernist orthodoxy, and reflects an understanding of Buddhism that is individualistic and disenchanted (to be discussed at greater length in the next chapter). The modernist interpretation draws a distinction between Zen vis-à-vis Pure Land Buddhism that is pivotal for how Zen practice relates to the identity projects of many of the adherents.[25] The process of distinction-making establishes an identity and purpose, set against the standard understandings and practices of Buddhism that are rooted in Pure Land Buddhism.

The idea of distinct schools of Buddhism has not previously been an important part of the way Buddhism was practiced in Vietnam, and most scholars writing about Vietnamese Buddhism acknowledge that Buddhism in Vietnam is a blending of the different schools (e.g., Thích Thiên Ân 1970). The notion of blending different schools is predicated on the understanding that there are distinctions between schools, a view that developed during the reform period and as part of the emergence of a global Buddhist orthodoxy. While the everyday practice of most people is not Pure Land Buddhism in the sectarian sense, "Pure Land Buddhism" has become the label that Vietnamese use for the standard devotional practices. From 1997, when I began research on Buddhism in Vietnam, to around 2005, when I first encountered Trúc Lâm, few people would actually volunteer the label when describing themselves, and they never made a distinction between their own devotional Pure Land practices as a distinct school, and particularly one distinct from Zen.

Practitioners at Sùng Phúc were therefore peculiar in pointedly defining themselves as Zen devotees and rhetorically drawing a distinction with Pure Land Buddhism as the "other." While not usually stated outright, Trúc Lâm adherents implicitly elevated Zen to superior status, seeing it as rational, as stressing the individual and self-reliance, and as based on the evidence of personal experience, compared to Pure Land's superstition (even while recognizing Pure Land Buddhism in its orthodox form), over-reliance on a supernatural being (Amitābha), and dependence on unverifiable faith.

These distinctions are explicitly taught by Thích Thanh Từ. He writes that Zen is the original root of Buddhism (Thích Thanh Từ 2002c, 174–183), and he compares the Zen and Pure Land schools in works such as *Phương pháp tu Tịnh độ tông và Thiền tông* (The methods of the Pure Land and Zen schools) (Thích Thanh Từ n.d.) and "Chỗ gặp gỡ và chỗ không gặp gỡ giữa Thiền tông và Tịnh độ tông" (Where the Zen and Pure Land

Schools meet and don't meet) (Thích Thanh Từ 2009b, 159–183). In the latter essay he writes:

> Firstly, as we know, in following Pure Land Buddhism faith is of foremost importance. In Pure Land Buddhism you need to have all of the following: faith [*tín*]; practice [*hạnh*]; and commitment [*nguyện*]. Faith is trust: trust that there is certainly a Land of Bliss [Sukhāvatī], trust that if you recite Amitābha's name [*niệm Phật*] he will guide you to Sukhāvatī. Only when you firmly believe can you begin to practice [*hạnh*] completely. When you *niệm Phật* you have to vow [*nguyện*] to be reborn in the Land of Bliss. Only then do you have enough of "Faith—Practice—Commitment." Of these, faith is the first step on the road to practice. The Zen school, on the other hand, doesn't rely on faith but on wisdom [*trí tuệ*] as the first step. [In Zen] we use wisdom to discriminate, but [for the Pure Land school] faith forms the basis for action. This makes the two approaches [i.e., Zen and Pure Land] different. (Thích Thanh Từ 2009b, 160)

He goes on to describe in subsequent pages how in the Pure Land school, the practitioner relies on an external force to guide him or her to the Pure Land, while Zen teaches the individual to rely on oneself by inquiring into one's own character through meditation. In doing so, he emphasizes the internality of Zen in contrast to faith in an external force as taught by Pure Land Buddhism (Thích Thanh Từ 2009b, 160–161). In *Phương pháp tu Tịnh độ tông và Thiền tông*, he explains that both paths are viable if done correctly, but he is clear that they involve very different processes, and he indicates that many people undertake Pure Land practices incorrectly and from a wrong understanding (Thích Thanh Từ n.d., 4–7). Thích Thanh Từ elaborated in a Dharma talk he gave at Thường Chiếu monastery in Đồng Nai Province in southern Vietnam in 2000:

> I ask, if a Buddhist falls ill they go to a monk to request prayers, but who will pray for the monk if he falls ill? Of course, he goes to the doctor. So, if that is the way it is, why don't the lay Buddhists just go directly to see the doctor? If the monk is sick, he can pray for himself. Monks and nuns can all pray for themselves; so lay Buddhists should be able to do the same. However, the monks go to the doctor while the lay Buddhists just go to the monks for their prayers. Can you believe it? Is this what you call wisdom? I have been talking about the living up until now, but let's turn our attention to the dead. If praying for salvation when someone dies was useful then why didn't the Buddha pray constantly, since liberation for all beings was his goal? If you read the history of the Buddha, though, does the Buddha ever go to funerals to pray for liberation for the dead? Never. The Buddha had great compassion and wanted to assist all living beings, but he never prayed like that. So, by praying we are basically claiming that we

are even more compassionate than the Buddha. We have misled lay Buddhists by teaching them to pray instead of teaching them the proper way to practice. (Thích Thanh Từ 2000a)[26]

The opinions of many of the practitioners at Sùng Phúc also reflect the distinction that Thích Thanh Từ makes between Pure Land Buddhism and Zen. Most consider meditation to be a more advanced Buddhist path than the devotional Pure Land practices in which most people engage. Echoing Thích Thanh Từ, an acolyte at Sùng Phúc juxtaposed what he called the "path of wisdom" with the "path of devotion" during our conversations. He would not go so far as to overtly assert meditation as a superior path, but he implied that it was preferable for those who are at a high enough level. "The Zen path is not better, but it is faster," he told me, implying that it was better for those who were at a sufficiently advanced level. Devotees at Sùng Phúc tended to talk about Pure Land as another path, a kind of lower form of meditation. In 2004, the vice abbot admitted that not all practitioners at Sùng Phúc adopted meditation as their exclusive practice and that some continued to practice devotional forms of Buddhism at other pagodas. His attitude toward this was that as their level advanced, they would be able to leave the devotional practices behind, but maintaining the practices in parallel was not an issue. This view, that everyone should find their own path and that all ways, including Pure Land Buddhism, were valid, was echoed by others at Sùng Phúc. Yến, a young woman in her twenties who managed the bookstore, explained it to me this way:

You asked me why people here sit in meditation and do the Penitence Rite, and elsewhere people chant sutras and recite the name of Amitābha [niệm Phật]. In reality, they aren't any different. It's like you riding a Honda Dream [motorcycle] and me driving a car, and both being able to arrive at Sùng Phúc. It is like that. They niệm Phật to make their hearts at peace and directed toward the Buddha. And as for me, I am a busybody, so I find meditation more suitable for me, but it is directed toward liberation in the same way.

What is notable in this exchange is that reciting the name of Amitābha is seen as being an equally valid form of practice and is not diminished in comparison to meditation; both are seen as techniques to make one's heart more peaceful, but without supernatural effect or assistance from an external being.

Others tended to conflate Pure Land Buddhism with the regular devotional practices and held a less favorable view of Pure Land Buddhism as a result. Three lay women I interviewed in 2004 used Pure Land as a way to talk about the reason they turned away from practice at regular pagodas and embraced a more orthodox Zen:

> Before [we started practicing Zen] our hearts were very small. We would go to Buddhist rituals and force the monk to read out individual names to wish for good things for us and our families.[27] If the monk did not read our names, we would start to complain: "Why aren't our names in there?" Now we are not like that and don't make wishes anymore. The Buddha taught us the Law of Causality: if you give good things, you deserve good things; if you do cruel things, then you will get the same back. Making wishes won't alter this reality. In our ignorance, we wished for everything and always complained. We brought small offerings but asked for the world, because our greed was enormous. If you don't give good things, how can you ask to expect good things? It is nonsense. . . . Now, even when people ask us to take part in Pure Land rituals, we say no.

These women distinguished their practice as being more advanced than the practice of Buddhists who engaged in devotional practices. Their distinctions were thus something of a performance aimed at building symbolic capital by identification with the elitist tropes of Zen as being for smarter, more cultured, more spiritually advanced beings. At the same time, there was also a sense in which attaching themselves to Zen was part of ongoing identity projects building their own sense of self-worth.

Dress is one of the most important external markers of distinction. In northern Vietnam, every pagoda has a group of dedicated Buddhists who gather to chant sutras four times a month. These more dedicated Buddhists identify themselves through their dress, donning brown robes when at the pagoda and usually wearing rosaries around their necks as markers of inclusion (Soucy 2012, 133–135). At Sùng Phúc, robes are used in a similar way, but rather than wearing the common brown robes used throughout northern Vietnam, they wear the gray robes that are more common in the south. While gray robes have no particular meaning in the south, as it is the color of robes worn by all Buddhists there, in the context of the north, the gray robes serve to differentiate followers of Zen at Sùng Phúc from the followers of Pure Land Buddhism everywhere else. This distinction is central to their identity as Zen practitioners, particularly since many followers at Sùng Phúc are not familiar with the practices of Buddhists in southern Vietnam. As one old woman explained to me when I asked the reason for the gray robes, "We wear gray robes because we follow Zen. Brown robes are for Pure Land Buddhists."

Many are heavily invested in their identities as Zen Buddhists. Once, I asked some followers about another follower (not mentioning who it was) whom I had seen wearing a mantle over her shoulders on an occasion outside of Sùng Phúc. When I posed the question, I assumed that it had something to do with Trúc Lâm. To my surprise, they were alarmed by what I had said. "Who is this woman?" they asked. "She shouldn't be wearing this if she is following the master. She must be following another monk as well. This is very bad." A few days later, at Sùng Phúc, I ran into one of them as she was speaking about this "problem" to another woman. Her description betrayed that being exclusive to Trúc Lâm was important to how she constructed her Zen identity.[28] This incident illustrates how for some people, there is a feeling that regular devotional practices should be discontinued once Zen practice has been adopted.

While there were a range of perspectives regarding Pure Land Buddhism, it was clearly important that the distinction be made as an identity statement, to distance practitioners from Pure Land beliefs and practices. In some cases, drawing these distinctions rhetorically created a normative Pure Land school that in reality does not exist. This allowed them to condemn the devotional practices that take place throughout northern Vietnam while not directly challenging the legitimacy of a normative Pure Land school. However, more often, Pure Land practices and beliefs were conflated with popular practices that were deemed to be superstition.

The layout of the Sùng Phúc compound and the activities that take place there say a great deal about the overall orientation of Sùng Phúc. First, they serve to establish Sùng Phúc and the Trúc Lâm organization as distinct from the regular form of Buddhism found throughout Vietnam. A rhetorical distinction is made between Zen and Pure Land Buddhism, though it is made with care in most cases. A more rigorous distinction is made between Zen, as the true Vietnamese Buddhism, and the practices of Buddhists most commonly found in Vietnamese pagodas, which Thích Thanh Từ and his followers condemn as erroneous:

> It very sad that there are many pagodas where people just rely on faith but don't use intelligence. They make offerings to the Buddha to get his blessings and to gain merit. Whenever they do anything, they first have to obtain blessings and protection from the Buddha. Afflicted by greed, hatred and ignorance, living in frustration and misery, they go to the pagoda to light incense and make wishes to the Buddha for him to relieve them of all their troubles. So, is this practicing with wisdom or is it just blind faith? If it is just faith, then it is not intelligent, and without using intelligence you

can't get awakening, and if this is the goal, what is the point? It often makes me very sad that Buddhists in Vietnam just rely on the monks and nuns. When they get sick, they ask monks to pray for them; when they die they ask monks to do a ritual for them. They just hand over money for the monks to pray for their peace and liberation. With that alone they feel satisfied that they have practiced well. (Thích Thanh Từ 2000a)[29]

This distinction between Trúc Lâm Zen in Vietnam and regular Buddhism is made through structures and practices unique to Trúc Lâm and Sùng Phúc, influenced by key elements of the Buddhist Reform movement, and are an outcome of the globalization of Buddhism. They include an emphasis on the historical Buddha; an attempt to purify Buddhism or to bring it back to an imagined original core of Buddhism, which usually involves a cleansing of elements that are seen as cultural accretions and as superstition; a rephrasing of Buddhism in a rationalist way that deemphasizes supernatural elements and secularizes Buddhism; and a view of Buddhism as a practice that saturates all elements of one's life and is relevant for practitioners of all ages rather than as confined to certain days and as being appropriate only for old people. Consequently, Trúc Lâm and Sùng Phúc make a strong effort to include activities and events that are directed specifically toward children and youths. Finally, these elements are packaged and given legitimation by both universalizing and internationalizing Trúc Lâm, while at the same time accentuating the nationalistic elements. These important aspects of Sùng Phúc will be discussed in greater depth in the chapters that follow.

PART 2

CHARACTERISTICS

CHAPTER THREE

||||||||

Secular Buddhism

Thích Thái Phước is a young-looking, friendly, and dynamic monk. When I first met him, he was notable for having started the youth group at Sùng Phúc. Since then, he has left Sùng Phúc to start a new monastery in Sa Pa, a hill town close to the Chinese border to the northwest of Hanoi, largely inhabited by the Hmong ethnic minority group and a major tourist destination in northern Vietnam. Thích Thái Phước had been attracted to the philosophy of Buddhism when he was young, but it was his life experiences as a businessman in Ho Chi Minh City that deepened his appreciation. He related to me that he had owned a successful wicker factory that did business with a Taiwanese company. He had been doing very well and had become quite wealthy, but misfortune made him realize that money was transitory:

> Like the Buddha said, life is impermanent [vô thường]. Like money: you have it, then you lose it. I understood this before, but I hadn't yet had the opportunity to really understand this truth at a deeper level. There were many years when I did business and had a lot of money. At that time, around 1989 or 1990, when I was doing business with a wicker factory partnering with a Taiwanese company, I was making 300 to 400 million VND [$130,000 to $176,000 US in 2017]. But so many times when I went to do business, people tricked me, and I ended up with nothing.

His misfortune caused him to reevaluate his life:

> So then I thought about what the Buddha taught, that money is not really yours. It really belongs to năm nhà. What is năm nhà? They are water, fire,

the king, thieves, and bad children who squander their parents' fortune.[1] So your assets really belong to these things, since they have the power to destroy your wealth. For example, the tsunami in Japan destroyed everything in an instant. These things belonged to water, so the water took it. For fire, if you save your fortune for hundreds of years but then the fire burns it all, you have nothing left. In a blink of an eye, you are left empty-handed. When you do something wrong and the government comes and takes everything away, then you are also destitute. When a thief steals your fortune, then you are also left with nothing. The last one is your children. If they become addicted to drugs or to gambling, then they steal your money to feed their addictions, and everything is, likewise, also gone. So the Buddha said that your wealth belongs to *năm nhà* and doesn't really belong to you. After I experienced this kind of loss, I realized that the Buddha was right. Then I decided that I needed to renounce. It was at that time that I decided to become a monk. I told myself that I had to bring the Buddha's teachings and my experience in life to tell young people. I had been there, so I understood all of these things and suffered when I lost everything. I was very miserable when I lost everything. Now I understand that fortune is empty of reality. If you are fated that way, then it will come to you, but when your good luck runs out, that's the end of it. It is the same with fortune or your wife and children. When you have enough good fortune [*có đủ duyên*] they come to you, and when you are out of good fortune [*hết duyên*], they are gone. Everybody has to die at some point. When the time is up for someone you love, then they die, and when they die, they are gone, despite your desire for them to stay with you for your whole life. These things I realized.

At the age of twenty-seven, he decided to renounce and become a monk. He was immediately attracted to Zen after reading Thích Thanh Từ's book *Ba vấn đề trọng đại trong đời tu của tôi* (Three significant issues in my life as a renunciate) (Thích Thanh Từ 1997). The book addressed some questions he had, including where humans come from and their reason for existence, whether there is life after death, and whether there is a solution to the problems of old age and death, and it had an important impact on him:

> When I read that book, I felt that the Most Venerable [Thích Thanh Từ] was a very wise teacher; very special. I felt that I needed to rely on him, to leave home and to study. The Most Venerable teaches very realistically [*thiết thực*], not in a superstitious way like other sects. His way is very compatible with science and with modern humanist thinking. The higher your education, the more you meditate instead of talking. So for the superstitious people, when they try Zen, it doesn't really penetrate [*không thâm nhập được*]. I decided that I had to follow this way. The Most Venerable Thích Thanh Từ is the greatest teacher for the twenty-first century.

Unsurprisingly, as a Trúc Lâm Zen monk and a teacher, Thích Thái Phước's descriptions of Buddhism and Buddhist practice reflected a modernist orthodox insistence that it was up to individuals to cultivate themselves. This came through particularly clearly in a lengthy discussion we had one day regarding the performance of mortuary rituals at Sùng Phúc, in which he distinguished the rationality of Sùng Phúc's practices from superstitious practices commonly found at most pagodas:

> Burning spirit money is not officially part of the Buddhist tradition. It is not part of the cultural makeup of Vietnam; it is actually Chinese. They created it and tricked us into adopting it. They created this practice in order to make money. Buddhism doesn't have a tradition of burning spirit money. So according to Zen, you have to practice Buddhism with wisdom. A Zen practitioner must use reason. That means you think about the true Dharma [Chánh pháp] and avoid conducting yourself in a misguided manner, like leading people to waste their time and money. For example, at Sùng Phúc, we direct them that rather than burning fifty or a hundred million đồng in spirit money for a ritual, they should instead use that money for charity. They could buy rice to give to poor kids or to some other charity, which has a positive impact in the real world. Our Buddhism teaches that you should do things that benefit everyone. You should not let people follow superstition. Buddhism doesn't have superstition.

Although he was not entirely secular in his view of Buddhism (believing, for example, that one of the purposes of conducting rituals at funerals was to teach the spirit of the dead the Dharma and that this would have a positive impact on their rebirth), in other ways, his view of Zen was that it was for the living. He pointed out that at Sùng Phúc, they gave Dharma talks at funerals primarily to benefit those still alive. He stressed that Zen was relevant for modern times and especially for young people (discussed further in chapter 7). His explanation of why he was drawn to Buddhism is classically orthodox, following the Buddha's own renunciation after experiencing the suffering in the world. Thích Thái Phước views Zen as beneficial from a soteriological sense, but he tended to stress how Zen is beneficial in a practical sense in everyday life.

The views that Thích Thái Phước expressed to me were different from those I had formerly encountered at pagodas around Hanoi, and they indicated an alternate way of practicing Buddhism and of understanding that practice. One of the most common religious acts in northern Vietnam is making offerings and reclaiming them as talismans that are believed to bring good luck.[2] The simple act of making these offerings is an essential element of interactions with the supernatural in Vietnam, whether in spirit-medium rituals, ancestor worship, communal house rites, or praying to the buddhas. The underlying notion is that there is a reciprocal relationship between humans and the supernatural, regardless of whether the supernatural power is a buddha, a bodhisattva, an ancestor, a god, a spirit, or a ghost. The supernatural are seen as either requiring, desiring, or deserving sustenance through offerings. In return, the supernatural is benevolent to humans, bestowing on them lives that are happy and lucky, wealthy and successful, and healthy and long. These qualities are represented by the gods Phúc, Lộc, and Thọ, who are deifications of these ambitions. Together, they underline the essential this-worldly nature of most religious practice in Vietnam. The giving and returning of gifts and the expectations of flows of benevolence show that relationships with the supernatural are understood as involving reciprocal ties between two parties. That is, relationships with the supernatural are built and maintained through the same mechanisms that govern human relationships, involving gift-giving and guided by notions of reciprocal obligation of moral debt (ơn) that serves to create affection and intimacy (tình cảm).

The buddhas and bodhisattvas are not commonly considered by most Buddhist practitioners in northern Vietnam to be qualitatively different from gods and spirits. In 2011, for example, I bought a statue of the Buddha in a store for my mother-in-law's birthday, and the store owner happily explained to me that "having a statue of the Buddha is good, because when you need good luck in business or anything else, you can pray to it and he will grant your wish." As another example, in March 2010, I went to the ancestor day ceremony at Vẽ Pagoda on the outskirts of Hanoi. Because the shrine room was already packed full, crowds of devout Buddhist women gathered outside the door to the main shrine, and they looked in as a ritual was being performed, many with their hands held together in displays of piety. As I stood outside with the crowd who couldn't get a seat inside, I watched as women came and went, usually bowing into the shrine room. What caught my interest was how several of them paused to stuff money into the hands of a statue of the bodhisattva Guanyin beside the door of the shrine, bowing and making wishes before going off to sit with friends, to buy something from one of the vendors of religious articles who had set up outside the pagoda gate, or to go say prayers and make offerings at the mother goddess shrine across the courtyard.

Understandings of Guanyin reflect the common understanding of the buddhas as embodying supernatural potency. The vast majority of supplicants who can be seen at Buddhist pagodas on the first and fifteenth of each lunar month, when supplications are understood as being more efficacious, would easily go to a spirit shrine in its stead and make the same kinds of requests.

Guanyin with a fistful of money at Vē Pagoda in 2010

The only distinctive feature of offerings to the buddhas as opposed to other supernatural beings is that the killing of living creatures is considered a moral transgression (*tội lỗi*), and therefore, offerings at Buddhist altars are vegetarian, mostly comprising fruit and cookies. Offerings are reclaimed as talismans (*lộc*) that are believed to bestow good luck. Some may be traded, usually with a representative of the pagoda who sits in a central location and distributes the pagoda's *lộc* before practitioners leave.[3] The *lộc* is then brought home and distributed to the family, with the idea that it will bring the whole family good luck and good health. There are, of course, other practices that take place in pagodas, such as sutra chanting sessions four times a month, but most Buddhist practitioners make these offerings as their only practice. Even for those who became more involved and participated in sutra chanting sessions, the explanations they gave for the motivations and expectations of their participation was not significantly different. Like the twice-a-month supplicants, they felt that their piety and actions would have the effect of bringing good luck, health, and fortune to their families.

In this worldview, time is seen as important, with certain times regarded as more efficacious than others. The beginning and end of the year and the first and fifteenth day of the month according to the lunar calendar (âm lịch) are understood as being especially potent. At these times, pagodas that are empty on most days suddenly teem with the devout seeking to take advantage of the day's supernatural potential. Daily life in Hanoi for most people, therefore, takes into account supernatural aspects of time. For instance, leaving the house at exactly noon is considered bad luck because this is when the streets are patrolled by the supernatural (quan đi tuần, the equivalent of the police in the supernatural realm), who can scoop up one's spirit, causing illness and bad fortune. When doing anything momentous—a business venture, marriage, funeral, moving to a new house, and so on—people usually consult a fortune-teller (thầy bói) to select appropriate times that are harmonious with their horoscopes. Certain spaces are also seen as being particularly powerful. The Vietnamese landscape is dotted with places marked by temples, pagodas, or shrines where the faithful can more successfully gain increased access to the supernatural to improve the chances for their wishes to be fulfilled.

We can generalize that the popular religious disposition in Vietnam is that the world is swimming with supernatural forces that must be navigated to avoid disharmony and to maximize chances for success. At Sùng Phúc, there is a break with this enchanted understanding. Instead, the practices, spaces, and schedules reflect modernist understandings of Buddhism as a religion, and the portrayal of Buddhism is rationalist in nature. The idea that the supernatural has an effect on our lives is denied, and Buddhist practice is reshaped so that it does not involve supplicating the buddhas for help but is instead directed toward perfecting the self.

This chapter will explore this radical reconstruction of Buddhism and how it relates to the influences of Buddhist globalization. I argue here that a prominent—perhaps central and defining—feature of this modernist discourse involves the secularization, disenchantment, or de-supernaturalization of Buddhism. This secularization recasts Buddhism as something more like a philosophy or psychology than a religion. This chapter will explore how the pronounced secularization of Buddhism has manifested itself in the Buddhist practices at Sùng Phúc and will explore the implications of this within the broader context of the globalization of Buddhism. I will start by explaining the sense in which I am using the idea of secularization and how secularization has defined the modernist understanding of Buddhism at a global level in the twentieth century. Then we will look more specifically at the shape it takes in the organization of the space at Sùng Phúc and in the practices that take place there.

SECULAR BUDDHISM

Charles Taylor has described the common understandings of secularism as a "subtraction story" (2007, 26–28), by which he means that secularism has been understood as what remains when religion is removed, leaving behind the truth of things. Religion, in this view, is seen as the froth, a cloaking, or deceptive effervescence that masks reality. While this popular understanding of secularism is implicit in much that has been written about secularization in the last century, Taylor points out that it is deeply problematic. The secular is itself constructed in opposition to religion rather than as something that is sui generis, and since religion as a category is a modern invention, the secular exists only as a counterpoint to it.

The reordering of Western thinking into sacred/religious and profane/secular and the subsequent globalization of this viewpoint has had a profound effect on how religion operates in contemporary global society. The impact of the secular is not simply that religion is separated from the non-religious but that religion as a category itself is invented, exported, and then taken up and employed by locals for their own political purposes (Picard 2017, 19).[4] The world becomes a disenchanted place that is no longer influenced by unknowable and unseen supernatural forces. The introduction of the notion of the secular has created the space where a distinction between the natural and the supernatural can be made, where in the past, this kind of distinction would have been inconceivable. As Taylor puts it, "One of the big differences between our forerunners and us is that we live with a much firmer sense of the boundary between self and others. We are 'buffered' selves. We have changed" (Taylor 2011, 38–39).

Disenchantment has also had a powerful effect on the reformulation of religion and views of ritual, so that collective ritual is marginalized and religious practice made into an optional practice chosen from a palette of possibilities, one of which is also non-participation. Ritual is transformed, according to Taylor, from an engagement with symbolic meaning through bodily actions that can have the real effect of provoking a supernatural response, to an inward transformation that is stimulated through symbols that are ultimately metaphorical (Taylor 2011, 51). It is precisely this shift toward internality that has been exported beyond the frontiers of the West in the construction of religion as a "function system" that stands distinctly apart from other function systems. Secularism created a space for people and institutions to operate outside the influence of supernatural forces. However, secularism not only operates outside religion but has also changed the inner workings of religion. Buddhism in particular has been profoundly shaped by the secularist way of viewing the world. What has emerged alongside the older, enchanted, and undifferentiated ways of practicing Buddhism is a new, modernist form that is secular in the sense that it has assumed a radical individualism, materialism, and humanist focus.

In sum, Taylor describes secularism as an entirely different way of thinking. The secular orientation that emerges in the modern period comprises five interlinking features: 1) personal commitment, referring to the expectation that religion is not just a matter of following along but that it demanded personal commitment or faith and that it was experienced individually; 2) disenchantment, meaning a fundamental shift to experiencing and explaining the world in a way that is utterly natural, of this world, and non-transcendent; 3) a drive to reform, or abolish, "false" religion or superstition; 4) disembedding of the individual from his or her social frameworks of family, clan, and society; and most importantly, 5) nonbelief as an option (Taylor 2011).

When I write about secular Buddhism, I am building on Taylor's ideas in referring to a fundamental shift in how Buddhism is practiced and how being a Buddhist is defined. This shift has several characteristics that correspond to Taylor's list, above: a conscious decision to undergo initiation and vows and to assume markings that define Buddhist identity and inclusion; an understanding of the teachings of the Buddha as being oriented toward self-cultivation and escape from the cycle of rebirth through techniques that are explained as psychological and scientific rather than as a means to improve the worldly situation of oneself and one's family (both dead and alive) through divine assistance; a conscious distinction between true, pure, or original Buddhism on one hand and superstition and cultural accretion on the other, achieved through systematic instruction of both monastics and laity; a view that Buddhism is a supremely individual act that can affect only one's own personal development and not one's community or family; and a view that Buddhism is commensurate with a humanist/scientific orientation.

This remaking of Buddhism to fit into the category of "religion" is now a discourse that has become globalized, though it is adopted and adapted in different ways at a local level. It is a discourse that originates from a Western, historically informed understanding of the world. It is therefore not surprising that the process of remaking Buddhism to be a religion also introduced a Western-derived framework of secularity and that this split between the religious and the secular informs how Buddhism is approached, conceived of, and practiced in contemporary Vietnam and elsewhere.

The evidence that I give here represents a profound internal shift in worldview, at least in the ways that people express and assert that view. Buddhism is being reshaped to be a religion both through the adoption of signifiers like the historical Buddha as a founder of the religion, but it also assumes a secularization that includes individual commitment and disenchantment. While rooted in Western historical dispositions and therefore prominent in Western approaches and interpretations of Buddhism (Scharf 1993), these modernist discourses of secularist Buddhism actually find their roots in Asian responses to the colonial encounter. It continues today in organizations like Trúc Lâm, which is converting Buddhists who had formerly practiced exclusively in a different way—in a communal way and in an enchanted way.[5]

Modernity is not uniformly experienced or expressed at a global level and cannot be simply reduced to a Western model; modernization is not just a synonym for Westernization. In the example of Trúc Lâm, we can see that rather than secularization being opposed to religion, it has been incorporated into Buddhism's conceptualization and practice. In this sense, some practitioners conceive of their participation in Buddhism as being entirely secular, while seeing no fundamental contradiction. In Vietnam, it is not usually the case that Buddhism is understood in this way, but in the construction of the Trúc Lâm space and the way they have altered practice, we see a pronounced movement in this direction.

The reconstruction of Buddhism that was discussed earlier was not merely a reaction to Western imperialism and Orientalist scholarship but was also an outcome of the ascendancy of secularism taking place in Europe and the Americas and its subsequent globalization. The spiritual crises in the West, brought on by the rise of scientific rationalism in the modern period, among other factors, created a disillusionment with religion that many felt would spell the end of religion. This was welcome by some, but for others, it created a deeply felt longing for some sort of noninstitutional spirituality (van der Veer 2014, 38). Buddhism was perceived by some Westerners, such as Paul Carus (1852–1919) and the Theosophist Henry Steel Olcott (1832–1907), as a religion for the modern times (Lopez 2008, 31; McMahan 2008, 97–107; Snodgrass 2009a, 54). Asian reformers had a different motivation, participating in this discourse as a way to resist Christian missionary pressures and recover from the wounds produced by the violent imperial encounter (van der Veer 2014, 56). A notable example was the Japanese contingent to the first Parliament of the World's Religions held in conjunction with the Chicago Fair of 1893, who argued that Buddhism's rational, experience-based outlook was more compatible with the modern scientific worldview than Christianity (Harding 2008, 65; Snodgrass 2003, chapter 9). To fulfill this role, Buddhism was altered by selectively stressing certain aspects while ignoring others in ways that amounted to an entirely new way of thinking of Buddhism, one that was greatly influenced by Western philosophy (Sharf 1993).

A new kind of Buddhism was born that shunned supernatural elements and the supplication of divine beings. Buddhism was demythologized, and its cosmologies reinterpreted as metaphorical. The demythologization and emphasis on the individual thereby internalized what were previously taken to be ontological realities (Bechert 1994, 255–256; McMahan 2008, 47). This "inwardness," Taylor points out, is an important aspect on the modern notion of the self, which has become dominant in the modern West and was subsequently globalized (Taylor 1989, 111).

In Mahāyāna Buddhism, the Pure Land sect confronted this shift by reinterpreting the Pure Land as metaphor. Thus, Taixu saw the Pure Land as something that could be created here and now (much like a utopia) rather than a place attainable after death with divine help. Taixu's interpretation was influential among elite Vietnamese Buddhist reformers, and there was considerable debate about whether the Pure Land was a place that actually existed. In the mind of reformers, what was at stake was a false reliance on the idea that if this world was not favorable, one could at least strive for the next. This, reformers felt, made Vietnamese overly compliant and unwilling to take action to bring about social change. So, for example, Thiện Chiếu, a reformist monk from the Mekong Delta region in southern Vietnam, published pieces in major Saigon newspapers that argued that the Pure Land was a state of mind rather than an actual place to be attained after death. However, this view was not universally held, and other Buddhists fought back by publishing vivid descriptions of the Pure Land, even in intellectual journals (Woodside 1976, 198–199).

In contrast to attempts to reinterpret the Pure Land as metaphorical and internal, Zen has been arguably more successful in realigning itself with the accent on internal transformation through one's own effort. D. T. Suzuki was the preeminent figure who has recast Zen as a practice that is singularly personal, making the individual more important than Buddhism itself

(Sharf 1993; McMahan 2008, 186–187). In one of Suzuki's earlier works, "Zen Sect of Buddhism," published in 1906–1907 in the *Journal of the Pāli Text Society*, he discouraged blind acceptance of external authority, like the sangha or texts, or reliance on the Buddha as a savior (Snodgrass 2009a, 64). Suzuki saw the Zen process as relying entirely on an intuitive exploration of one's own mind and on face-to-face transmission from master to student. In doing so, he decentered the focus of Orientalist scholarship so that its emphasis on texts, and especially the Pāli texts that were considered the most authentic, was challenged (Snodgrass 2009a, 63).

The modernist reconstruction of Buddhism also historicized the Buddha and presented him as a human example rather than as a cosmic being. Orientalist scholars like Rhys Davids took the position that the Pāli tradition was the nearest representation of the original Buddhism of Siddhārtha Gautama, while Mahāyāna was viewed as akin to Roman Catholicism (from a Protestant perspective) (Hallisey 1995, 34; Harding 2008, 96; Snodgrass 2007, 192). This Orientalist preferencing of an imagined original Buddhism also profoundly affected Buddhist reformers in Asia, who upheld and promoted the centrality of the Buddha in the new restructuring of Buddhism as a religion. The mythology of the Buddha was stripped away to supposedly reveal a biography of the Buddha as an extraordinary and exemplary man. The Buddha, in the modernist interpretation, has been redrawn, in the words of Winton Higgins, to be "like a contemporary Greek philosopher addressing human predicaments in turbulent times, attracting a following which forms communities committed to living by his teachings" (2012, 117).

Other aspects of Buddhism were demythologized as well. Shaku Sōen, the Japanese reformer and teacher of D. T. Suzuki, went to the World's Parliament of Religions held in Chicago in 1893 and portrayed Buddhism as being simultaneously compatible with Christianity and superior to it in Buddhism's ability to coexist with science by, for example, deemphasizing literal rebirth while emphasizing that the universe is run by the natural laws of cause and effect (McMahan 2008, 68–69).

In this new form, Buddhism has been reshaped and promoted as a psychology rather than a religion. Take, for example, this account of the interaction between one of the earlier proponents of a modernist Buddhism, Anagārika Dharmapala, with the noted religionist and psychologist William James, sometime between 1902 and 1904:

> In Boston [Dharmapala] wished to attend one of the classes which Prof. William James, the celebrated psychologist, was holding at Harvard University. The yellow dress that he had adopted after his return from the

Parliament of Religions made him a conspicuous figure in the hall, and as soon as Prof. James saw him he motioned him to the front. "Take my chair," he said, "and I shall sit with my students. You are better equipped to lecture on psychology than I am." After Dharmapala had given a short account of Buddhist doctrines the great psychologist turned to his pupils and remarked, "This is the psychology everybody will be studying twenty-five years from now." (Sangharakshita 1952 [2008])

Buddhist reformers in Vietnam also participated in this rephrasing of Buddhism in scientific terms. Reformist magazines published a number of articles starting in the 1930s that tried to show the compatibility of Buddhism with modern science. Nguyễn Thị Thảo shows that from the period from the early 1930s to after the Second World War, many of the magazines published articles that tried to explain the soul, the Pure Land, and hell from a scientific viewpoint (Nguyễn Thị Thảo 2013). Claims of the compatibility of Buddhism and science remain strong today, with international figures like the Dalai Lama stating that if science were to uncover anything that contradicted Buddhist ideas, then those Buddhist ideas must be discarded in favor of science (McMahan 2008, 115–116), and even scholars like B. Alan Wallace (2003) contributed to it by publishing academic accounts of how Buddhism is a kind of protoscience, uncritically participating in modernist Buddhist discourses that claim authority and legitimacy through highly selective comparisons.

The new emphasis on individual experience made meditation central to Buddhists influenced by modernist discourses, especially in the West. Its importance in Asia, while not pervasive, has also become more prominent and continues to increase. It would be a mistake, however, to think that it is merely Western predilections for meditation practices and toward Zen as a tradition that has bounced back to Asia. In fact, the constructions of Buddhism that emphasized meditation and the individual experience were formulated by Asian Buddhist reformers and then brought to the West. The rarity of meditation in Buddhist Asia before the reform period illustrates the extent to which its importance is a product of Buddhist modernism. Dharmapala tried in vain to find a monk who could teach him meditation in Sri Lanka and eventually had to travel to Burma to find an old monk to teach him (Sangharakshita 2008). The heir of the modernist discourses within Theravāda Buddhism has gone on to even more radically decouple other Theravāda practices like *dāna* (cultivating generosity through giving, particularly to the sangha) and merit transfer (whereby the monastic sangha is seen as a field of merit that can be transferred to the laity) from the centrality of meditation, seen particularly in the *vipassanā* meditation of Insight Meditation and Goenka (McMahan 2020).

What emerges is a kind of Buddhism that is uniquely secularized and disenchanted. Meditation as a technique is offered up as a replacement for chanting sutras, and an emphasis is placed on instruction rather than ritual. A Buddhist view of karma and rebirth is maintained, but with a strong rationalistic portrayal and an emphasis on moral action rather than the possible outcome in future lives. Rituals and chanting are not entirely abandoned, but their significance is reinterpreted as metaphorical rather than instrumental, as paying respect rather than supplication, or for increasing an understanding of the Buddha's teachings rather as magical incantation. The Buddha himself is historicized and taken as a human exemplar rather than as an active force.

While this is primarily how Buddhism is interpreted and portrayed by Trúc Lâm, there remain areas of ambiguity that contrast with the more complete secularization of Western Buddhist practitioners. For example, Shambhala Buddhists I have spoken with articulate that Tibetan Buddhist deities are representative of psychological conditions and should not be seen in a literal way, or a Western follower of Thích Nhất Hạnh who insisted that her Zen was a practice rather than a religion. These points of ambiguity are important, too, for understanding the popularity of Zen in contemporary Vietnam.

SECULAR BUDDHISM AT SÙNG PHÚC

The modernist secular interpretation of Buddhism at Sùng Phúc can be seen in the teachings, rituals, and practices that take place there. Sometimes it comes through forcefully, for instance in the writings of Thích Thanh Từ, which frequently reflect the modernist, reformist discourse that separates Buddhism from superstitious practices and beliefs:

> The Buddha's way of teaching was practical, there was nothing magical or superstitious about it. So today we shouldn't put up with practicing in blind faith without trying to gain an understanding [of what the Buddha taught]. People shouldn't believe that the Buddha will grant wishes, or assist us in our lives, or give us protection. Instead, we need to carefully scrutinize ourselves in order to apply the Buddha's teachings to eradicate our delusions. (Thích Thanh Từ 2000a)[6]

Thích Thanh Từ's secularist view of Buddhism accentuates inner transformation (rather than worldly gain or improved rebirth) through individual effort (rather than the assistance of the buddhas). It is systematically presented to the lay followers of Trúc Lâm at Sùng Phúc not only in Dharma talks and in the writings of Thích Thanh Từ but also in how the rituals are constructed and in the practices that are sanctioned and taught. Sùng Phúc has created a space that denies opportunities for engaging in reciprocal relationships with the buddhas. For example, there is no opportunity to make offerings and receive *lộc* (reclaimed offerings considered to be talismans that conveys the buddhas' blessings), which is how Buddhism is generally practiced in northern Vietnam. The layout of the shrine provides no place to assemble offerings, and the altar is supervised constantly by monks, which precludes devotees from placing offerings on it.

The unique and persuasive identity of Trúc Lâm is partially established through the distinctions it makes in relation to the regular form of Buddhism practiced in Hanoi. This modernist discourse is one of the more attractive elements for youths and men, who are more averse to supplicative practices they see as lacking an independent reliance on self and devoid of the goal of inner transformation. As one man in his seventies explained, its brand is so successful that it is changing the way regular pagodas are presenting themselves:

> When Zen came to northern Vietnam, it developed very strongly and also affected other schools, like Pure Land and Tantrism. Monks here have had to change because they always have to adopt and learn new things to adapt Buddhism to social trends. Therefore, now in pagodas in the north, monks are starting to improve. Before that—the truth is—they mixed superstitions with non-superstition [i.e., Buddhism], so that is what people followed. For example, they burned spirit items and spirit money, which is wasteful. At Sùng Phúc, there is no superstition [like at regular pagodas]. We don't burn spirit money here. Now monks elsewhere are slowly changing, too, and they are advising followers to not be wasteful.

The contrast between the spaces and supplicative religious practices at other pagodas and those at Sùng Phúc is instructive. At Sùng Phúc, on the first and fifteenth of the lunar month, there is no discernible increase in lay traffic to the monastery. On one sample morning in October 2011, a day that corresponded with the auspicious first day of the lunar month when other pagodas would have swelled with devotees, only a few lay Buddhists trickled into the compound at Sùng Phúc. In the meditation hall, I saw a couple of young people seated on the floor, one sitting facing a wall in meditation. The only movement in the ancestor hall and the main shrine was the volunteers doing their daily task of cutting and arranging flowers for the altars. The few lay Buddhists who passed through the main shrine, perhaps ten or so all morning, made no offerings; they merely paid respects to the statue of the Buddha, with the monk in attendance hitting the bowl gong once when the devotees bowed to the altar. Then they got on their motorcycles and left. Incense was not put into incense holders, nor were offerings of fruit and money made. No spirit money was burned. No *lộc* was received. While the buddhas were dispensing blessings at other pagodas in Hanoi that morning, none were available at Sùng Phúc. One layman explained it this way: "The abbot said that Śākyamuni statues are only made of earth and wood. I really respect Śākyamuni for what he gave humanity. But that was the end of it. He is dead. He knows nothing, so why do you burn sprit money for him?"

Not only was the traffic of devotees small in comparison to the crowds of devotees that I saw flowing through the gates of the regular pagoda a kilometer down the road, but unlike other pagodas, Sùng Phúc offered no special program to mark the first and fifteenth as unique. While other pagodas follow the lunar calendar for all festivals and ritual activities, Sùng Phúc holds a regular program based almost entirely on the solar calendar. There, lectures are offered three times during the week, on Tuesday, Wednesday, and Thursday afternoons at 2:00, attended by some of the monks and nuns and by a number of lay people. Every night there is a Penitence Rite, and on the weekends, there are activities for adults on Saturday and another for youths and children on Sunday. In response to my questioning about the lack of specific activities on the days usually considered more potent, one woman who had been involved at Sùng Phúc for over five years said to me:

> At Sùng Phúc, the monks have a very busy schedule. They get up every morning at three and meditate and then they have a rigid daily regimen, so they are always busy. At normal pagodas, they don't do anything except on the first and fifteenth. So at Sùng Phúc, they don't need to do anything special on the first and fifteenth. They are already busy every day.

This was the most common explanation given when I asked about this issue of sacred time. Another frequent explanation was that it was done this way to accommodate the work schedules of the devotees, which was important because, unlike at regular pagodas where attendees tended to be older and retired, many of the devotees at Sùng Phúc were younger and had work and school obligations. An older man who lived in a neighborhood near the Đuống Bridge (not too far from Sùng Phúc) explained it this way:

> Pure Land pagodas only follow the lunar calendar, so they don't have so many followers. Students or kids cannot go, so pagodas are nearly empty.

Chanting sutras and reciting the name of Amitābha [niệm Phật] is a little different from meditation; it doesn't allow you to release the heaviness inside [xả tâm]. So the activities at Sùng Phúc are very suitable with intellectual people, office workers, and laborers. There is an entire company where all of the employees come to Sùng Phúc. If the main day for rituals, meditation, and Dharma lessons fell on a day other than Saturday, they wouldn't be able to come. So at Sùng Phúc, they don't completely give up the lunar calendar. On the first and fifteenth, the monks still light incense and chant sutras like normal, but they don't have activities for regular lay Buddhists.

Both of these explanations were adequate to rationalize how the activities at Sùng Phúc were scheduled, though the frequency with which these responses were given to me and their similarity indicated that perhaps my interlocuters were repeating Trúc Lâm talking points. The reasonableness of the explanations obscures a fundamental switch in the way time and space have been radically reconceptualized at Sùng Phúc. By structuring activities according to the solar week and ignoring the supernatural potency associated with the lunar calendar, Trúc Lâm is not merely making things more convenient for their younger, working (or studying) followers; it is fundamentally altering the relationship between the Vietnamese people and the supernatural world. Time becomes a practical consideration, something used to ensure maximum participation, while the concept of a potent, supernatural time during which the buddhas are more responsive and supplication more efficacious is rejected. This is a drastic switch from an enchanted to a disenchanted worldview.

Trúc Lâm's bias against the common practices of supplication of the buddhas is synchronous with dominant orthodox discourses. The normative Buddhist institution that has driven the creation of a Buddhist orthodoxy holds the modernist view and disseminates these views through magazines available throughout Vietnam and online. Ironically, scholars who have studied Buddhism, both in Vietnam and internationally, also reproduce a view that dismisses supplicative practices as being something other than Buddhist (usually relegated to a category like folk religion or superstition). This judgment, at least on the part of supposedly objective scholars, represents a bias toward authoritative, orthodox, modernist understandings of Buddhism proposed by those who have a power stake in asserting this stance.[7] While it is important to avoid the bias toward orthodoxy, it is also crucial to recognize how Western (and Vietnamese) scholarship on Buddhism both mirrors and participates in discourses of orthodoxy that are central to the reconstruction of Buddhism as a religion. The rich and penetrating worldview of the supernatural most commonly held in Vietnam serves as the necessary rhetorical counterpoint for this modernist orthodoxy that Trúc Lâm Zen puts forward:

> First, we need to know that superstition is blind faith without reason or objective truth. I will give some examples for clarity: belief in spirit mediums, divination and fortune-telling, lucky or unlucky days, the predetermination of fate, palmistry and physiognomy, the efficacy of sacrificial rites, putting faith in protective talismans and exorcists, supplicative offerings to get through calamities or illness, and so on. These kinds of beliefs are unreasonable, lack evidence, and are without use, and that is why they should be called "superstition." (Thích Thanh Từ 2010b, 15)[8]

This secular rhetorical position, which refutes the efficacy of the buddhas' blessings, is a distinctive characteristic of Trúc Lâm. It is one that links the views of the Buddhist Reform movement, the Communist critique of religion, the orthodoxies that have been supported by the often unreflexive academic construction of Buddhism, and globalized discourses of Buddhist modernism.

SÙNG PHÚC AS A SECULAR SPACE

In chapter 2, I described the layout of Sùng Phúc as being very different from the regular pagodas in northern Vietnam. Though some of these differences represent the influence of Buddhist spaces from southern Vietnam, from where all the monks at Sùng Phúc come, there are substantial differences even from southern pagodas that mark this place as having a distinct worldview that is buffered and disenchanted. There is also an intentionality in the choices that the designers have made in the creation of this space that indicates not only a distinctive perspective that guided its construction but also a desire to discursively influence the users and visitors of the space.

As mentioned in chapter 2, the historical Buddha is the central focus at Sùng Phúc within an overall iconographic narrative that links Sùng Phúc and Trúc Lâm through the Chinese Chan lineages and back to the original Flower Sermon of the historical Buddha. We have already seen that by secularizing and humanizing the historical Buddha, he is erected as the unifying symbol of Buddhism as a global religion. The Buddha, as a teacher and an example, is a person, however extraordinary. From this viewpoint, while respect is owed him, making offerings and supplication is not seen as resulting in the Buddha's granting wishes for worldly benefit or salvation. The Buddha taught about karma, but he has no capacity to change karma.

Starting with the Buddhist Reform movement, Buddhist elements that create something identifiable as a unified religion were accentuated, while elements perceived as extraneous cultural accretions outside of the orthodoxy were weeded out. These excluded elements were pejoratively described as being "cultural" or "superstitions" and were assigned a value different from elements that were considered strictly part of Buddhism. More usually, they were condemned as superstition and discouraged. At Sùng Phúc, there is an absence of any physical aspects or spaces associated with what people in Hanoi commonly call the "spirit side" (*bên thánh*) (see Soucy 2012, 25–31). So while mother goddess shrines (*nhà mẫu*) are standard features at pagodas in northern Vietnam, they are missing at Sùng Phúc. Some of the only non-Buddhist iconography in the Sùng Phúc compound is in the communal house, which, although it is on the grounds of the monastery, is understood as belonging to the village rather than Sùng Phúc, and is usually closed. The only other non-Buddhist iconography is a small statue of the earth god (Ông Địa) placed under a bonsai tree near the guest reception room. The abbot insisted to me, however, that this statue, which is found in shops and homes throughout Hanoi and to whom offerings are made for good luck, is only decoration and not for worship.[9] This assertion was borne out by the fact that offerings were never made and incense never burned at the statue. Another missing element is a furnace for burning spirit money, a common religious practice in Hanoi but banned at Sùng Phúc. (Even the central pagoda, Quán Sứ, which discourages the practice, has a pair of furnaces for burning spirit money on either side of the main pagoda gate.)

The discouraging of these kinds of practices by altering the architectural elements that are usually part of pagodas in the north reflects anti-superstition rhetoric that has been a part of the Buddhist Reform movement since the very beginning and has been maintained by the Buddhist institutions of South Vietnam during the war and by the Communist state in the north since 1954. It is also reflective of the Western views and practices of Buddhism that have sought to return Buddhism back to its imagined essence and avoid practices that are seen as being culturally grounded rather than part of the "proper" Buddhism.

Burning spirit money (*vàng mã*) in one of the
purpose-built furnaces at Quán Sứ Pagoda, 2007

SECULAR PRACTICES

Zen Buddhism as it is presented by the Trúc Lâm organization and at
Sùng Phúc is rationalized and secularized. In contrast with Buddhism as
it is generally practiced in the north, Trúc Lâm stresses the importance of
individual action, comprehension, and inner transformation rather than
divine assistance. Until the last decade, efforts to educate lay Buddhists in
the north have been limited. In 1997–1998, when I began my research in
Hanoi, Buddhist lectures where given only at Quán Sứ Pagoda and Bà Đá
Pagoda, the headquarters of the Buddhist Association of Hanoi (Thành
hội Phật giáo Hà Nội). Although called "lectures" (*giảng*), these gather-
ings often amounted to little more than recitations of sutras, and most attendees were more interested in gaining merit from attendance than in
gaining knowledge from listening. The sutras themselves were written in

Sino-Vietnamese in modern romanized script (*quốc ngữ*), making them difficult for most practitioners to understand. By contrast, the sutras and rituals at Sùng Phúc use colloquial Vietnamese so that everyone can understand them. Furthermore, every opportunity is taken to teach Buddhism through Dharma talks, whether at a Sunday program for youths or a mortuary ritual.

Trúc Lâm's program comprises four main practices: meditation, study, moral behavior, and ritual. While none of these is unique to Trúc Lâm Zen, their manner of presentation and practice, naturalistic explanations, and disassociation from the supernatural constitute a rephrasing of Buddhism as distinctly modernist and secular. All are seen in terms of individual striving and internal transformation.

Meditation as Secular

Meditation was not an important—let alone, central—Buddhist practice before the advent of global Buddhism. As Lopez points out, in China, around 80 percent of monks lived in hereditary temples where their mainstay practice consisted of rituals dedicated to the dead; in Japan, this is still the case (Lopez 2002, xxxviii). In Theravāda countries, where meditation is considered a core element along with scriptural study, it is the scriptural study that is most highly esteemed; meditation monks are held in low regard and generally thought to be incapable of study (Lopez 2002, xxviii). Needless to say, lay Buddhists, whether Theravāda or Mahāyāna, did not meditate at all, while only a few monks meditated as part of their regular practice. Only in the modern period has meditation becomes central: "In keeping with the quest to return to the origin, Modern Buddhists looked back to the central image of the tradition, the Buddha seated in silent meditation beneath a tree, contemplating the ultimate nature of the universe" (Lopez 2002, xxxvii).

In Vietnam, meditation has also not been an important part of practice for the vast majority of Buddhists. To be sure, there have been monks throughout the centuries who practiced meditation from time to time and followed Zen teachings, but as Cuong Tu Nguyen has stated, these individuals were, and still are today, exceptions (Nguyen 1995, 113; 1997, 98). Before I was introduced to Sùng Phúc, I had not met anyone in northern Vietnam who meditated. When people did occasionally speak about meditation, they described it in its symbolic status, held up as an ideal practice of Buddhism rather than as something that people actually did, an activity that was practiced by mummified monks of the past, not living Buddhists today. By 2004, I had begun to see books on meditation in bookstores around Hanoi. Still, some people felt that teaching meditation to lay

Buddhists was inappropriate, even recklessly dangerous. One monk in Hanoi told me a story of a lay Buddhist who had not been properly prepared and had sunk into a deep trance from which it had taken days to revive. The story was used specifically as a criticism of Thích Thanh Từ for indiscriminately teaching meditation to lay Buddhists; the monk who related the story did not meditate himself and felt that meditation was a mystical practice that should not be undertaken by those who were not properly conditioned.

Although meditation is a central practice at Sùng Phúc, it is notable that it has been largely stripped of mystical connotations. Rarely did my informants say anything about meditation having a supernatural transformative effect. The textual manifestation of Zen in Vietnam, particularly as seen in the *Thiền uyển tập anh,* often stressed the supernatural powers of eminent monks. While Trần Văn Giáp tended to overlook this aspect of the text, displaying the magical powers of eminent monks seems to have been centrally important to the writers of the *Thiền uyển.* The biography of Trí Nhàn, for example, focuses on the mystical powers gained through meditation rather than its potential for achieving enlightenment or improving mental health:

> After comprehending the essence of the teaching. He went directly to Mount Từ Sơn and lived under a tree. During the day he chanted the sūtras, and at night he practiced meditation, devoting himself diligently to austerities. He vowed to keep this up for six years.
>
> One day he was sitting in meditation when he saw a tiger chasing a deer toward him. Trí Nhàn said to them: "All sentient beings cherish their lives—you should not harm each other." The tiger bowed its head to the ground as if he were taking refuge [with a teacher], and then went away. (C. T. Nguyen 1997, 193)

The potential for meditation to generate magical ability is excluded in the modernist view. Instead, meditation is seen in scientific and secular terms as affecting one's psychology and improving one's outlook on life. As Thích Thanh Từ stresses, it is meant to make one wiser and more peaceful:

> This meditation method follows the tradition of Vietnamese Zen, including a number of basic stretches and exercises that we have developed over time for monks and nuns to practice at our Zen monasteries, as well as for interested lay Buddhists. We have found through careful testing that these practices have the following results: the body and mind [*thân tâm*] gradually become calm [*an định*], wisdom [*trí tuệ*] increases, so that your

life becomes pure [*thuần*], virtuous [*thiện*] and peaceful [*an lạc*]—this manifests in actions of self-sacrifice, for the peacefulness and well-being of friends, family and society. (Thích Thanh Từ 2010a, 3–4)

One of the most common ways that meditation becomes secularized is in a belief in its health benefits, a value that practitioners stressed to me. Good health was probably the most frequently cited reason for involvement in this form of practice and also one of the main factors that initially attracts many followers to Sùng Phúc. Mrs. Tuyết, whom we will meet in chapter 5, expressed several times that her health was the main motivation behind taking up meditation. A young student of medical anthropology whom I interviewed in 2004 also said that one of the reasons she became involved in Trúc Lâm Zen was related to the health benefits of meditation, but with the twist of wanting to learn to harness the power it generates to heal others:

In fact, the reason that I meditated at that time [when I first became interested] was I had a class that was called "Meditation for Healing." They use the method of meditation to open energy points in the body for the purpose of healing sickness in others. That is, they gain the ability to make energy that can then be transmitted through their hands. They lay their hand on the energy points of the other person's body to open these energy points and are able to cure the person of a number of ailments. At that time, I attended that class and the teacher of that class really liked me. He said that I had an aptitude for doing this. In fact, I didn't like it much myself because before starting I was a Buddhist and had been reading books on Buddhism since I was young. . . . If you do normal meditation, it will take you ten or twenty years to get this kind of energy, and you will have to retire to a forest cave. But with the method they were teaching, the teacher helps [by giving some of his power] so that your energy can flow more quickly. However, there is a shortcoming, which is that they don't concentrate on controlling your breath, and if you can't control your breath, then you can't regulate your heart/mind [*tâm*].[10] I also wanted to regulate my heart/mind because in Buddhist meditation, like in Indian yoga and in other kinds of meditation, they all speak about controlling the heart. I felt that the teacher was not paying attention to regulating the heart/mind, so I switched to Buddhist meditation. That is what pushed me to study Zen, though actually, I have been a Buddhist since I was very young.

While she seems to be speaking of meditation as a way to gain access to spiritual healing, these kinds of healing practices are typically seen in Vietnam in scientific terms, as medicine rather than religion, in much the same way that spiritualists in the nineteenth century viewed their practices as "a secular truth seeking, experimental in nature and opposed to religious obscurantism and hierarchy" (van der Veer 2014, 38). The scientific view of meditation was also clear in a description of meditation that was given by an older male practitioner at Sùng Phúc:

> Sitting [i.e., meditation] closes your blood circulation in your body. The blood pumps to your brain, and therefore your brain cells receive more blood, making you more intelligent. So you will become more tolerant than regular people. We only spend one-tenth of our brain cells. So when we sit in meditation, all the blood that is blocked in your lower body is diverted to the brain, allowing it to open. It means the brain cells are open, and this gives you more energy, making you smarter, more consistently intelligent. If you sit like that for hours, it is wonderful. It means you become liberated, but you also have good health. When I was in the army, I had a skin disease, but after four years of meditating, my skin problem was cured. That disease really made me suffer, and medicine didn't work. But when I went to the Zen center to meditate, it changed my hormones because of the meditation. It made my immunities stronger, my liver, heart, lungs heathier. I sleep better now. So it's very good. My blood pressure is normal, lung and heart and liver are good. It's good for your health; it's also good for your mental health [tâm lý] and for your intellect [trí tuệ].

The health benefits of meditation are used as a lure to attract new followers. An acolyte at Sùng Phúc suggested in 2004 that I would benefit greatly from meditation, since the life I was living was filled with stress. Meditation, he felt, was the best way to relieve some of this stress and improve my health.

The association between health and meditation extends beyond Trúc Lâm Zen and is pervasive in representations of meditation in popular culture and self-help literature. Books are now available in Vietnam that reinforce the view of meditation and Buddhism as something other than a traditional religion. Representative of this growing body of literature was a book I saw on display at a bookstore in Hanoi in 2004 whose cover featured a Shaolin-type monk in a martial arts stance and whose title was *Phật giáo và sức khỏe* (Buddhism and health) (Dương Quốc An 2004). This way of viewing meditation, and Buddhism more generally, mirrors meditation as it is presented in the West.

It might be surmised that medicine and health practices are becoming popular in response to the state's withdrawal of free medical care. As in the West, however, it is often those with more disposable income and leisure time who have the luxury of becoming engaged in activities like meditation or aerobics. The practitioners at Sùng Phúc seemed to be those who would not have suffered most from the withdrawal of state support for public health care. Instead, the focus on meditation as beneficial for health represents the impact of global constructions of Buddhist meditation that increasingly portray meditation in natural and scientific terms, detached from the religious aspects (McMahan 2020).

Secularization of Ritual

The Penitence Rite is performed every evening at Sùng Phúc and is a main part of the regular program on Saturdays, along with meditation and a Dharma talk. It is also expected that lay Buddhists will perform it at home as a core part of their practice (along with meditation). The Penitence Rite along with the occasional rituals are, like meditation, viewed in a secular way. They show the fundamental shift in worldview that sees rituals as bringing about inner transformation.

The Penitence Rite

The Penitence Rite at Sùng Phúc differs substantially from the Penitence Rites usually performed at other pagodas, where they are called Sám Nguyện. The liturgy that is usually used at regular pagodas involves chanting sutras and reciting the names of buddhas and bodhisattvas. The primary goal for most people is to secure the buddhas' blessings and thereby bring material benefit to themselves and their families in their daily lives. People also frequently explain that they need to perform the Penitence Rite because of their karmic burden, usually referring to their need to be pardoned. They feel that their participation would help ensure that the Buddha would absolve (xá) them of their sins (tội lỗi).

At Sùng Phúc by contrast, the Penitence Rite was explained as being focused solely on individual cultivation. Yến, for example, a woman in her twenties who worked in the bookstore and practiced Zen at Sùng Phúc, denied that the Buddha's forgiveness is of any importance for the Penitence Rite:

> So, when you have sinned, you take refuge, recite the Five Precepts, and the Penitence Rite. It's as if I have done something against you, and when I meet you, I say sorry. You can also use the term "sám hối." If I think I am wrong, I meet you and say I am sorry, and you accept the apology, right? You have forgiven me for my infraction. But if when I have finished apologizing, I then go somewhere and do something bad again, then was my apology of any use? When you participate in the Penitence Rite, you have to be penitent about all of the things you have done wrong, and then you have to correct them and don't repeat the offense, and only that way is it of any use.

Her explanation regarding the Penitence Rite shows a de-supernaturalization of ritual, whereby it is no longer believed that an external

supernatural entity responds to the performance of a ritual with benevolence that then brings good luck in her material life. Instead, the focus is
shifted to an internal transformation through rigorous practice, in the
way that Schwenkel and Leshkowich describe as central to neoliberal discourses of moral personhood (2012). Thus, we see that the Penitence Rite
is taught at Sùng Phúc as an opportunity for self-cultivation. This self-
cultivation will ultimately result in a more harmonious family life, perhaps, but not through divine favor or good karma. Rather, through
self-cultivation, the practitioner will have rooted out negative emotional
responses that are at the root of conflicts in the home, and their equanimity will serve as a good example for other members of the family to emu-
late. I only rarely encountered this view at other pagodas, and mostly by
men who were invested in distinguishing themselves from women by being more doctrinal.[11]

Weddings and Funerals

The two most frequently practiced occasional private rituals are weddings and funerals. Weddings are not an explicitly religious ceremony
in Vietnam. Standard weddings do not involve religious specialists,
and the religious element usually involves only the bride and groom
paying respect to each other's ancestors. The central focus of the wedding is the feast, which lacks any religious elements whatsoever. The
performance of monk-officiated wedding ceremonies at Buddhist pagodas is a very recent development that I have not seen elsewhere in
the north. Even at Sùng Phúc, such ceremonies are usually supplemen-
tal to the standard wedding rather than a replacement for it. Furthermore, none of the Buddhist weddings I witnessed involved full
families, whereas regular weddings are focussed more on the extended
family than about the bride and groom. In some cases, parents did not
attend the Sùng Phúc ceremony, though a scattering of other family
members would usually be there. The religious aspects of the ceremony included the officiating monk chanting, followed by an exchange
of rings, a Dharma talk, and photographs. The external form made it
appear to be modeled on a Christian wedding. However, there were no
implications that the Buddha blessed the union or that by doing the
service at a pagoda, good luck would be bestowed on the marriage.
Rather, the participants merely expressed that as Buddhists, they
thought it was appropriate to have a Buddhist service. In this way, the
weddings at Sùng Phúc represent shifts from the group to the individual and from a largely secular ritual to a religious one, albeit one that
was de-supernaturalized.

Memorial services are an entirely different story. They have long been the staple of Buddhist monastic service to the laity at all pagodas, and monastics are involved in many of the steps taken during the long process of mourning. The main reason for ritual interventions in common Buddhist mortuary rites is to assist the passage of the soul of ancestors through the process of the expiation of sins in the underworld and subsequent rebirth. This assertion that rituals and offerings can supersede the actions and intentions of the dead person, on whose behalf the rituals are performed, contradicts orthodox assertions of the cause-and-effect process of karma. This contradiction is underscored by Thích Thanh Từ's assertion that the Buddha never prayed on behalf of dead people.

At Sùng Phúc, the long ritual process is stripped down, and instead of the three-year process common in northern Vietnam, only a memorial service is performed at the monastery on the thirty-fifth day after death. Aside from chanting, there is very little in the way of ritual. No petitions (*sớ*) to the kings of hell are read and incinerated, and no spirit items (*hàng mã*) for use by the dead in the underworld or spirit money (*vàng mã*) are burned. Another difference is that teaching is made an important part of the service. The vice abbot at Sùng Phúc explained it this way:

> Thích Tĩnh Thiền: Hell [*địa ngục*] is in your heart. "*Địa*" is a place. "*Ngục*" is the form of suffering. . . . When one suffering in our heart ends, another begins. That is hell. In this place, our conscience, one state of suffering continuously gives rise to another without end. That is the feeling of hell from inside yourself. If you leave this body, then you will leave that feeling of suffering behind.
>
> Me: After you die it is still suffering?
>
> Thích Tĩnh Thiền: You suffer in your heart.
>
> Me: Not externally, but in your heart, is that right? You punish yourself?
>
> Thích Tĩnh Thiền: That is, the suffering of everyone is hell. So, the end of this suffering is the beginning of another. It is continuous.
>
> Me: So, if it's like that, does performing rituals for the dead achieve anything?
>
> Thích Tĩnh Thiền: Performing rituals for them, keeping vigil for them, changes the feeling in their hearts. It is like in the morning, they are sad; when they arrive [at the pagoda], they forget their sadness and their suffering ends. So, they change their hearts.
>
> Me: I understand everything you are saying, but according to Vietnamese traditions, you have to burn spirit money for the dead, right? Because they have to buy a house, pay off the kings of hell, or buy things like a motorcycle, TV, or a computer in the underworld.
>
> Thích Tĩnh Thiền: That is superstition. Here we don't burn spirit money.

Study and Comprehension

As we have seen from the funeral, ritual is seen as less important than teaching, studying, and learning about the Dharma. Most of my interlocuters at regular pagodas insisted that it was the act of chanting or sponsoring a ritual that was important and that the karmic benefits of chanting were not conditional upon comprehension. Rituals themselves are usually conducted either by monastics or ritual specialists (*thầy cúng*), and attendance even by the ritual's sponsor may be unnecessary for the ritual to produce a positive effect. At Sùng Phúc, monks insist that comprehension is the only important thing, and most of the lay practitioners agree (an objective enhanced by the use of colloquial Vietnamese, as explained above). One lay man explained: "Chanting sutras is also good. It is a kind of meditation. The purpose of chanting sutras is also to gain realization. But in the Trúc Lâm Zen school, the sutras are translated to Vietnamese. In Pure Land, they cannot translate everything, so they have to use [sutras written in] Sino-Vietnamese, and they just chant without understanding the meaning." He still saw value in chanting sutras without comprehension, but only because it was a form of meditation. He pointed out to me that understanding the meaning of the sutras was not just important but was also both more modern and doctrinally correct.

This stress on intellectually grasping the Buddhist teachings meant that every opportunity is taken to teach the meaning of Buddhist teachings to the laity and to junior monastics, with classes held in the afternoons and a certificate awarded to participants. Monks give Dharma talks at virtually all events—even at weddings and funerals. Furthermore, lay Buddhists are encouraged to study at home. The presence of the bookstore, with its large collection of books, CDs, and DVDs attests to the importance placed on studying as a central practice for all lay Buddhists.

The assiduous use of vernacular Vietnamese in Trúc Lâm liturgy speaks to the didactic importance they place on chanting sutras. As an example, the Penitence Rite includes reciting the Three Refuges. The version of the Three Refuges as recited at Sùng Phúc spells out, in very approachable and specific language, both what it means and what it entails:

We resolve for the rest of our lives to take refuge in the Buddha, the Dharma and the Sangha.

- Taking refuge in the Buddha is: Henceforth we will honor, worship, respect and follow Śākyamuni Buddha, our clear sighted and enlightened master.

- Taking refuge in the Dharma is: Henceforth we will honor, worship, respect and follow the clear Dharma that came from the golden mouth of the Buddha.
- Taking refuge in the Sangha is: Henceforth we will honor, worship, respect and follow the monastics who cultivate the right and clear Dharma of the Tathāgata (the One who has thus gone).
  * Having taken refuge in the Buddha, we will not worship or follow God, spirits, ghosts or animals.
  * Having taken refuge in the Dharma, we will not worship or follow other religions and heresies.
  * Having taken refuge in the Sangha, we will not honour or follow wicked friends or evil groups. (Thích Thanh Từ 2009a, 16–17)[12]

By comparison, the language used in regular pagodas in Hanoi for the Three Refuges is more technical and less informative:

- I take refuge in the Buddha, may all beings be able to follow the Unsurpassed with their whole hearts.
- I take refuge in the Dharma, may all beings clearly understand the sutras, endless wisdom like the sea.
- I take refuge in the Sangha, may all beings unceasingly foster the Great Assembly without fear.
(Nghi-thức tụng-niệm của Gia-đình Phật-tử 1960, 19)[13]

Not only does the Trúc Lâm formulation make it entirely clear what is expected by taking refuge in the Buddha, the Dharma, and the sangha, but it also does something else that is peculiar to Trúc Lâm: it makes Buddhism exclusive. It prohibits the practice of other religions and worship of spirits, which is an important part of regular religiosity in northern Vietnam, thereby structuring Buddhism as a modern and global religion by differentiating it in the way discussed in the introduction.

The de-supernaturalization of space is also notable in the explanation of Yến, who worked in the bookstore. She explained that if one were unable to get to the monastery to participate in the Penitence Rite, one could do it at home in front of one's own Buddha statue, and even if one lacks a Buddha statue, one can still do it because "penitence is in your heart, and if your heart tells you that you have done something wrong—for example, if you short-changed someone and pocketed the cash—you know that this is stealing, and in your heart, you feel that you wouldn't dare do this again to someone else."

Moral Practice

Moral practice is an important aspect for all Buddhists, and it is no different at Sùng Phúc. The centrality of the Penitence Rite as the main ritual performed at Sùng Phúc as part of the Trúc Lâm program underscores the importance of morality as a central Buddhist action in the program. Morality is highlighted as a core part of being a lay Buddhist in several ways. Unlike at most pagodas, a vegetarian meal is served at Sùng Phúc every week on Saturdays as part of the monastery's weekend activities, and lunch is open every day to any who happen to be at the monastery. By doing this, the importance of vegetarianism—already something closely associated with Buddhism in Vietnam—is reinforced. The meal itself is ritualized, starting off with prayers and with a symbolic offering to animals and wandering ghosts. The meal is eaten in silence, and following the meal, another prayer is said followed by recitation of the name of the Buddha: "Nam Mô Phật Bổn Sư Thích Ca Mâu Ni."

Several other regular practices at Sùng Phúc are emblematically identified with Buddhist practice. Following all services and meditation sessions, the karma generated by the activity is ritualistically shared with the universe. On important festival and ritual days, living beings are released (usually small birds released from cages). Before lunch, a small ritual called Cúng Đại Bàng (Offering for eagles) is performed that symbolically feeds wild animals. Morality is understood at Sùng Phúc as being an essential part of self-cultivation, while the importance of generating karmic merit is downplayed. So while symbolic rituals are performed regularly, they are understood as cultivating mercy but not as being capable of intervening in the karmic path of other beings.

Taken together, the rituals and practices performed at Sùng Phúc as part of the Trúc Lâm program displace the supernatural influence in the lives of the practitioners. In their modernist view of Buddhism, a sharp distinction is made between worshiping the Buddha and merely acknowledging the role that the Buddha played in discovering the truth of things and in passing on his great discovery. This is in contrast to Buddhism as practiced at most pagodas, where Buddhists see the Buddhist pantheon as a source of potent benevolence that can aid them with the problems of material existence. Of course, there is also a sense that Buddhism teaches important truths about how to live a moral life and how one might one day perfect oneself, but when I asked people at regular pagodas why they performed rituals (and especially the standard Penitence Rite), people explained that they did it to get good luck and health for themselves and their families. They said that it improved their karma or that the Buddha would forgive them for their moral failings. People sponsor memorial services to speed the souls of their dead relatives through hell to a favorable rebirth. They sponsor rituals to bring good luck for their businesses and their careers. This remains the primary way that most Buddhists in Vietnam (by which I mean people who engage with Buddhist ritual and Buddhist spaces and who consider their actions to be Buddhist) engage in Buddhist practice today and understand the purpose of those actions.

At Sùng Phúc, we see a substantial shift away from understanding actions as being supplicative in nature. Instead, everything is framed in terms of striving for self-perfection. Even the spaces are set up in such a way as to dissuade typical practices that denote reciprocal relationships with the Buddhist supernatural. There are no places available for people to engage in the typical practice of burning incense and making offerings in the way that forms the core of most Buddhist practice at other pagodas in Hanoi. There are no trays provided for offerings. No incense is lit by visiting laity. The altars are constantly policed by monks who make sure that these practices do not take place. There is no furnace in the courtyard for burning spirit money as there are at every other pagoda in Hanoi. There is not even the common donation box (*hòm công đức*) where people can make donations to gain merit (the literal meaning of *hòm công đức* is "merit box"). In short, there are no opportunities at Sùng Phúc for lay practitioners to "worship" the Buddha by giving offerings in exchange for favors.

Rituals at Sùng Phúc serve an entirely different purpose than they do at regular pagodas. There is a distinct deemphasis and even a discourse against the notion that the Buddha can play an active role in people's lives. Instead, the focus is resolutely on cultivating an inner awareness of one's actions and one's mind. Rituals are not performed to harness, invoke, or supplicate the buddhas and bodhisattvas. Instead, the purpose of the rituals is to evoke an inward gaze to compel individual cultivation, whether it is through meditation or the moral practices that are reinforced by the main Penitence Rite.

Part of this secularization of Buddhism in Trúc Lâm and in other forms of global, modernized Buddhism is the presentation of Buddhism as being scientifically based and capable of solving rational problems. The concept of causation has certainly always been a part of Buddhist philosophy, but the people at Sùng Phúc do not tend to speak of it as a motivation for their Zen practice. Thích Thanh Từ, in his explanations of Zen, explicitly evokes the parallels between science and Buddhism. For example, in *Thiền tông Việt Nam cuối Thế kỷ 20* (Vietnamese Zen in the late twentieth century),

Thích Thanh Từ draws specific ties to the process of achieving enlightenment and scientific discovery. He cites examples of Archimedes and Newton before drawing this conclusion:

> These two stories illustrate that scientific invention came by focusing all of their energy on the problem until light shone on a solution. It's the same with a Zen practitioner who, when confronted by a problem, focuses on thinking about it ceaselessly until they have a sudden moment of awakening. This awakening is a scientific reality, not some kind of occult mystery. Therefore, the goal of a Zen practitioner is to find realization. Realization is a creative invention, not something impenetrable, where you will only know the results of your spiritual practice after you die. So, I am telling you practitioners that you have to be determined, courageous and persistent, to brave death in order to live. Zen is for training heroes who are inventive and creative, and that is the core of the path to enlightenment and realization. (Thích Thanh Từ 2001, 28–29)[14]

By saying that Zen as presented at Sùng Phúc has become secularized, I do not mean it in the sense that van der Veer (2014) describes spirituality, as a way to seek religious truths without the obscurantism of institutional religion. If anything, Trúc Lâm Buddhism has a more rigid hierarchy and organizational structure and a more rigorous program than would be found in regular pagodas in northern Vietnam. Instead, the secular Buddhism I have described in this chapter changes Buddhism along the lines of what Charles Taylor describes. Devotees make a conscious choice to be Buddhist. Practice is transformed into an internal, psychological process focused on individual transformation. The trappings of Buddhism remain, but they have been disenchanted, or de-supernaturalized, and converge with neoliberal notions of self-improvement, so that religious practice continues even though the practitioners have been rhetorically turned into buffered selves. Their practice does not include the possibility of supernatural forces shaping their lives either positively or negatively. Instead, practice is an individual act that demands rigorous self-cultivation, which is seen as scientific in both approach and effect.

This is not to say that this secular, rationalist discourse of Buddhism is overtaking more common religiosities in Vietnam. In fact, while a dominant modernist Buddhist discourse is certainly gaining traction globally, particularly with young people and men who find devotional, enchanted Buddhism antithetical to their identity project, there is simultaneously an astounding rebound in a thoroughly enchanted religious orientation. The construction of Buddhism—and of religion generally—is fluid and historically contextual. Even in the time I have been doing research in

Vietnam, I have seen a significant shift. Women still continue to engage in regular practices that were targeted as non-Buddhist by the Buddhist reformers and is perpetuated by the state-controlled Buddhist institution. Nonetheless, there is a shift by many toward practices such as Zen meditation that are seen as more orthodox and more doctrinally correct. Even ideas like realization have been secularized, as this explanation by a retired army officer who practices at Sùng Phúc, named Mr. Xuân, shows:

> *"Giải thoát"* [*vimokṣa*, release, liberation] doesn't mean you are not going to die. If I am upset about something or someone, and I recite the name of Amitābha [*niệm Phật*], it calms me down. That is liberation [*giải thoát*]. Liberation is not something so formidable to achieve. For example, when you are upset about something or something is bugging you, you meditate for a few minutes; you are liberated. When you work hard for the full week, you go to the pagoda to meditate; it means that you release your stress. Don't think about liberation as some momentous event. It is very ordinary, simple. It is just a good feeling, that's all. For example, if I am a little angry with my wife, I remind myself that I am a Buddhist, so I have to be tolerant and search for the root of my anger. Doing this, I have become liberated on my own.

It is worthwhile making a final note about the extent of this secularization of Buddhism. Although Trúc Lâm engages in an extensive rhetorical effort to assert a modernist, secular, and humanistic approach to Buddhism, the transformation was not entirely complete in practice. The secular rhetoric did not entirely blot out a more enchanted way of practicing Buddhism. The collection of relics in the meditation hall is one instance. Another is the transfer of merit that is done at the conclusion of the meditation. However, these could be described as vestigial, at least from the perspective of the dominant discourse. When I asked the monks at Sùng Phúc about these things, they always explained them in secular terms. Of course, at the level of individual practice, the success of the secular discourse depended very much on the individual, as we will explore in part 3.

CHAPTER FOUR

||||||||

Nationalism and Internationalism

In previous chapters, we have seen that there are reoccurring expressions of nationalism that emerge at Sùng Phúc. This is primarily seen in the employment of Trúc Lâm and Trần Nhân Tông as symbols of a uniquely Vietnamese Buddhism. The thematization of Trúc Lâm—embedded in the architecture, rituals, and activities and in the repetitive utterances at Sùng Phúc—can be seen as a form of marketing, making this kind of Buddhism more attractive by branding it as the authentically Vietnamese Zen tradition and distinguishing it from regular pagodas. (From a Buddhist perspective, it might be seen as "skillful means" [S. *upāya*; V. *phương tiện*], an instrumental approach to teaching that recognizes the need to teach in a way that reaches the level of the audience.) Thích Thanh Từ writes, "To speak of the Vietnamese Zen school is to speak of Vietnamese Buddhism" (Thích Thanh Từ 2001, 5), as though most Buddhists in Vietnam are not practicing Vietnamese Buddhism.

The nationalistic face of Zen presented at Sùng Phúc is seemingly incongruent with another core discourse that positions Buddhism as a world religion. As I mentioned in the introduction, reformers transformed Buddhism into a world religion by drawing boundaries around a particular set of beliefs and practices (Đạo Phật, the way of the Buddha, or the Phật giáo, religion of the Buddha), and turning the Buddha Dharma into Buddh*ism*. One outcome of this process was that reformers made international connections and stressed the underlying unity of the various Buddhisms that were found in South, East, and Southeast Asia and that were beginning to spread to Europe and North America. This internationalism was prominent in South Vietnam through the 1960s, with many of the leading monks of the time studying overseas and participating in international Buddhist meetings. In North Vietnam in this period, there was considerably less engagement with other Buddhist countries. Since the Renovation in the late 1980s, when Vietnam liberalized its economy and opened its doors to the world, Buddhism has taken an increasingly prominent role as a tool of international relations while simultaneously gaining prestige at home.

The nationalist distinctions and the internationalist engagements are evidently in some tension and even appear to be in contradiction. On one hand, claims for Vietnam's having a unique tradition are a central Trúc Lâm narrative; on the other hand, Trúc Lâm's aspirations to be an international Buddhist organization requires that it sometimes overlook what is unique in order to build pan-Asian connections and inter- and intra-community ties in the diasporic context. Trúc Lâm therefore advances discordant discourses, claiming to be uniquely Vietnamese while having considerable ambition to be an international Buddhist organization whose monasteries and centers represent this ostensibly uniquely Vietnamese Zen around the world. The involvement of reform Buddhists in nationalism is not isolated to Vietnam. In fact, it is a prominent feature of the reform movements in all Buddhist countries. Lopez points out that many Buddhist reform leaders, like Dharmapala in Ceylon, Taixu in China, Shaku Sōen in Japan, Ledi Sayadaw in Burma, and more recently, the Dalai Lama, were also very involved in independence movements. Simultaneously, though, they were also forming transnational networks of like-minded Buddhists from around the world (Lopez 2002, xxxix).

This chapter will examine this tension between Trúc Lâm's construction as a uniquely Vietnamese school of Zen and one that is also actively involved in forming international networks. I will start by describing how the nationalist and internationalist discourses are manifested at Sùng Phúc before turning to examine how these two discourses coexist and are even complimentary aspects of the discourse that emerges from the globalization of Buddhism.

BUDDHISM AND NATIONALISM IN THE TWENTIETH CENTURY

Buddhist monks have always been involved in politics. However, their premodern and modern involvements differ in important ways. In the medieval period, the sangha was closely associated with the political elite, serving as advisers in the court; as Keith Taylor notes, in premodern Vietnam, religious and secular affairs were undifferentiated, as all affairs were considered religious (K. Taylor 1990, 150). In the modern period, especially in the twentieth century, Buddhism was fundamentally reshaped as a religion that was distinguished from the political function system, which created a structural tension with imperatives for Buddhists to take political nationalist stances. Vietnam was a colony that was being squeezed by the French for its natural resources and labor and experiencing a "racial diarchy," whereby Western-educated Vietnamese who had been exposed to concepts like liberty and equality were frustrated by persistent colonial structures built on an ideology of racial inequality (Luong 2010, 80–81). Foreign domination and colonial rule led to deep soul searching. Vietnamese intellectuals responded in a variety of ways, ranging from calls for a return to an imagined glorious Confucian past to modernist movements (like Communism) that advocated total abandonment of traditional culture and institutions (Marr 1981; McHale 2004; Woodside 1976). The latter, what Chatterjee calls "Eastern nationalism," arises from a sense that the backwardness they perceive in their own culture because of globalized standards flowing from the West cannot be addressed by imitating a fundamentally alien culture. Reformers searched instead for ways to regenerate a "national culture, adapted to the requirements of progress, but retaining at the same time its distinctiveness" (Chatterjee 1993, 2).

The Buddhist response to colonialism and the pressure of Catholic missionization was to create associations that sought to modernize Buddhism. This response, which emerged in the 1920s and was deeply influenced by modernization projects taking place in other Buddhist countries, came to be called the Buddhist Reform movement (Chấn hưng Phật giáo). Reformers in Vietnam were in fairly close contact with other reformers internationally and regionally, particularly Taixu (one of the most prominent reformist monks in early twentieth-century China), whose essays were frequently reprinted in the magazines published by the reform organizations in Vietnam beginning in the 1920s (Devido 2007).

The Reform movement in Vietnam was not overtly political. Instead, it aimed at building associations, opening temples to the public, educating about Buddhist doctrine, and turning monks into a resource for the laity beyond the ritual functions that they had previously fulfilled. These organizations tended to be elite and based in the urban centers of southern, central, and northern Vietnam. The reform organizations prioritized the education of monastics and established monastic schools that assumed a Westernized, rational model. They were also interested in educating the laity, so they held public Dharma talks and published material in the romanized Vietnamese script (quốc ngữ).[1] The focus of this intellectual activity was on discovering Buddhist history, elucidating Buddhist philosophy, and creating—restoring, in their view—a Buddhist orthodoxy by separating what was conceived as true Buddhism from "merely" cultural practices (*phong tục văn hóa*) and superstition (*mê tín dị đoan*). Taixu's ideas in particular shifted the emphasis of Buddhism's aim from personal transformation to transformation of society. In this second goal, nationalism was baked in, to the extent that there was a constant nationalistic undertone to the discourses of orthodoxy that continue today through the national Buddhist association.

Main and Lai argue that the understanding of Buddhism as needing to be socially engaged arises out of a redefinition of political space, which created mutually constituted differences between religion and secularism (2013, 9). The movement in Buddhism toward social engagement was, therefore, in some sense a resistance to secularization (Main and Lai 2013, 21). This new activist Buddhism spread the view that it was no longer enough for monastics to be cloistered and focused solely on personal attainment, inner cultivation, and interacting with the laity only when performing funerary rituals and memorial services. The Buddhist Reform movement called on the monastic sangha to be fully engaged with society and with teaching the Buddha's Dharma while being concerned with all forms of human suffering, not merely the spiritual or that conceived of in the abstract.

Buddhist reformers of the twentieth century saw suffering as more than an inevitability of the human condition. Instead, suffering of all kinds—but particularly human physical suffering—became for them the object of religious practice. Taixu felt that Buddhism in its decline had become preoccupied with funerals and rituals for the deceased and that was aimed at transferring merit to ancestors. He argued that the living were in the best place to generate merit and that the focus of Buddhism should therefore be the world of the living (Pittman 2001, 180). Taixu called for monks to open the doors of their temples and become involved in society. He criticized standard interpretations of the Pure Land as a place to be attained by faith in Amitābha and reinterpreted the Pure Land as a state created in this world through social action. He called this reoriented form of Buddhism "humanistic Buddhism" (Renjian Fojiao, though usually termed Rensheng Fojiao by Taixu [Chandler 2004, 43]), translated in Vietnamese as Nhân gian Phật giáo.

While the initial impact of the Reform movement in Vietnam was limited to urban elites, the long-term effects of their activities have been profound and continue to reverberate in the way that Buddhism is transforming in Vietnam in the twenty-first century. The delay in their effect is largely a product of historical circumstances already discussed. The Second World War and the Japanese occupation, followed by the protracted war of resistance against the French after the war, limited the reformers' resources and curtailed their activities. When the dust settled after the French withdrew from Vietnam in 1954, the country had been split in two. In the north, the Communists stifled all religious practice. While Buddhism was not suppressed to the extent that folk religious practices and Confucian institutions were, all religious practices, including Buddhism, were discouraged. Real Buddhist reform in North Vietnam stagnated until the 1990s and did not really accelerate until the start of the twenty-first century. In 1981, the government formed the Vietnamese Buddhist Association, under the umbrella of the Fatherland Front, as the only legal Buddhist organization, and while the government continued to sanction reformist ideas, they did so because such ideas coincided neatly with Communist ideology. Superstition, for instance, was a prime target of the state campaign against religion, this focus also aligning with reformist concerns with modernizing and purifying Buddhism by drawing distinctions between true Buddhism and folk degradations and superstitious practices.

Meanwhile, in the south, Buddhism developed quite differently under conditions of relative freedom of religion, though it encountered discrimination under the regime of the Catholic president, Ngô Đình Diệm. The situation became serious in early 1963 when all flags but the state flag were banned by the state. The law was ignored with impunity by Catholics celebrating the Catholic bishop's birthday (Diệm's brother), but when Buddhists flew the international Buddhist flag a few days later at the celebration of Buddha's birthday (Lễ Phật Đản), the police fired on the crowd, killing nine and wounding fourteen (Phạm Văn Minh 2002, 187). This led to Thích Quảng Đức's self-immolation on June 11, 1963, on a street in Saigon. This shocking act, and Malcolm Brown's photograph of it, galvanized the country and led, barely five months later, to a coup d'état and the overthrow and assassination of Ngô Đình Diệm. Thích Quảng Đức's act was felt internationally as well, as many Americans realized that their government was supporting an oppressive regime.[2] The episode also had the effect of bringing together disparate Buddhist groups and creating a unity—along with an awareness of the political power that they held—that had eluded the Buddhist reformers of the earlier generation. The result was the politicization of Buddhism in the south and the formation of the Unified Buddhist Church, later called the Unified Buddhist Church of Vietnam, or UBCV. It is notable, however, that while the political nature of his act was apparent, Thích Quảng Đức wrote of his sacrifice in very religious terms in his final testament, saying that his intention was "to cremate this temporary body as a sacrifice to Buddha in order to merit virtue and to promote the preservation of Buddhism" (Miller 2014, 47).

The connection between the earlier reform movement and the UBCV is direct; virtually all the leaders in the Struggle movement, as the UBCV's cause came to be known, attended the educational institutions that had been set up for monastics by the Buddhist reformers in the 1930s and 1940s, including prominent monks like Thích Trí Quang, the leader of the UBCV, and Thích Nhất Hạnh.[3] These figures actively promoted the values first put forward by the earlier reform movement, particularly a focus on education, an orthodox understanding of Buddhism, a modernist and rational model for new institutions and organizations (with committees, presidents, secretaries, etc.), and above all, a commitment to political and social engagement. They were also concerned with unifying Buddhists and creating international links.[4] These guiding values, in short, exhibited the outward-facing orientation typical of Buddhist globalism.

Following its victory in dislodging Ngô Đình Diệm in late 1963, the UBCV continued its protests, which culminated in a major Buddhist uprising in 1966.[5] The focus shifted from a basic defense of Buddhism from the Catholic assault of Ngô Đình Diệm to a more political protest against American involvement in the war and the puppet presidents the Americans backed and controlled. While the public was deeply sympathetic to the resistance of Ngô Đình Diệm's oppression of Buddhism and felt that it was justified, public support was not as strong for the subsequent political protests in which they were engaged. The opinion of many was that the protests had become too deeply political and self-serving (Topmiller 2002, 63).

The Struggle movement ultimately failed to end the war, and its activism culminated in a major clash with the government in 1966 that brought their movement to an end. Nonetheless, it had achieved a unity that hitherto had not existed. After reunification of North and South Vietnam under the Communist government in 1975, the UBCV eventually emerged as an outlawed Buddhist group opposed to the Communist control of religion. The leaders of the UBCV in Vietnam have since spent much of their time either in prison or under house arrest. While they are able to make periodic statements and take actions to reify their opposition to the state control of religion in Vietnam, they are active mostly overseas. Through its Paris-based spokesman Võ Văn Ái, the UBCV continues to speak out against the Vietnamese Communist government. Meanwhile, since 1981, the Communist state-supported Vietnamese Buddhist Association (Giáo hội Phật giáo Việt Nam) functions as the unifying organization in Vietnam.

We can see that nationalism has played a major role in Vietnamese Buddhism throughout the twentieth century. Buddhism in the Trần dynasty (1225–1400) was also remade by nationalist thinkers—Lê Văn Phúc, Phan Kế Bính, and Phạm Văn Thụ prominent among them—by developing the argument that the Trần repelled the Chinese (Yuan) invasion because "people followed Buddhism and were thus more altruistic, daring, and patient. They were willing to 'sacrifice themselves to save the world'" (Kelley 2015, 1990). Thích Thanh Từ, as a young monk during the turbulence of the Struggle movement, was an heir to these ideas. I have not seen any mention that he was involved with these political aspects, though it is hard to imagine that he did not take part in some way given that until 1959, he studied at Ấn Quang Pagoda, one of the main political pagodas in Saigon. However, the motivation to recreate the only Vietnamese Zen school certainly arose from the cauldron of nationalist, reformist, and activist impulses that were brewing in Saigon at that time.

The motivation for Thích Thanh Từ to focus on Trúc Lâm Zen is rooted in the discourses of nationalism that have been a part of Vietnamese Buddhist reform since the 1920s. Trần Văn Giáp established the history of Buddhism in Vietnam through a Zen lens, but the disjuncture between this supposed history and how Buddhism was actually practiced caused consternation for Thích Thanh Từ:

One time I was going to Japan, and on the ship, I met two or three people also going to Japan. I got to know them and asked why they were going to Japan, to which they replied that they were going to study Zen. Not long after I heard a report that a Japanese monk had started a Zen center in Paris, France. During a break in the summer this monk went to visit a number of countries in Southeast Asia. When he got back, he told all of the Zen practitioners about Buddhism in countries like Sri Lanka, Burma, Thailand. Among them was a Vietnamese Buddhist, who asked: "Master, did you visit Vietnam?" When he replied that he had, the Vietnamese Buddhist asked him what he thought of Buddhism in Vietnam. The Japanese monk laughed loudly and exclaimed: "It's mixed up!" When I heard this, I was very sad. When In Japan, I saw that there were clearly differentiated Buddhist sects. If it was a Zen temple, then the teachings were properly Zen. If it was Pure Land, then followed the Pure Land doctrine. If you entered the gate of one of these sects, then you leave from that gate.[6] Coming back to Vietnam I felt it is a lost cause because we don't know what teachings we follow, so we follow all of them. Why was Buddhism transmitted to Japan five hundred years after Vietnam, and yet their understanding has surpassed ours? The Zen sect has been in Vietnam for such a long time but no one has a desire to study from us. Even worse, we go to Japan to study. Isn't it lamentable? This is something that I find really sad.

Because of this, after I finished my regular program of study, I swore an oath that I would concentrate on researching about Zen, especially Vietnamese Zen. (Thích Thanh Từ n.d., 11–12)

THE EMBLEMATIC KING

With the Vietnam War (known in Vietnam as the Resistance War against America—Kháng chiến chống Mỹ) ongoing, the narrative of the re-created Trúc Lâm Zen school stressing its links to Vietnamese resistance against overwhelming foreign military forces—whether Chinese, French, or American—had deep resonance. As mentioned in chapter 1, the Trúc Lâm school was founded by a former king of Vietnam, Trần Nhân Tông, who defeated the Mongol invaders with the help of another important historical hero, his general and cousin Trần Hưng Đạo. For his role, Trần Hưng Đạo was remade into a hero as part of a self-conscious building of nationalism in the late nineteenth and early twentieth centuries (Kelley 2015). King Trần Nhân Tông has not received the same attention as Trần Hưng Đạo, but he shares in the narrative as the king who led his people in defending the nation, and he draws symbolic power from it.

The modern Vietnamese construction of history focused on Vietnamese heroic figures who could serve to catalyze the Vietnamese. Marr writes that in the 1920s, "young Vietnamese intellectuals . . . rediscovered Vietnamese heroes, most obviously the leaders of ancient struggles against the Chinese and the Mongols, but increasingly those that fought the French as well" (1981, 252). These heroes include mythic figures like Bà Triệu (ca. 226–248 CE) and the Two Trung Sisters (Hai Bà Trưng, ca. 14–ca. 43), who rebelled during the first and second periods of Chinese domination; Ngô Quyền (897–944 CE), who defeated the Southern Han kingdom at the Battle of Bạch Đằng River in 938 CE; and Lê Lợi (ca. 1384–1433), who led a campaign from 1418 to 1427, defeating the Ming and founding the Later Lê dynasty (1428–1788). The choice of Trần Nhân Tông and Trúc Lâm Zen therefore participates in this construction, both reinforcing the nationalist narrative, but also benefiting from it.

The symbolic importance of Trúc Lâm is not uniquely held by Thích Thanh Từ's Trúc Lâm organization but is also widely acknowledged by Vietnamese scholars and Buddhists. Even Thích Nhất Hạnh has acknowledged the importance of Trúc Lâm Buddhism, saying that "Bamboo Forest Buddhism [i.e., Trúc Lâm] is a kind of engaged Buddhism" (Hunt Perry and Fine 2000, 37). Websites created by overseas Vietnamese repeat the claim that Trúc Lâm Zen is the quintessential Vietnamese Zen school. The site www.buddhismtoday.com, for example, has a short history of

Buddhism in Vietnam, written by a monk from Ho Chi Minh City, that ascribes Trúc Lâm's importance to its being "the first Vietnamese Chan Sect that had ever been founded and the king was consecrated as the first Patriarch" (Thích Minh Chau 1994).[7]

For Vietnamese Buddhism as a whole, Trúc Lâm's value is its symbolic role in nationalist assertions that take China as a counterpoint for proving Vietnamese uniqueness and merit. This view is echoed in Thích Thanh Từ's writings:

> An independent country must be independent politically, militarily, culturally and economically. The Trần dynasty was an era of victory over the Yuan Mongolian invasion of our country. The Trần kings were able to fight against the enemy, bringing great honor to the country, politically and militarily. In regard to culture in the Trần dynasty, if you reread the Trần texts, you see that the Trần kings had a specific idea that we could not continue to borrow Chinese culture to build a Vietnamese culture. Writing is one way to express one's culture. So, although the Trần dynasty studied Chinese characters, they wanted to translate them into a Vietnamese writing system and decided to adopt Nôm [demotic characters]. Although Nôm existed previously, it was during this time that the writing system developed. So, when King Trần Nhân Tông became Emperor, he wrote a morally valuable text that we still have today . . . completely in Nôm. Thus, he desired not just military and political independence; but also independence from China in all cultural matters. That's what I find very awesome and venerable. (Thích Thanh Từ 2000a)[8]

On the village ancestral day, I had a discussion with a small group of men and women at the communal house on the Sùng Phúc monastery compound. One of the women said to me, "Pure Land Buddhism is from India and is foreign, but Vietnam's roots are Zen, from King Trần Nhân Tông on Mount Yên Tử." The group of villagers said that Xuân Đỗ Thượng was proud to have the Zen monastery there, but they admitted that many in the village went to a regular pagoda in a neighboring village. The conversation was peppered with expressions of needing to remember their roots (nguồn gốc, an expression often used in nationalistic propaganda) and references to Trần Nhân Tông. Their pride in Trúc Lâm centered on nationalist themes. The conversation soon moved to a comparison of how friendly (tình cảm) the Vietnamese are compared to foreigners.

THE TRÚC LÂM ZEN BRAND

References to Trúc Lâm as the uniquely Vietnamese Zen Buddhist tradition are systematically reiterated at Sùng Phúc in both overt and subtle

ways. The very name of the organization, Trúc Lâm, evokes this history.
We have also seen how Trần Nhân Tông is present in the architecture
and objects at Sùng Phúc, as with the ancestor hall's focus on the patriarchs of Trúc Lâm and the poems reproduced on the large bronze temple bell. This propensity to look to history for authority is a common
feature for all religions. It serves as a resource for self-understanding by
piecing together a coherent narrative, often by glossing over discrepan-
cies and discontinuities in the process. It is done in such a way that innovation is often cloaked as a return or recovery of an original past
(Beyer 2006, 119). Nonetheless, Thích Thanh Từ has been fairly transpar-
ent about the fact that that his recreation of Trúc Lâm is not entirely a
faithful continuation.

Thích Thanh Từ's intention to recreate the spirit rather than replicate
the original Trúc Lâm Zen school is recognized in websites dedicated to
the school (see Hoang 2002). Thích Thanh Từ himself is also quite clear
that the form of Buddhism that he is calling Trúc Lâm is actually his own
construction:

> Regarding Zen Buddhism in Vietnam in the late twentieth century, I am
> talking about the way we practiced Zen at Chân Không Monastery from
> 1970 to 1986 and at Thường Chiếu Monastery from 1974 to now. This is the
> method for practicing Zen that I taught. I didn't follow the teachings of the
> Chinese Zen lineages like Tào Động [Ch. Cao Dong 曹洞; J. Sōtō], Lâm Tế
> [Ch. Linji 臨濟; J. Rinzai], Qui Ngưỡng [Ch. Gui Yang 潙仰; J. Igyō], Vân
> Môn [Ch. Wenyan Yunmen 雲門文偃; J. Ummon Bun'en] or Pháp Nhãn
> [Ch. Fayan 法眼; J. Hōgen]. I just combined three important aspects of the
> historical traditions that were transmitted from China to Vietnam.
> The first of these is from the second patriarch, Huệ Khả [Ch. Huike 慧可],
> the second is from the sixth patriarch Huệ Năng [Ch. Huineng 慧能] and
> the third is from founding monks of Trúc Lâm. They converge to a place
> of discernment, enlightenment and practice of these three ancestors to be-
> come a method of practice that we use today at our monasteries. (Thích
> Thanh Từ 2001, 46)[9]

The invented nature of this tradition is nonetheless overshadowed by the
massive number of references to Trúc Lâm and Trần Nhân Tông.

The nationalist sentiments are overt in the new Trúc Lâm school. The
literature produced by Thích Thanh Từ and other senior leaders in the
organization frequently focuses on the historical patriarchs of the Trúc
Lâm school. The shelves of the bookstore at Sùng Phúc are lined with
books describing this early history. Thích Thông Phương, who was the
abbot at the Trúc Lâm Monastery at Yên Tử, the historic center of the Trúc
Lâm school, has written several books specifically on the topic, with titles

such as *Trần Nhân Tông với Thiền phái Trúc Lâm* (Trần Nhân Tông with the Trúc Lâm sect) (Thích Thông Phương 2008) and *Thiền phái Trúc Lâm Yên Tử* (The Trúc Lâm Yên Tử Zen sect) (2003). Thích Thanh Từ has also written many books detailing the life of Trần Nhân Tông and creating links between his historical Buddhist school and the modern organization; his book *Hai quãng đời của sơ tổ Trúc Lâm* (Two stages of life of the founder of Trúc Lâm) (2002a) is a good example.[10] The importance placed on this history was also repeatedly stressed by devotees with whom I spoke who evoked Trúc Lâm as the one uniquely Vietnamese school of Zen, founded in northern Vietnam and not transferred from China.

Rebuilding at Mount Yên Tử

The symbolic value of Trúc Lâm has led to a successful effort to reestablish a Trúc Lâm Monastery at Mount Yên Tử, where the sect was originally founded by Trần Nhân Tông.[11] There has been an interest in Yên Tử as a pilgrimage destination for a long time, though its isolation means that it was not often visited until recent decades. It was of sufficient interest, however, for Nguyễn Thiện Chính to write a poem about it that was published in the Buddhist reformist journal from Hanoi (*Đuốc tuệ* [The torch of wisdom]) in 1936 (Nguyễn Thiện Chính 1936, 21).[12] The poem does not mention Trúc Lâm or Trần Nhân Tông, but it includes references to some of the main sites along the pilgrimage trail up the mountain, maybe indicating how the Trúc Lâm narrative has risen in importance only later in the twentieth century.

Thích Thanh Từ, in recreating Trúc Lâm and establishing a monastery at Yên Tử, is tapping into the "Golden Age of Buddhism" myth. His reimagining of Yên Tử as a center of Vietnamese Buddhism comes from ideas of Buddhist reformers. Trí Hải, the most prominent Buddhist reformer from the north, also had visions of renovating and expanding Yên Tử Pagoda because of its fame as the historic site of "national Buddhism." He found it in a decrepit state, with many of the structures having collapsed from neglect and disrepair. He started reconstruction in 1940, using cement instead of wood, with the intention of adding a school and a rest home, but he was unable to complete the project (DeVido 2007, 267), likely due to the outbreak of World War II and the Japanese occupation of Vietnam.

During the Vietnam War, Yên Tử was closed off and used as a military base, but by the 1980s, it was beginning to get increased religious attention and pilgrim traffic. Since then, pilgrim traffic has grown, from ten thousand in 1992 to more than a million in 2015 (Lauser 2015, 12), at least in part because of the enormous Trúc Lâm Yên Tử Monastery complex that was built by Thích Thanh Từ's disciple Thích Thông Phương. The addition of a cable car in the early 2000s for pilgrims who prefer not to hike to the top of the mountain and a colossal fifteen-meter statue of Trần Nhân Tông built in 2013 certainly add to the site's attractiveness as a tourist/pilgrim destination. However, it is likely that Thích Thanh Từ had wanted to reestablish a Trúc Lâm monastery there for a long time before it was actualized. When he founded his headquarter monastery in Đà Lạt, his original intention was to call it Trúc Lâm Yên Tử Monastery, but he hesitated because he felt that it would be wrong for geographical reasons; instead, he shortened the name to Trúc Lâm Monastery (Thích Thanh Từ 2002a, 7).

Mount Yên Tử holds symbolic importance for Trúc Lâm as the geographical center of Vietnamese Buddhism. As such, Yên Tử is frequently evoked in conversation, in writings, and in Dharma talks. It is also depicted in the Sùng Phúc space, through murals depicting Thích Thanh Từ on pilgrimage there, and in the altar carvings of the burial stupa of Trần Nhân Tông.

Language

Earlier, I quoted Thích Thanh Từ's comments about how much respect he had for Trần Nhân Tông's gaining symbolic independence from China by writing in Nôm demotic characters and trying to strengthen a specifically Vietnamese culture. The use of language is an important way that Thích Thanh Từ asserts cultural independence from China. He therefore made sure that all the sutras used at Sùng Phúc were written in vernacular Vietnamese. He recognized that when the sutras were written in Sino-Vietnamese, monks and laity alike failed to understand the meaning of what they were chanting. He describes this situation of cultural "dependence on China" as "painful" (đau đớn) and "sad" (đáng buồn) (Thích Thanh Từ 2000a; 2000b, 58–59). While the use of vernacular Vietnamese makes Buddhist liturgies intelligible, it also serves to assert Vietnamese identity and to step beyond cultural reliance on China.

Thích Thanh Từ's other battle with Chinese language is with the syntactic vestiges it has left, particularly in the phrase for reciting the name of the Buddha. At Sùng Phúc, practitioners intentionally use the idiosyncratic phrasing "Nam mô Phật bổn sư Thích Ca Mâu Ni" (homage to the Buddha Śākyamuni), with the word for "Buddha" (Phật) in the middle of the phrase rather than at the end, which is the norm (Nam mô bổn Sư Thích Ca Mâu Ni Phật). Thích Thanh Từ's explanation for adopting this word order is as follows:

Remember, in Chinese language the common noun in the sentence is always at the end of the sentence and the proper noun comes before it. So, in the phrase, *"Nammô Bổn sư Thích-ca Mâu-ni Phật,"* "Śākyamuni" is the proper noun and "Buddha" is the common noun. The common noun goes after, and the proper noun goes first. That way conforms with Chinese syntax. However, in Vietnamese, the common noun is placed first, while the proper noun comes after. For example, if we want to introduce a Venerable named Chân Tâm, what do we have to say? Is it the "Venerable Chân Tâm" or "Chân Tâm the Venerable"? If we say Chân Tâm the Venerable, people will laugh, right? That is because "Venerable" is a common noun and "Chân Tâm" is a proper noun. Following Vietnamese syntax, we say Venerable Chân Tâm. In this way, Vietnam should be true to Vietnam. Why do we depend on them for everything, including words and grammar? Why don't we have the courage [to go our own way]? (Thích Thanh Từ 2000a)[13]

The ties between Buddhism and nationalism are not unique to Trúc Lâm, nor are they unique to this period of time, or even to Buddhism in Vietnam. The reform movements throughout Asia were entangled with nationalism from their inception. They arose out of the colonial encounter as a Buddhist response to national crises brought about by the pressures of aggressive Western imperialist expansionism and Christian missionary efforts in the nineteenth century. We see a strong nationalistic sentiment expressed by Dharmapala in Ceylon (now Sri Lanka) and in how the Japanese Shin Bukkyo movement backed Japanese imperialism early in the twentieth century and supported the Japanese state in the Second World War.

Vietnam was no different. The roots of this activism, at least in the modern period, come from Buddhist involvement in resistance against French colonialism. At times, this came in the form of direct participation in fighting (for example, during the so-called Monk Revolution of 1898 led by the monk Võ Trứ in Bình Định and Phú Yên Provinces); at other times, resistance was expressed by sheltering fighters in pagodas (Nguyen Tai Thu 1992, 378). Less directly, the Buddhist Reform movement that began in the 1920s was also inherently political, an intellectual attempt to resist Western colonial hegemony—French colonialism specifically—and aggressive Christian missionization that were inherent in European imperialism. It involved a reworking of Buddhism to be a thoroughly modern world religion as part of a nationalist apologetic. In the process, Buddhism was transformed to conform with Western expectations of the category of religion in the ways described above. While there was a long history of resistance against the state, direct political activism became the hallmark of Buddhist identity in South Vietnam in the 1960s (Topmiller 2002).

Trúc Lâm's allure for many of its followers is that it is a distinct Vietnamese school of Zen. This is important for many because there is a strong current of nationalism in Vietnam that comes out of their experience of colonialism and wars of resistance. There is a history of nationalism inherited from the Southeast and East Asian Buddhist reform movements, and Thích Thanh Từ picked up on this, almost certainly as a young monk in Saigon around the time of the Struggle movement. As such, he was open about wanting to re-create Trúc Lâm as the Vietnamese Zen for the modern period. However, while there is a strong current of nationalist sentiment, there is also an international orientation that would seemingly be in opposition to the barriers that nationalism tends to throw up.

TRANSNATIONAL TRÚC LÂM

Lay practitioners at regular pagodas with whom I spoke did not typically report holding global aspirations for the spread of Vietnamese Buddhism. On the other hand, some of the monastics, including the vice abbot at Sùng Phúc, proudly informed me that Trúc Lâm Buddhism was spreading around the world and produced a list of contacts in Western countries to illustrate the extent to which it has already spread. Indeed, the vice abbot's willingness to give his time to me was, by his admission, partly motivated by a hope that my research would help make the world aware of Trúc Lâm Zen.

There are currently fifty-four Zen monasteries (*thiền viện*) and meditation centers (*thiền tự*) in Vietnam and around the world. While most are in Vietnam, there are many international locations, including in Australia, the United States, France, and Canada. Tu Tam Hoang, who has translated some of Thích Thanh Từ's books, writes of Từ's intentions, "His primary goal is to renovate Vietnamese Zen Buddhism, and make it beneficial to all of us, regardless of our ethnicity" (Hoang 2000, 9). There is a strong missionary outlook to Thích Thanh Từ, who sees it as his responsibility to spread Trúc Lâm Zen:

> I cherish the wish that you will light your own torch and let it shine so that you can give your brightness to many people. Bring it all over to clear everyone's delusion. Bringing an end to everyone's delusion means aiding with the suffering of all living beings, so that light will not only be for a short period of ten, twenty, thirty or forty years. Truthfully, that light is not just from my torch, for one day it will dim and extinguish. I want it to be passed on to others to keep it going, so that before it burns out with one person it is transferred to others, until the world is no longer in the dark. That is my wish, dream and my cherished goal. (Thích Thanh Từ 2000a)[14]

The proliferation of monasteries across Vietnam, and particularly the expansion of Trúc Lâm to return it to its birthplace in northern Vietnam, is surely part of this vision. It appears, however, that success in attracting Western converts has been limited.[15]

Other Asian-based Buddhist organizations have also encountered barriers to spreading the message of their organization beyond their ethnic group. For example, Tzu Chi and Buddha's Light International Association, both centered in Taiwan, have been largely unsuccessful in gaining converts outside ethnic Chinese communities overseas. These organization face the dilemma of either maintaining a core of supporters by preserving an integral ethnic identity or making adaptations that could attract converts, a strategy that runs the risk of detracting from the cultural aspects that appeal to the ethnic community. The result is that the international part of the organization continues to be propped up by the overseas Chinese community, especially those originating from Taiwan (Chandler 2004, 6). By Chandler's estimate, as much as 80 percent of funds raised for Hsi Lai Temple in Los Angeles come from key Taiwanese donors who visit periodically from Taiwan (2004, 266).

Thích Thanh Từ's construction of a Vietnamese Zen is rational and secularized, making meditation the central practice and focusing on the historical Buddha. These aspects have proven particularly attractive to Buddhist converts in the West, and yet Trúc Lâm has not been attractive to Western converts. One explanation for this difficulty may well be that the nationalistic elements present in Trúc Lâm Zen hold far more meaning for overseas Vietnamese than for Westerners who come from a non-Buddhist background. Another is that the monastics overseas are uncomfortable speaking in languages other than Vietnamese. However, the reformed nature of Thích Thanh Từ's Trúc Lâm Zen is likely attractive to overseas Vietnamese who have had more contact with Western styles of Buddhism. The nationalist elements of the school are also a draw, stirring feelings of patriotism without the negative associations of the Communist regime of the north. Without a more thorough investigation than I have yet been able to undertake, however, this remains speculation. I have visited Trúc Lâm centers in Canada, France, and California but have come across only one non-Vietnamese (Caucasian) follower in Canada. When I interviewed him, he said that he had been introduced by Vietnamese friends and that he was an avid meditator. Nonetheless, he had no particular interest in either Vietnam or in the lineage. Although anecdotal, his case suggests that the nationalistic rhetoric that is a part of Trúc Lâm may not be compelling to converts.

Thích Thanh Từ himself, it seems, has long been oriented internationally, as the reformers and their heirs tended to be. Unlike the two other
monks who have introduced Vietnamese Zen to the West, Thích Nhất
Hạnh and Thich Thiền An, Thích Thanh Từ never studied overseas. He
has nonetheless traveled extensively. He first went to Cambodia in 1956
and then to India and Japan in 1965. He was not to travel again until after
the Renovation brought Buddhism back into state favor and loosened
travel restrictions. In the 1990s, during the period of expansion of his vision and organization, he went to China (1993), Switzerland (1994), Indo-
nesia (1996), the United States, Canada, and France on numerous occasions
from 1994 to 2002, and Australia on several occasions from 1996 to 2002.[16]
Old age and ill health have limited his travels in recent years.

The outward-looking orientation is a prominent part of Sùng Phúc.
Several months before I began my research there in 2011, an Indian monk
had stayed at the monastery. While no foreign visitors came while I was
there, it seemed that the monks and lay followers from Sùng Phúc were
constantly traveling abroad to visit sites in India and China, making connections with monks in Burma, or visiting Trúc Lâm centers that had
been established overseas. Taken as a whole, this marks a significant shift
from the insular orientations typical of most pagodas. As economic prosperity has grown in Vietnam, many more people are traveling internationally to visit Buddhist sites as pilgrims, with the main draw being to
visit the sites from the life of the Buddha in India and Nepal; companies
have appeared in recent years that cater specifically to this religious clien-
tele. Nonetheless, most pagodas in Vietnam are not concerned with creating linkages or expanding beyond their own communities. Sùng Phúc
has a missionary mandate, premised on the idea that Buddhism is a
global world religion, which makes linkages important. It also indicates
a view of Buddhism that sees missionary expansion of Vietnamese Zen as
a central programmatic element.

The Trúc Lâm organization presents two seemingly contradictory tendencies. The first is seen in the nationalistic sentiment that it mobilizes to
attract Vietnamese practitioners to Zen. The systematic branding of Trúc
Lâm as *the* uniquely Vietnamese school of Zen clearly strikes a chord with
many Vietnamese today. The tension between Vietnam and China in the
Spratly and Paracel Islands in the South China Sea in recent years has
sparked a sense of nationalism greater even than the state has been able to
generate through propagandistic appeals. Indeed, the nationalist sentiment that burst onto the streets in 2014 was too intense even by the state's
standards. Despite echoing nationalist discourses that the state uses to

maintain legitimacy, the state could not tolerate challenges to its strict control of social spaces, especially when rioters started to vandalize foreign-owned companies thought to be Chinese (though the mobs sometimes mistakenly hit companies that were not).

Since the Renovation opened the doors of Vietnam to the world in the late 1980s, there has been a sense of angst that foreign ideas and values will have a corrupting influence, especially on young people (we will see this concern expressed by young adherents in chapter 7). One of the answers has been to harness icons of Vietnamese culture to strengthen a sense of Vietnameseness, and Buddhism has been one site of this expression of "tradition." The government has supported the declaration of historical pagodas as recognized historical sites (*Di tích lịch sử—văn hoá*). In some cases, the state supports reclamations of pagoda lands that were lost to encroachment during periods when Buddhism was undermined by Marxist policies (during the post-1954 period through the war and up to the Renovation). The lotus was adopted as the national flower in 2011, and the state periodically praises Buddhists for their contributions to the country. In a more unusual move, a provincial government has sponsored the rebuilding of a Buddhist pagoda on one of the Spratly islands that has been occupied by the Vietnamese in an attempt to anchor their claim over the islands to a historical and cultural basis (*Đạo Phật ngày nay* 2012).

It is against this backdrop of increasing nationalism, untethered from the mechanisms of state propaganda, that the allure of Trúc Lâm as uniquely Vietnamese begins to make sense. The use of this trope by the Trúc Lâm organization is intentional. The stress on Trúc Lâm's Vietnamese origins is seen in the organization's emphasis on the historic founders of Trúc Lâm, as the ancestors in the rituals, in discussions, and in the prominent placement of their statues in the space most often used for activities. Likewise, this Vietnamese Zen is frequently evoked by the youth group in its name (Trần Thái Tông Youth Group, named after the grandfather of the founder of Trúc Lâm). When a two-day youth event was organized, it was similarly called the Vạn Hạnh Zen Youth Jamboree after the eminent Vietnamese monk from the tenth century.

Contradictions do arise from Thích Thanh Từ's construction of Trúc Lâm as the Vietnamese Zen school. The first is that the re-created Trúc Lâm school is beholden to the reformist discourses that emerged in response to pressures from colonialism in the first half of the twentieth century. More recently, it has been influenced by globalized Buddhist trends popular in the West and by the changes that have taken place in overseas Vietnamese Buddhism. In this way, Thích Thanh Từ's "true Vietnamese sect" is largely invented and is influenced at least as much by global forces as by Vietnamese historical precedent. A second contradiction is that while appealing to nationalist sentiments by claiming Trúc Lâm as a Vietnamese Zen school, imagined or otherwise, the organization also holds aspirations for global expansion. The school's English-language website has been set up at the direction of Thích Thanh Từ by one of his followers in California, who is also translating Thích Thanh Từ's books into English and distributing them for free. Thus, while nationalistic sentiments are frequently evoked, there is simultaneously a strong sense of internationalism as well, inherited from the Buddhist Reform movement and the cosmopolitanism of Buddhism in the south before reunification in 1975.

The practice of meditation, along with a culturally neutral type of Zen, have represented dominant trends in Buddhist globalism. While the Buddhists in northern Vietnam are also influenced by these global trends, other factors play a role in attracting them to Zen. For a fuller understanding of their motivations, we now turn to an exploration of some of the participants at Sùng Phúc.

PART 3

PARTICIPANTS

CHAPTER FIVE

||||||||

Zen Women

In her essay "Lin-chi (Rinzai) Chan and Gender: The Rhetoric of Equality and the Rhetoric of Heroism," Miriam Levering describes how the message of Chan teachers since at least the eighth century has been unambiguous in stating that gender is not a factor in ability to attain enlightenment. Nonetheless, the language they used was heavily gendered, describing the heroic nature of Zen in thoroughly masculine terms. She writes, "When the rhetoric is masculine, and when the model of the spiritual path is presented in imagery with such a strong masculine ring to it, it seems to 'fit' naturally with our expectations for men" (Levering 1992, 150). Levering concludes that the rhetoric of masculine heroism in Chan literature "never allowed women's experience and language to have anything like an equal influence on its expressive form" (1992, 151).

This view, from a textual reading of Chan literature, should imply that Zen would not be attractive to women in Vietnam, since the language of self-reliance and cultivation resonates with Vietnamese masculine discourses, as in Thích Thanh Từ's exhortation for practitioners to be "courageous" and "heroic." Consequently, it would be easy to see how Sùng Phúc would be a space primarily for men—and in many ways, it is. Monks hold the central positions in rituals, sit at the main table during meals while nuns sit off to one side, and reside at Sùng Phúc while nuns live in a residence off-site. The murals and statuary exclusively show men in meditative positions. The mural of Bodhidharma meditating in a cave for nine years (so long that he left his shadow permanently on the wall) is a particularly poignant example of the heroic masculine practice about which Levering was writing. Despite the prominence of masculine symbols and patriarchal structures, women outnumber men at Sùng Phúc, as is the case at all pagodas in Vietnam and Vietnamese pagodas abroad. It is notable, though, that Zen does appear to have a special appeal to men, resulting in a proportionally larger number of men going to Sùng Phúc and practicing Zen than would typically be seen chanting sutras at a regular pagoda. This chapter and the next will look further at how gender plays out in practice in Trúc Lâm and at Sùng Phúc and will explore how individuals approach Zen and what motivated them to go to Sùng Phúc.

In my previous book, I explored how women and men approached Buddhism differently (Soucy 2012). Many men, and especially those in positions of authority at the pagoda, held views that reflected the modernist interpretation of Buddhism put forward by the Buddhist reformers in the early twentieth century. Their view of Buddhism and of being Buddhist was more rationalistic and more individualistic. Most women I encountered did not hold this view, instead expressing that their activities had repercussions that reverberated throughout their social network. Women tended to feel, for example, that their own Buddhist practice would benefit their entire families, regardless of whether the ones for whom they were praying practiced or believed. This social benefit tended to be their main motivation for participating in pagoda activities. Men, by contrast, stressed that their practice brought about individual cultivation only and that the laws of karma meant that doing rituals on another's behalf was a waste of time and a misunderstanding of the Buddha's teachings. Both men and women, therefore, selected certain practices over others and interpreted those practices in different ways. Neither approach represents a more orthodox or "correct" approach to Buddhism. Rather, they are grounded in cultural, contextual, and historical ways of being that are deeply rooted in gender structures.

My analysis of gender and Buddhist practice in *The Buddha Side* was predicated on the differential participation of women and men in Buddhist practice specifically and in religion more generally. I argued that women became Buddhist practitioners more frequently and to a greater extent than men because Buddhism had been constructed in Vietnam as a quintessentially female practice and that the pagoda was viewed as a feminine and feminizing space. Young women make offerings to emphasize their femininity and especially as a display of sexually attractive feminine weakness and submissiveness (*hiền*), or they do so as an act of selfless caring for the family. For married women, Buddhist practice was—and usually still is—constructed as an extension of women's role as family caregivers. When men get involved, mostly in old age, they tend to disassociate themselves from the practices of women and step back from a devotional understanding of Buddhism. Men often described to me that when they chanted sutras (*tụng kinh*), for example, they did so to learn about the teachings of the Buddha, and they downplayed the notion that chanting had any supernatural effect, such as bringing good luck to the family.

Discourses of religion versus superstition are gendered and reflect an overall hegemonic structure that subordinates women to men in Vietnamese society. The rituals, imagery, historical narratives, and hierarchical structure all serve to push men into the center and women to the periphery. This is done quite literally at Sùng Phúc, where the monks always take the central position and nuns are physically relegated to the side.

The religion/superstition binary leans heavily on Orientalist constructions that view Asian tradition as static and backward while positively equating modernity with the West. These broad stereotypes that were rhetorically used to subjugate the East to Western colonial powers have been replicated in gender discourse such that in the reformation and modernization of Buddhism in the twentieth century, women's practices were equated with a debased superstition, while men were seen as pursuing a higher and more developed path. For some men, this expressed itself as a complete denial of all religion and an assumption of an atheist and rationalist humanism, particularly as set out by Communism. For others, like the Buddhist reformers, it was a rejection of older forms of religiosity that were holistic and enchanted and that did not make the secularist distinctions between the supernatural and the natural worlds. This general view of traditional versus modern expressions of religious practice was also largely juxtaposed with gender structures, so that women and women's religiosity was equated with the superstitious past, while the reformulated Buddhism-cum-world-religion was equated with a modern, international, and universalist practice properly oriented toward a masculinized individualistic quest for personal salvation. In Charles Taylor's terms, this discourse turned the Vietnamese modernists into "buffered selves" as opposed to the "porous selves" of the premodern Vietnamese (Taylor 2007, 37–38). This discourse, in Orientalist fashion, was equated with Western-styled progress and modernity, while the East was seen as backward, undeveloped, and corrupt, and therefore in need of being fixed. Not incidentally, it also drew on Confucian ideals of self-perfection that were closely tied to elite constructions of masculinity.

One of the most notable aspects of Sùng Phúc is that its constituents are quite different from those at regular pagodas. As already stated, my experience at all Buddhist pagodas, both overseas and in Vietnam, has been that it is primarily women who practice. When men do practice Buddhism, they tend to carve out roles as ritual experts, which elevates their position in the pagoda and differentiates their practice from women's (Soucy 2012, chapter 9). While in overseas communities, male participation seems to be higher (perhaps constituting 20 percent), in Hanoi, most rituals see only around 10 percent male participation, and I have often attended rituals where there were no men present. Furthermore, while male practitioners often take leadership roles in the pagoda despite their disproportionately low numbers, women are the ones largely responsible for Buddhism's practical maintenance; they do the lion's share of volunteer work for the upkeep and cleaning of the pagoda, and they are the main financial supporters, often motivated by competitive displays of piety (Soucy 2012, chapter 7). The gender imbalance is so self-evident that Hickey, Jamieson, and others have ascribed an idealized religious landscape of the Vietnamese village as being divided between the male space of the communal house (đình) and the female space of the Buddhist pagoda (Hickey 1987, 5–7; Jamieson 1986, 99–100; 1993, 31, 36).

This book has largely focused on how a new kind of modernist Zen has come about and how it is being presented by the Trúc Lâm organization as authentically Vietnamese, particularly in the local context of Sùng Phúc in Hanoi. That is, I have been discussing the intentional presentation of a modernist, secular, and nationalistic form of Zen Buddhism as it is constituted by those who possess the greatest portion of symbolic capital and have the means to control the message. However, following from my earlier critique, we must recognize and validate the ways people interpret that discourse and interact with it. The consumers of the spatial and rhetorical discourses have agency, which they use to take possession of these discourses and use them for often unintended purposes. As such, this chapter and the next will look at the different ways that Trúc Lâm Zen is experienced by men and women, how it fits into their lives, and what this says about gender construction and individualization in Trúc Lâm. To understand not just how Trúc Lâm Buddhism is presented but also what it looks like in practice, we must also understand something of how it is appropriated by its followers, how they reorganize and use those teachings in ways that resonate with their lives, and how these actions fit into their identity projects. This chapter and the next two look at how Trúc Lâm is practiced on the ground and explores what it is about Trúc Lâm Zen that attracts and opens a space for a diverse consistency of participants—men, women, old people, and youths.

Unlike the previous chapters, the final chapters will focus on anecdotal descriptions of some of the participants. Some have been chosen because they are representative, others because they illustrate something interesting about the way people engage in Zen and how their participation fits into their identity projects and social interactions. In the next chapter, I will turn my attention to the men at Sùng Phúc, examining how the modernist construction of Buddhism in the form of Zen is particularly appealing. In the final chapter, I will look at the involvement of young people at Sùng Phúc. Here, I will look at Sùng Phúc's women. Given that women are the mainstay of and most prevalent participants in Buddhism in Vietnam, their presence in Trúc Lâm is not surprising. What is noteworthy, however, is their high level of participation within the context of Trúc Lâm's stress on a masculine, modernist interpretation of Buddhism that deemphasizes many of the aspects that are important for feminine identity construction as it usually relates to religious practice.

THE WOMEN AT SÙNG PHÚC

As with regular forms of Buddhism, most practitioners at Sùng Phúc are women, and most of these are older women who have practiced devotional Buddhism for many years. Some still continue to participate in devotional rituals and merely add Zen meditation as an addition to their array of practices; others switch to Zen exclusively. The reasons why women are attracted to devotional forms, as articulated elsewhere (see Soucy 2012), are rooted in pagodas being constructed as feminine spaces and devotion being a feminine activity imbued with tropes of self-sacrifice, emotionalism, and care of the family. The rationalistic and desupernaturalized reconstruction of the modern Zen presented by Trúc Lâm would therefore seem ill-fitted with women's way of practicing Buddhism. Given the rationalist interpretation that Trúc Lâm takes, which denies the notion that participation has a positive effect extending beyond the individual, and particularly to the practitioner's families, the most pressing question is why Zen is attractive to them.

There are, of course, a range of motivations and constellations of factors that attract women to Trúc Lâm. For some, an important draw is the significant prestige attached to Zen and the potential that participation will increase symbolic capital within the context of competitive religiosity that is common in women's communities in Vietnam (Soucy 2012, chapter 7). For others, the message of Zen resonates with a modernist construction that has a progressive feel. These discourses of Buddhist modernism are compelling, since they have been reiterated by the

Buddhist institution for close to a century and have been reinforced by the state (especially in its Marxist form), by the media, and by the academy. For others, as in the concluding example of this chapter, the main motivation can be idiosyncratic, but it nonetheless draws on prominent aspects of Thích Thanh Từ's teachings, in particular the nationalist message.

Mrs. Tuyết's Inclusive Religiosity

I first met Mrs. Tuyết in 1997, and I know her to be a fairly typical lay Buddhist woman. She was intensely devout, and she practiced Buddhism in ways that were typical of older women in Hanoi. By this I mean that I had known her to go twice monthly to pagodas to make offerings and to make offerings at her home altar. Whenever she could, she went on pilgrimages and attended Dharma talks and special events at places like Quán Sứ Pagoda, the largest pagoda in Hanoi and the headquarters of the Vietnam Buddhist Sangha. Her Buddhist practice can be characterized as being devotional, inclusive, syncretic, and impregnated with popular beliefs.[1] Thus, while she recited sutras and listened to Buddhist lectures, she also sought advice from fortune-tellers and gave offerings to gods, goddesses, ancestors, spirits, and ghosts to ensure her family's good luck and protection from bad influences. She described her practice as typical, saying, "All women in Vietnam go to pagodas to make wishes for everyone in the family, to bring them good things and good luck."

It was therefore unexpected when in 2005, she began to practice the orthodox Zen of Trúc Lâm. Her participation appeared to be a part of a broader intensification of her Buddhist practice. This increased investment in Buddhism was not viewed favorably by her family, who complained to me that she was donating too much of the family savings to monks whom they strongly suspected of being charlatans, or at very least of taking advantage of credulous and gullible old women. They also resented that she seemed to be more focused on her Buddhist practice than the family, leaving her retired husband to do the cooking and cleaning and to care for the grandchildren while she "went off to pagodas." Mrs. Tuyết told me that her health was the first motivation for taking up meditation. The first time she mentioned this, she said, "I meditate to calm myself, make myself healthy and not worry about things." She repeated this a week later, though with a slight rephrasing: "I meditate to understand about the Buddha and to improve my health." This connection between practicing meditation and improving health was a recurring theme in conversations with several individuals during interviews and conversations, which I will discuss further below.

Her attachment to the Zen monastery and the master, however, was not as exclusive or as intense as it was for many other followers. While she was enthusiastic enough about meditation to sit a few times a week at her home and although she clearly respected the master, her deepening involvement had not resulted in her severing ties with other Buddhist leaders. Furthermore, while she claimed to meditate, her home practice consisted predominantly of chanting sutras. After fifteen years, she continues today to remain engaged with other Pure Land pagodas, especially with Quán Sứ Pagoda, while also going to Sùng Phúc. Her activities have slowed somewhat in the last few years because of age and health, but while her pagoda activities may have been reduced, and by 2018 she was not meditating as frequently, she nonetheless continues to be religiously active. She could still be heard chanting sutras in her house every day, the rhythmic tok tok of the wooden fish that keeps pace with her chanting drifting through the neighborhood's evening air.

This brings up an important point regarding the motivations for becoming involved with Zen. In *The Buddha Side*, I showed that women's participation in Buddhist rituals was closely tied to performances of femininity. For married women, participation invoked the ideal of women as selfless caregivers for their families. Buddhist practice was seen as a supernatural extension of the more general performative expectation that women place care of family above all else as a measure of their worth as a wife, mother, or grandmother. Their claims that their Buddhist practice brought good luck, health, and prosperity to their families were predicated on the underlying view that they could perform this supernatural labor as a surrogate for others. Trúc Lâm teaches that participation in Buddhist chanting or meditation will not bring good luck to oneself, never mind one's uninvolved family members. The teachings at Trúc Lâm instead emphasize, as we have seen, that only individual striving will bring spiritual advancement and that the goal is self-perfection and self-realization rather than material reward. This emphasis on individualistic self-cultivation fits very well with masculine rhetoric of self-reliance and heroic effort, but it is utterly at odds with the usual feminine-based construction that stresses practice as resonating through women's social networks. Yet despite this seeming incongruence, we see that the demographics of the participants at Sùng Phúc, where most practitioners are old women, are not radically dissimilar from those at other Buddhist spaces in Vietnam. The fact that it also attracts men and youths does not nullify the need to explain why women like Mrs. Tuyết are involved with this modernist form of practice that denies her practice there as benefiting anyone other than herself. Clearly, the rationalistic view and masculine rhetoric of individual striving does not have a deterring effect.

There are, of course, several factors at play. To begin with, the masculine rhetoric of individualism, positing that everyone can only be responsible for his or her own spiritual progress and that praying for material benefit for others is not a part of Buddhism, was lost on, or ignored by, many of the older women with whom I spoke. Others appeared to adopt this rationalist interpretation of Buddhism and viewed their previous practice and understanding as misguided and misinformed. However, it also seems that participation in Zen gave them a sense of identity that distinguished them from other Buddhists in Hanoi. Although none of the women with whom I spoke would have admitted to choosing to practice Zen because it made them look good in the eyes of their peers, their performance and display of their Zen identity attested to its symbolic value and to the capital that could be accrued by association with it.

The rising popularity of Zen in contemporary Vietnam is a result of converging discourses of modernity and legitimate practice that have come about because of the globalization of Buddhism and ingrained elite biases. This has led to a valuation of Zen above devotional practices. There are a variety of reasons why my informants have become involved in the Trúc Lâm organization and took up meditation as a central Buddhist practice. However, it often appears to be much less about the intellectual content of Zen than about the aura of Zen and the resonance it has with contemporary identity projects. This has to do with wanting to be simultaneously associated with modernity while connecting with what is seen as a valuable Asian—and specifically Vietnamese—tradition.

Trúc Lâm's denial of the supernatural web of interconnections with the human world and the possibilities that common understandings of devotional practices offer for supplication on behalf of a woman's network of human relationships, challenges some of the important implications of Buddhist participation as part of a more holistic religious practice. This holistic religious practice generally extends past Buddhism to involvement in an array of practices and locations, including spirit mediumship, communication with the dead through spirit-calling rituals (gọi hồn), geomancy, fortune-telling, ancestor worship, pilgrimages, and making offerings and supplications at a variety of spirit shrines (đình, đền, miếu, phủ, điện, and so on).

The solution for women like Mrs. Tuyết is to supplement their regular practices rather than to replace them. For them, Zen represents an adjunct rather than a total practice—an attitude that flies in the face of how Trúc Lâm is positioned by its elite. Thus, Mrs. Tuyết will present herself as a

Trúc Lâm adherent by donning the gray robe when she goes to Sùng Phúc, but she maintains another brown robe for when she chants sutras at other, more typical, devotional pagodas. The fact that the standard religious practice follows the lunar calendar but that Sùng Phúc follows the rhythm of a regular, solar-based workweek makes it easy to maintain other practices while adding practices at Sùng Phúc. For these people, the emphasis on meditation as a health practice with a Buddhist flavor does not challenge their holistic worldview. Zen is clearly valuable for them, but it is not everything.

This double-dipping is not necessarily seen as a problem. The vice abbot related that he was aware that some followers went to other pagodas and chanted sutras rather than exclusively practicing meditation at Sùng Phúc. He was not particularly concerned with it, but his comments implied that he saw chanting sutras as a lower form of practice and believed that people are at different spiritual levels. Other practitioners I spoke with were less sanguine about the issue, expressing alarm when I mentioned that some followers at Sùng Phúc were also participating in rituals and activities at other pagodas. I inferred from this that people who participated in both were not necessarily open about it.

Mrs. Thật: Identities and Distinctions

I arranged to meet Mrs. Thật at a location outside of Sùng Phúc to have a conversation about her participation in Trúc Lâm Zen. Despite the non-Buddhist context of our meeting place, she met me wearing gray, loose-fitting, monastic-style clothes. Her narrative expressed how Zen had changed her life:

> I didn't know anything about Zen before I started. Inside me there were a lot of bad things such as greed and attachment. When I initially followed Zen, I learned my body is not mine and my soul is impermanent. This realization helped me let go of greed, anger, desire for revenge, and even love and hate. I realized that nothing is real, and this idea freed me. . . . Before that, my life was not going very well. Now I have let go of worries and don't get upset. I have followed Zen for nine years. After three years my family changed dramatically. Before [I started practicing Zen], there was a lot of discord. My husband and I fought, and we both were unwilling to back down. Now I understand that everything is empty of reality and I let things go, so that now we don't fight at all.

Mrs. Thật's body language was calm and measured and she presented herself using the props of monastic-style clothing.[2] In doing so, she performed her Zen identity for me. Her story emphasized the transformative effect that Zen has had on her life, describing how she had divested herself of three stores that she owned so she could concentrate on practicing Zen at home. She expressed how she had developed a distaste for money and had moved away from her earlier attachment to worldly wealth. The transformation she had experienced by following Zen had also extended to her family. She related with evident pride how two of her children had renounced and become monks. Mrs. Thật's presentation followed a pattern of creating distinctions that I often encountered with followers of Trúc Lâm Zen and, as we have seen, reflects the way that Trúc Lâm is presented at Sùng Phúc by distinguishing itself from what representatives of Trúc Lâm considered the superstition-laden practices at the other devotional pagodas. Zen, for Mrs. Thật, represented a totalizing practice that was distinct from a Buddhism practiced only at certain places on certain days, and the appearance of being and sounding Zen-like were central to her identity construction.

Competition in Vietnamese pagodas for practitioners to be recognized for their piety can be fierce and ongoing. I have referred to this dynamic as "conspicuous devotion" (Soucy 2012, chapter 7).[3] Older women, particularly, compete to be recognized for their devotion through the displays of objects, dress, and behavior, such as having the biggest home altar or the nicest robe, going on the most impressive pilgrimages, or giving large donations to pagodas and monastics. Actions like these constitute a prominent performative element of Buddhist practice for many, building symbolic capital in the community and contributing in important ways to the identity projects of many individuals. But why Zen, specifically? The crowd of mostly women who were meditating at Sùng Phúc were demographically indistinguishable from the crowds of women whom I would normally see taking part in devotional rituals; it was only the object of their intensity that distinguished them, having been redirected from devotional practices to meditation. The answer, I think, can be found in the way Zen is layered with multiple symbolic meanings laden with elite connotations.

Zen has long been associated with elite intellectual culture throughout East Asia, including Vietnam (C. T. Nguyen 1997, 54). The cultural valuing of Zen over other forms of Buddhism in Vietnam is particularly evident in the transmission-of-the-lamp stylings of the *Thiền uyển tập anh,* modeling Buddhist history in Vietnam as Zen. The intention of this was to confer legitimacy on Vietnamese Buddhism by association with Chinese elite Chan culture (C. T. Nguyen 1997, 99). It led the author(s) to cloak stories of eminent Vietnamese monks, who frequently exhibited the tendencies of popular practice, with Zen tropes and to frame Vietnamese Buddhist history as the story of Zen lineages, particularly of three schools: Vinītaruci, Thảo Đường, and Vô Ngôn Thông.

While Trúc Lâm is not framed as one of the three main Zen schools in Vietnam of the medieval period in the *Thiền uyển,* its importance arises in the Trần dynasty as the first attempt to establish a genuinely Vietnamese Buddhist school (C. T. Nguyen 1997, 20), which occurred at around the same time that the *Thiền uyển* was written. Trúc Lâm's association with elite culture stems from its founding by a former king of Vietnam. The fact that King Trần Nhân Tông is also credited with defeating a major Chinese Yuan dynasty invasion adds to its symbolic potency (Dutton, Werner, and Whitmore 2012, 316). The romanticized view of Trần Nhân Tông and Trúc Lâm reinforced the elite presumptions of Zen and has made Trúc Lâm a lodestone for Vietnamese Buddhist reimaginings. So, for example, Thích Nhất Hạnh wrote a book called *Am mây ngủ* (Thích Nhất Hạnh 1982—later translated as *Hermitage among the Clouds*) that gives a romantic account of Trần Nhân Tông as an exemplary Vietnamese Buddhist figure (Thích Nhất Hạnh 1998b). The unmistakable elite nature of the scenes pervades the entire book, depicting him as not only a wise holy figure but also a former king who continues to be sought for guidance by the royal court, reinforcing tropes of Zen as elite.

Zen's elite nature is further accentuated by distinctions drawn between Zen and normal Buddhist practice, with the latter typically viewed as infused with superstitious, non-Buddhist elements. In this way, practitioners elevate Zen by drawing on global discourses of religion and modernity, combined with engrained elite views that draw distinctions along lines of orthodoxy and heterodoxy.[4] Reformers and apologists in Vietnam reacted to French colonialism by wanting to modernize Vietnamese society. A marker of this modernity was the distinction made between superstition and religion, equating the former with typically Vietnamese folk practices and the latter with the world religions. In doing so, they were assuming globalized discourses of Buddhist modernity that, Nedostup notes, were drawing as much from Protestant Christian sensibilities as from local biases (2009, 7).

While these global discourses are important for understanding the currents that brought Trúc Lâm Zen into existence and explain its teachings, it does less to explain how women who were formerly engaged in regular, devotional Buddhism are now attracted to the more austere and secular modernist Buddhism of Trúc Lâm. After all, as the example of Mrs. Tuyết showed, practitioners do not necessarily replace their more holistic understandings of the spirit world with the buffered, secularized view that Trúc Lâm advocates as Buddhist orthodoxy. There are other factors at work as well.

The cultural prestige that women accrue by associating with Zen and the hegemonic modernist discourses that it represents is also a significant motivation for adopting Zen practice. Zen is more than just an activity in their lives, and it can become central to their constructed identities as moral and modern selves. Zen practice at Sùng Phúc reflects what Erving Goffman, in his analogy of social practice as dramaturgy (1959), has characterized as a social "performance" involving actors, audiences, and props. Distinctions are drawn between Zen and standard Vietnamese Buddhist practices as part of this social performance. As we saw with Mrs. Tuyết, drawing distinctions was not always part of everyone's practice, but it was crucially important for some and a prominent element in many followers' practice. This was the case for Mrs. Thật, who was resolute in not participating in devotional Buddhist practices. She repeated a line that I frequently heard at Sùng Phúc that there was nothing wrong with Pure Land Buddhism but that Zen was more appropriate for some people, implying that Zen was for more advanced beings, like herself.

Participation in Buddhism yields less Bourdieusian profit for men and young people than it does for older women. This is because older women's communities, social lives, and identities frequently turn on their Buddhist practice, whereas for men and young people, this is not usually the case. This Buddhist community life, furthermore, often increases in importance for women as their children grow up. The social importance correspondingly accentuates competitive behavior. Because the stakes are higher, socially speaking, competition among women increases, and so they invest more in their performances. Some women at Sùng Phúc competed to wear the best robes that featured elaborate embroidery in off-tone gray. The demand for such robes drew vendors of religious wares to the gate on busy days and drove a proliferation of Buddhist supply stores in the neighborhood. Some women would wear pins that indicated that they had visited a particularly important pilgrimage site. Pilgrimages to India to visit the main sites of the historical Buddha were seen as the most prestigious.

There were also conspicuous displays of Zen practice. Whereas women at regular pagodas were competitive in their devotion, telling rosary beads and chanting audibly, at the Zen center, many women made a show of their meditation. Some would arrive early and start meditating in the main shrine room when no one else was doing so or would meditate by themselves in front of a wall in a visible location on a high-volume day. The conspicuous nature of these meditative displays was presumably intended to show religious virtuosity or diligence, replacing the conspicuous displays of piety in devotional performances at regular pagodas.

Lay woman at Sùng Phúc meditating in front of a wall before the Penitence Rite, 2011

Another example of conspicuous practice could be seen in another follower whom I visited at home. Having set herself up as the leader of a group of neighborhood women who went to Sùng Phúc, she built a special room in her home and regularly had everyone over to meditate. In return for her volunteerism, she gained access to the monks, which in turn built prestige among her peers. She displayed this with pictures prominently framed on the walls of the main room in her house showing her posing with various notable monks of the Trúc Lâm movement, including one with the founder, Thích Thanh Từ.

As for Mrs. Tuyết, she had an elaborate altar that, unusually, had no Buddhist icons or statues but instead featured two small crystal pagodas that she claimed held relics of the Buddha, which she would proudly show visitors, particularly if they were monastics. While there were multiple complex motivations for both Mrs. Thật's and Mrs. Tuyết's participation in Zen practice at Sùng Phúc, it was apparent that an important one was the symbolic capital conferred by Zen practice, which was a more advanced form of Buddhist practice in the eyes of many.

Zen practice is loaded with symbolic capital that is reinforced by its positive representation in the media and by state recognition.[5] At the same time, Zen escapes some of the negative connotations that adhere to devotional practices, which are equated by some, particularly men, with superstition.

The prestige of Zen is therefore a big draw for women whose identities are closely tied to peers' viewing them as exemplary Buddhists. Whereas in the past, Quán Sứ Pagoda was especially attractive to those who wished to gain symbolic capital within their Buddhist communities, now, as a politically central pagoda in Hanoi, Quán Sứ's attractiveness has been partly displaced by the rise of Trúc Lâm Zen and the Sùng Phúc Monastery.

Mrs. Minh and the Vietnamese Buddha

I first met Mrs. Minh in 2011. Mrs. Tuyết had just introduced her to Sùng Phúc, and Mrs. Minh had become interested in meditation. Mrs. Tuyết made a point of telling me that Mrs. Minh had just started coming to Sùng Phúc and practicing Zen, so she was not sure if I should bother interviewing her. Nonetheless, I explained that discovering what attracted people to Trúc Lâm was also important to me, so she proceeded to make the introduction.

Mrs. Minh was in her late fifties when I first met her. As a girl of five or six, she would accompany her grandmother to the Buddhist pagoda, particularly on the first and fifteenth of the lunar month. At the time, she felt that there was something special about the place. She continued to practice as she grew older, going to pagodas when she had the chance in order to wish for peace (cầu an), luck and benefit (phúc lộc), and auspiciousness (tốt lành). She also went to spirit-possession rituals to worship the spirits (thờ thánh). In other words, she practiced Buddhism, like most people, as part of a more holistic religious practice.

Mrs. Minh's motivation for practicing Zen at Sùng Phúc was surprising. She stated that her main affiliation was not to Buddhism but to a new religious movement, called Đạo Hồ Chí Minh (or colloquially, Đạo Bác Hồ), that was devoted to worshiping Hồ Chí Minh as a national hero and a god. The religious movement is predictably nationalistic, with "Uncle" Hồ worshiped as a god and savior of the nation. Unsurprisingly, she was particularly drawn to the nationalistic aspects of Trúc Lâm. She explained that according to the religious texts of her religion, Uncle Hồ taught that Vietnamese must worship the Vietnamese spirits.[6] She said that before the year 2000, she worshiped "foreign" buddhas like Śākyamuni and Guanyin, but she now felt this to be inappropriate:

> Śākyamuni Buddha was the son of a king in India. He became a buddha there . . . Vietnam also has a buddha-king named Trần Nhân Tông, who also ruled the country for several generations. After that, he abdicated the throne and gave the crown to his son. Then he became a monk on Mount Yên Tử. And what did he follow? He followed Zen. That is the main thing

I want to say to you, that this [Trúc Lâm] is Vietnamese Zen. So India has Zen, China has Zen, Vietnam also has Zen.

In our discussions, Mrs. Minh emphasized that Trần Nhân Tông was a national hero who defeated the Chinese before becoming enlightened and that he was therefore worthy of being worshiped by the Vietnamese. Her feeling was that Śākyamuni, while perhaps an enlightened being, was the buddha for the Indians, while Trần Nhân Tông was the buddha for the Vietnamese. This fundamentally nationalist view was not entirely divergent from prominent discourse in the Trúc Lâm literature and marketing, and it was one of the key elements that drew her to Sùng Phúc, though her interpretation and selective practice was idiosyncratic:

So now I will tell you. Because I understand already, when I go to Sùng Phúc Monastery, I don't chant "Nam Mô Phật Thích Ca Mâu Ni." I still go, but when I go, I just chant one phrase: "Xin quy hòa Phật"—like Uncle Hồ taught—"Xin quy hòa Phật," Đức Chúa Trời [Virtuous God of Heaven], Đức Mẹ Địa [Virtuous Mother Earth], Đức Ngọc Phật [Virtuous Jade Buddha]—which is also a title for Uncle Hồ—Đức Ba Cha (that is the three times father was born), Đức Thánh Mẫu (that is the three mothers); Đức Tam Tổ [the Virtuous Three Ancestors]. The three ancestors of Vietnamese are who? They are Trần Nhân Tông, Huyền Quang, and Pháp Loa [the first three patriarchs of Trúc Lâm]. They are called Đức Tam Tổ. So, together, these are the virtuous buddhas, spirits, and gods of Vietnam. In this way, we chant clearly for the gods of Vietnam. All of the foreigners—Australians, Americans, English, French—came to Vietnam and asked why we don't have a Vietnamese buddha. Uncle wanted Vietnam to have its own identity. In one of his speeches, he said he was very sad because the Vietnamese buddhas have a lot of merit but are not worshiped, or they are just put on a side altar, while the foreign buddhas get the main spot on the main altar. This is [regrettably] still the way it is now.

Because of her belief that Trần Nhân Tông is the Vietnamese buddha and that Śākyamuni was only the buddha for the Indians, when Mrs. Minh went to Sùng Phúc, she avoided entering the main shrine dedicated to Śākyamuni. Instead, she went straight to the ancestor altar, where the statues of Trần Nhân Tông and the other two patriarchs of Trúc Lâm are located, and she engaged in her own private prayer. While she meditated and wore the same gray robe worn by everyone else, and while she even participated in the usual recital of the Three Refuges and the Five Precepts, she engaged in these activities on her own terms, holding a parallel symbolic meaning that did not conform with the official orthodoxy put forward by the Trúc Lâm institution.

Mrs. Minh had moved on by the time I met her again two years later. I was told that she had become more involved in the Uncle Hồ religion and was no longer interested in Buddhism. Nonetheless, Mrs. Minh is an example, albeit, perhaps an extreme one, of the nationalist sentiment that Trúc Lâm intentionally evokes by drawing on a partially invented history of Zen-ness of Vietnamese culture, and particularly of Trúc Lâm Zen as a uniquely Vietnamese school of Zen Buddhism. The nationalist sentiment that was central to Mrs. Minh's motivation for becoming involved with Buddhist practice at Sùng Phúc and the symbolic significance that she attributed to that practice were also often expressed by both the laity and monastics at Sùng Phúc. As the only native Zen school, Trúc Lâm was a source of pride for the people at Sùng Phúc. Most people did not place Trần Nhân Tông above the historical Buddha and proclaim him as the buddha for the Vietnamese people, but many did express to me that they felt that he was a buddha. The organization actively used this nationalist sentiment as a marketing tool to make Trúc Lâm Zen attractive to the Vietnamese people, systematically branding their organization and activities and incorporating this construction into its space through its layout and iconography. Mrs. Minh shows that messaging is not always received passively but may instead be reinterpreted and used in idiosyncratic ways.

The motivations for Buddhist lay women tend to be more varied than they are for men. The female practitioners at most pagodas stress external performance and belief over inner cultivation and comprehension. Furthermore, devotional practices often revolve around supplication, making offerings, and obtaining talismans that can be distributed to family members. Most describe the purpose of their religious practice as bringing benefit to their family in the form of wealth, health, and harmony in their relationships. As such, their religious activities are in large part an extension of women's expected caretaker roles for their family. The meditation practice and the teachings at Sùng Phúc stress a much starker individualism and deny the community elements that are so central to women's usual forms of Buddhist practice. Practitioners at Sùng Phúc are taught that the benefits of meditation do not transfer to family members except insofar as the practice improves one's character, which can then improve family relationships and smooth family dynamics—a natural rather than supernatural process. It is thus the practitioner, not the Buddha, who brings benefit. This being the case, it is somewhat surprising that so many women are nonetheless interested in Trúc Lâm Zen. As Mrs. Minh showed, the reasons that they gave were sometimes quite idiosyncratic.

For some, participation at Sùng Phúc did not preclude other forms of religious practice or even Buddhist practice at other pagodas. Certainly, the prestige of Zen was a motivating factor since it elevated their own image as devout Buddhists and built symbolic capital within their communities. Thus, while at first glance it may be surprising, there are nonetheless ample reasons why they would be attracted to Zen.

CHAPTER SIX

||||||||

Zen Men

While most practitioners at Sùng Phúc on any given Saturday are women, lay Buddhist men make up a higher percentage of the sangha there than at regular pagodas, constituting around 30 to 40 percent of the laity who attend events as opposed to the 10 percent or so at regular pagodas. This chapter will look at the motivations of these men to participate at Sùng Phúc. Zen for them is constructed in a way that creates an opportunity to be involved without compromising their masculinity, by drawing on specific tropes of masculine self-reliance and cultivation.

The complicated construction of religion through the last century or so placed it in juxtaposition with the rational, modernist discourses that held hegemonic sway. Men, as a whole, have benefited from aligning themselves with these modernist discourses and avoiding religion, which in the media is associated with women, irrationality, and premodernism and often undifferentiated from superstition (Soucy 2012). Those few who did become involved in Buddhism practiced, and conceived of their practice, differently from women. The pagoda was seen as a feminine space, particularly when juxtaposed with the masculine space of the communal house (đình) (Jamieson 1993, 12–16). Its ascribed feminine character meant that it was also perceived as threatening to their masculinity (Soucy 2012, 70).[1] A common theme that emerged when speaking with male participants at Sùng Phúc was that notions about male participation in Buddhism is changing and that such notions are accompanied by a reorientation of the symbolically gendered notion of the space as no longer challenging to masculinity. The term they employed also marked this change; the usual label for a Buddhist space—pagoda (chùa)—was replaced by a grander designation with more prestige: Zen monastery (*Thiền viện*). One of the draws of Trúc Lâm for these men was the strong anti-superstition element that characterized its presentation of Buddhism. That is, what attracted many men to Sùng Phúc was that the Buddhism practiced there had been reconstructed as a religion, with the legitimacy accorded it by alignment with the modernist discourse of the Vietnamese Buddhist institution, supported by international agreement of Buddhist orthodoxy that draws distinctions between a global Buddhist religion and heterodox local practices. These elements can be discerned in an explanation given to me by a man at Sùng Phúc:

> Men are now starting to follow Buddhism. In the feudal past, it was divided, so that women would go to the Buddhist pagoda [*chùa*], while men went to the communal house [*đình*]. The communal house is where men discussed important issues and made decisions, like policy in the village, but women were forbidden from entering and excluded from making these big decisions. Women would go to the pagoda with their families, but they could not go to the communal house. Therefore, before the Renovation, there was no equality. After, men started to realize that the pagoda is actually a place that is very calm, a peaceful place for practicing Buddhism and worshiping the Buddha. So now [that Buddhism has been reformed], it is one hundred percent a religion [i.e., not superstition]. It isn't fiction.

His implication was that Buddhism had been purged of superstitions, presumably by men's participation. Buddhism, as a result, was now a properly differentiated religion rather than a mix of Buddhism and superstitious beliefs and practices.

What follows is a description of the relationship between masculinity and religion in Vietnam, which will lead to an exploration of how three lay men at Sùng Phúc relate to Zen Buddhism and how their experiences there diverge from what I observed at regular, devotional pagodas in Hanoi.

MALE SKEPTICISM

During the colonial period, masculine modernity was largely tied to a humanist, materialist, rationalist, and scientific viewpoint that led many to turn their backs on religious ritual and scorn religious practice as backward superstition (Luong 1993, 286; Malarney 1993, 281; 2002, 103). The apogee of this was the rise of the Marxist worldview and the suppression of religion under the Communist state from 1954 in northern Vietnam and after 1975 in the south (Choi 2007, 103–104; Kleinen 1999, 171; Larson and Endres 2006, 152–154; Luong 1993, 285; Malarney 2002,

80–85; P. Taylor 2007, 13). The state paid particular attention to dismantling institutions that they felt challenged their authority and represented the corrupt feudal society of the past. Particularly targeted were the institutions of local power. For that reason, communal houses, where the village tutelary deity was worshiped and where the council of elders made decisions at the local level, were thoroughly dismantled. The family was another institution that was targeted, with the state particularly concerned with the lifecycle rituals of weddings and funerals because they were seen as being wasteful and because they offered prominent opportunities for conspicuous consumption and the building of status at the level of the village (Malarney 1996). These moves indicate the concern of the Communist Party to undermine and replace ties to "more intimate collectives" (Appadurai 1996, 162) in the interest of the fragile abstraction of the new nation.

Much as in the Chinese campaign to destroy superstition in the 1920s to 1930s (Nedostup 2009, 15), wastefulness and superstition were central polemical targets that were used in attempts to subvert all manifestations of religious expression. Divination, fortune-telling, spirit channeling, geomancy, and possession rituals were particularly targeted and made illegal, and the police heavily enforced this ban by arresting and harassing anyone who participated, though some officials did it with more vigor than others.

Religiosities that had been categorized as officially recognized religions, especially those that had been identified in this way by the Western academy and that had been reshaped to fit the category by reformists and reform movements in Asia, were allowed to continue, though their activities were curtailed.[2] The Catholic Church was permitted to exist, though the power of the Vatican was usurped by the Vietnamese state (Keith 2012, 248; Matthews 1992, 70). Buddhism was recognized and allowed to continue on an official level but was controlled in various ways; some pagodas had their properties confiscated, major rituals were curtailed, and their role in performing funerals was, for a while, taken away. The Buddhist following was essentially reduced to a few old women chanting sutras a few times a month, who, because they were seen as non-threatening—they included the mothers and grandmothers of some officials—were allowed to quietly continue their practices.

While the hard power of the state was exercised against religious practitioners, there were other persuasive ways in which the negative attitude toward religions was perpetuated. The media published stories that alternatively criticized and ridiculed religious practice as wasteful, superstitious, and backward remnants of an oppressive feudal past.

Cartoons still appear that poke fun at practitioners engaging in practices that are seen as superstitious, and while male ritual specialists are sometimes featured, often portrayed as shifty characters with sunglasses and pencil mustaches, most of the deluded participants are depicted as women. The Vietnamese academy, too, participated by recognizing certain religiosities as being proper religion and others as being backward and corrupt superstition.

Membership in the Communist Party was given only to those who were declared atheists. To progress in a society where businesses were all state owned, membership in the Communist Party was effectively mandatory for anyone who wanted to advance in their careers. This was more a concern for men than for women, which led men to adopt dispositions that completely scorned all religious practice, including Buddhism.

The overwhelming discourse was therefore against religion generally and Buddhism specifically. Until the Renovation in the late 1980s, most people avoided religious spaces. Given that the ramifications for engaging in religious practice during this period were severe, it is no surprise that involvement with Buddhism was limited to those who were already economically marginalized—primarily old women who were unemployed. After the Renovation, this freeze on religious practice continued for quite a long time, and the anti-religious disposition still persists today, although it is declining.

The anti-religious discourses were demonstrably gendered. Many of the practices that were criticized as being superstitious, premodern, irrational, and backward were ones in which women engaged as part of their responsibilities as caretakers of the family. The fact that some of the practices that were deemed superstition were made illegal (though in practice, they were informally tolerated) only served to reinforce hegemonic constructions of gender that viewed—and shaped—women as emotional rather than rational, and as constitutionally "premodern."[3] It also served to make religious practice antithetical to masculine gendered identity and identity projects. So, for example, one old man I knew, a former intelligence officer, became interested in Buddhism as he neared retirement but would only interact with monks away from Hanoi and hesitated to participate in Buddhist rituals until after he retired (Soucy 2012, 159–160).

When I began fieldwork in Hanoi in 1997, very few lay men could be found participating in any capacity at Buddhist pagodas. Young men may have brought their girlfriends there to make offerings and supplicate the buddhas for help, but the men usually waited outside the pagoda. Old men sometimes practiced Buddhism but tended to do so only if they were involved as part of a ritual group or were leading the chanting sessions.

In the 1990s, and to some extent even today, men who were interested in Buddhism—particularly young ones—were seen as effeminate; jokes about the sexual orientation of monks can still be heard. In general, Buddhist pagodas continue to be seen as women's places, and participation in Buddhist activities challenges masculinity. The discourse against Buddhism, while losing some of its forcefulness today, has been sustained for almost sixty years in northern Vietnam.

In the last fifteen years or so, there have been changes in attitudes toward religion. Shrines to earth gods have appeared in entrance areas to businesses, and village festivals have been enthusiastically resurrected. Young men sponsor rituals performed by spirit mediums to improve their business prospects, though this is still avoided by a majority of them. At Buddhist pagodas on the first and fifteenth of the lunar month, some men can be seen making supplications at the Buddha altars. They are still vastly outnumbered by women, but their presence is evidence of a substantial shift in attitudes and perceptions.

The reasons for this shift are complicated and not easily explained. It seems to be the case that businessmen in particular have reengaged with the supernatural. One young man I know who in 2005 expressed skepticism toward all things religious, saying that it was all superstition, was by 2013 sponsoring spirit-medium rituals to improve his luck in business. While his wife was the primary impetus for this, he had become a compliant participant. He explained to me that he now believed more than he used to because he had received help from the gods. He still retained some skepticism, but he said that he was willing to do whatever it took to succeed, including engaging with the supernatural. While he usually left his wife to organize and perform most of the rituals, he said that he felt more secure knowing that he had sponsored rituals that could be beneficial. This view seems to reflect the kind of magical thinking for gardening and deep-sea fishing that Malinowski noted in the Trobriand Islands, where ritual was used specifically for instances where there was a greater element of chance (Malinowski 1948).

However, the re-enchantment of Vietnam extends beyond businessmen trying to guard against the vagaries of doing business in the current freewheeling economic context of Vietnam. There is a general shift at all levels toward a more positive view of religion and religious practice. This may be led by the state, which is no longer as devoutly anti-religious as it had once been. Religion has become emblematic of a Vietnamese traditional culture and has become more closely associated with statements of nationalism (as evidenced, for example, by Vietnam's recent adoption of the lotus as the national flower, mentioned earlier).

This re-enchantment of Vietnam is selective in several ways. First, the more devotional practices that are aimed primarily at harnessing the promise of potency for personal benefit—frequently in an amoral way—are more often attractive to businessmen than to people from other walks of life, especially since doing business can sometimes challenge moral behavior (Weller 1996). Most men are still prone to expressions of skepticism and a reticence toward religious involvement. Where men do take part in religious practice, however, it is usually selective. Politicians pay respect to national heroes, like the Hùng kings, the mythical rulers of the primordial Vietnamese kingdom of Văn Lang, though they would usually phrase their actions as remembering or paying respect rather than worshiping. They would also not voice an expectation that their actions will result in receiving benefit from the supernatural. Village men typically take part in village festivals and rituals related to the tutelary god of the village, though this is often seen as tradition (*truyền thống*) or custom (*phong tục*) rather than religion (*tôn giáo*). The forms of religion that are usually avoided by men in Hanoi are those that have in the past been seen as superstition. Spirit-possession rituals (*lên đồng*) and "soul-calling" (*gọi hồn*) séances are examples of these. However, in a general sense, religious activities that focus on supplication are seen as being irrational and emasculating, and they continue to be viewed skeptically, particularly by men.

Josephson-Storm has presented an interesting argument that is worth considering here. He demonstrates that disenchantment was nowhere nearly as complete as modernist claims have stated, declaring that both disenchantment and modernity are myths (2017). Myths, however, have power. While a disenchanted modernity might never have been as complete or as inevitable as social theorists presumed, that does not detract from the compelling nature of this hegemonic discourse that has dominated for the last century. One of the effects was that it ascribed social capital to secular performances while marginalizing religious expression. The extent to which the discourses were fully realized is less important than that people engaged with the discourses, for they compelled many to think and act in new ways, regardless of their being incomplete and sometimes ambiguous and that they were contradicted by sporadic expressions of irrationality.

These contradictions between dominant discourse and actual practice are also present in Buddhism, which holds an ambiguous position in Vietnam. Buddhism is often seen as a women's religion, partially because most people have no depth of Buddhist knowledge and because the media in northern Vietnam has for half a century portrayed it in a mostly negative light. Buddhism is therefore commonly associated with people making wishes and asking for assistance from the buddhas. This devotional reliance runs counter to tropes of male self-reliance that are based in the modernization that Josephson-Storm underplays as "myth," and therefore, men have generally avoided Buddhist spaces. Furthermore, the idea of seeking supernatural assistance was criticized widely by Marxist-humanist views that sought to undermine the idea that lives were determined by unseen forces.

On the other hand, in recent years, the media has increasingly portrayed Buddhism positively. The state has praised Buddhists for their role in building the country and has positively associated it with Vietnamese history and tradition. Interlocutors equated the Zen mummies that I described at the beginning of the book with a high level of Buddhist achievement that reinforces the notion that Vietnamese culture stands equal to and independent of China's. In promoting Vietnamese culture and values, Buddhism has been seen as having a significant symbolic role but only after having been remade in a modernist way, with devotional practices and reliance on the supernatural subsumed under discourses of individual self-cultivation. Looking at Buddhist journals from the Reform period before the Second World War to the post-Renovation period shows a noticeable decline in emphasis on Pure Land Buddhism and an increased highlighting of the Zen school and meditation.

THE MEN OF SÙNG PHÚC

Despite the increased participation of men in religion in general, there remains a persistent unwillingness by many to become Buddhist. While not as stark as when I started my research in the 1990s, there is still a substantial imbalance between male and female followers of Buddhism. Zen seems to be an exception, particularly as it is structured in the context of Trúc Lâm's globally influenced modernism. The rationalistic and individualistic expressions of Buddhism avoid many of the negative associations of superstition and blind faith that seem to be obstacles to men's participation in more devotional forms of Buddhism.

The rest of this chapter will look at three men's participation in Trúc Lâm. The first two are retired lay members who attend rituals weekly. The third is a lay devotee who is living as an acolyte at Sùng Phúc while he decides whether to become a monk.

Mr. Thiệu, the Confucian Scholar

Mr. Thiệu is a bright, friendly, and energetic man whom I met at Sùng Phúc one day in 2011 near the beginning of my research trip. He made a point of coming to greet me to tell me how happy he was that a foreigner was interested in Vietnamese Zen and then invited me to come to his house. Several days later, I arrived at his house around lunchtime. His wife had prepared a feast with six different dishes, including fried spring rolls and a square sticky rice cake (*bánh chưng*) that was out of season (as it is more usually served around Tết Nguyên Đán, the lunar New Year). He was neatly dressed in dark slacks and a button-down short-sleeved shirt. His house was small, well kept, and filled with books. Mr. Thiệu and I sat together to eat the delicious lunch, while his wife left to eat in the back, leaving us to talk, eat, and drink alone.

Mr. Thiệu was clearly a proud man who wanted to be known for being refined and cultivated in a sense that resonated with a Confucian ideal of scholarly elitism. A good portion of the conversation that day revolved around his activities as a poet, his membership in the Poetry Society (Câu lạc bộ Thơ), and the book of poems that he had published. He began a lengthy conversation by asking for my astrological sign, and when I told him I was born in the Year of the Monkey, he immediately exclaimed that we were fated (*có duyên*) to meet and that our astrological signs were very compatible. He then explained his motivation for approaching me at Sùng Phúc, saying, "When I saw a foreigner was interested in Buddhism [*có tâm với đạo Phật*], I felt very close to you [*rất tình cảm*]."[4] He felt compelled, he said, to be an ambassador for Vietnam and for Vietnamese Buddhism and therefore invited me to his home.

Mr. Thiệu took refuge, thereby officially becoming a Buddhist, about a year before I met him. He said that he was initially attracted to Buddhism because his wife had not been well for several years. Finally, some medicine he bought seemed to help her, and when her health returned, she said to him, "I am doing well now because we were lucky to get the right medicine. The gods and buddhas gave me my health back. Now you and I should go to a pagoda to take refuge in the Buddha." Previous to that, he had an ancestor altar at home (as is customary) but had no involvement in Buddhism and knew nothing about it. However, he explained, "after my wife was cured because the gods and buddhas took care of her, I started to go to the pagoda to take refuge and was given a Buddhist Dharma name. Then I started to do the Penitence Rite and listen to the monks teaching about the Buddha Dharma."

Mr. Thiệu was typical of many of the Buddhist men with whom I have spoken. He felt that one of the most important things about being a Buddhist was to understand the dharma, for without understanding, there was little point in being Buddhist. He explained:

> Truthfully, many people go to the pagoda without understanding [about Buddhism]. But when you go to pagoda and you chant sutras, it doesn't achieve anything if you don't understand what you are chanting. It doesn't help anything at all. When you enter the pagoda, first you have to thoroughly understand the five precepts of the Buddha.

This rational understanding of Buddhism is the typical view of older men at pagodas, whether they follow Zen or Pure Land Buddhism. Elsewhere I show how men distinguish their practice from women's by accentuating the importance of comprehension over ritual and by engaging in performances of knowledge (Soucy 2012, chapter 9). This view also aligns them with the intellectual elite who led the Buddhist Reform movement and is therefore a position that held cultural dominance. They typically try to show themselves to be not only knowledgeable but also experts. Within the context of Pure Land devotional Buddhism, this can be done by joining the group that leads the rituals (*ban cúng*). The men who follow Zen also frequently accentuate this rational aspect of Buddhism, similarly aligning themselves with the Buddhist reformers and the view that is commonly upheld by the Buddhist institution. In doing so, they realign Zen as being suited to masculine dispositions. In its Zen guise, Buddhism is no longer femininizing. Reflecting this, Mr. Thiệu held that Zen was particularly suited to men:

> Zen is especially suitable for men because it stresses self-reliance. In the Zen school, if you want to do something, you have to do it yourself. Therefore, if you want to follow Zen, the first thing is that your mind/heart [*tâm*] has to be pure. The basic characteristics of men are that they drink alcohol, eat a lot, talk loudly, and so on. After you take refuge [*quy y*, i.e., become a Buddhist], you have to talk gently and with wisdom. You have to speak from a position of self-awareness and try to understand others. You have to understand that desire, anger, and ignorance [*tham, sân, si*] are a part of human nature. Therefore, the people who really have desire, they can't follow Buddhism. After you take refuge, you have to avoid getting angry [which is a stereotype of men]. For example, you have to solve issues in the family appropriately. If, say, your children are rude and disrespectful, talking back to you, can you get angry? Normally fathers would admonish them for being so rude. But I won't say that. [Because I am a Buddhist], I have to explain to them according to the Buddha's teachings,

telling them that they should do good things to be moral, and teach them about dharma and how they will be punished if they act that way because of the law of cause and effect.

This was a view expressed to me by a number of people, though Mr. Thiệu was more forthright about it. Zen for Mr. Thiệu fit with his self-image as a poet and an intellectual. For him, the point of meditation and of participating in Buddhism had to do with improving knowledge. Conversely, he downplayed devotional Buddhist activities that do not involve understanding Buddhist philosophy:

> Zen is very suitable for me for this reason: it is more practical than just chanting sutras and reciting the name of Amitābha. If you want to meditate, you have to have *bodhicitta* [*tâm bồ đề*—the awakened mind, an alignment toward achieving enlightenment]. Only with the buddha mind [*tâm Phật*] can you meditate. If you don't have *bodhicitta*, then you can't meditate. . . . Of course, people who don't understand about spirituality go to the pagoda but don't comprehend anything at all about the Buddha Dharma. If you don't understand the Buddha Dharma, then going to the pagoda doesn't resolve anything at all. It's useless.

After our discussions over lunch were concluded, Mr. Thiệu took me to where he writes. It was in a separate house not far from the apartment where we had eaten. The house was set up to be a scholar's studio. There was a sitting area next to a big desk where he did his writing and studying. The room was decorated by a large statue of Di Lạc (Maitreya) and a stone mountain with a fountain that he explained was for feng shui. His apartment was decorated with Chinese calligraphy and a large photograph of him being celebrated by his poetry club. It seemed important for him to show me that he was a scholar and a poet, and he claimed that he came from a cultured family (*gia đình văn hóa*). He translated the Chinese calligraphy hanging on the wall, showed me his book of poetry, offering me a copy, and played a DVD that showed a festival in his home village in Hưng Yên Province. The importance of showing me that he was a poet with a depth of cultural knowledge indicated that having me at his house was part of his identity project, building his own sense of self-worth and his self-image as a Confucian-style scholar. There was also a public aspect to my visit, as he took considerable time introducing me to his neighbors and explaining that I was a professor of Buddhist studies from Canada. None of this diminished the sincere generosity and friendship that he extended to me. Rather, it was an indication that his participation in Zen at Sùng Phúc was part of a larger identity project of constructing and presenting himself as a model Confucian scholar and as a cultured man: "Zen is very suitable in society today," he explained, "because it combines the study of the Dharma and training yourself to be calm through meditation, which helps to improve self-discipline. It also helps your health, improves your mind, your body, your heart. . . . Therefore, Zen is very suitable for men."

Mr. Xuân, Retired Army Officer

I was introduced to Mr. Xuân in 2013. When I met him, he was seventy-one years old. He had been well educated, having studied political science, and had become a regimental commissar in the army. He explained to me how he began practicing Zen at Sùng Phúc, which he had been doing for around five years:

> When I started following Buddhism, I went directly to the Zen monastery [Sùng Phúc]. I was first introduced by the women of the Buddhist lay group in this area. One old woman liked me and urged me to go to the Zen monastery. At that time, it was after Tết [lunar New Year] and, coincidentally, when I came back from my home village, my wife told me that since I didn't have anywhere else to go and had some free time on my hands, I should go to visit this pagoda because it is the most beautiful. She took me to Sùng Phúc Monastery. When I went there, I saw the events calendar, so I secretly registered the next day for the meditation class and started meditating right away. I have had an affinity for Buddhism for a long time, but never acted on it until this point.

Mr. Xuân quickly became a devoted practitioner of Zen, "meditat[ing] every day without fail." He began by meditating for half an hour but now meditated for an hour a day. When I asked about meditation, he went on at length about the benefits to health, character, and intellect:

> When you train in meditation, you sleep really well. I am seventy-one this year, and I feel my mind is very clear. I still drive a motorcycle at full speed, haha! No problem! I still feel I am very active and agile. That is the most valuable thing. I have a few grandsons who go to Sùng Phúc with me. I directed them to meditate. I told them that if they meditated, they would study better. If someone goes to meditate, if they can't sit still, then they won't study well, and the ones who can sit still will study well. They will be more patient and motivated. But the ones who fidget will lack motivation. If you are a little bit uncomfortable and you give up, it's because you lack patience and motivation, so then you will be a loser in life. Meditation is good. It cures disease, makes you healthier, and resolves all your issues, so you will lead a better life. In the family, everyone lives in a loving environment—the

young ones, the elders, are all loved. So now I can talk to the younger people. They listen to me. I can talk to the kids, the elders, to everyone.

Mr. Xuân understood Zen to be an elite religion, and this was perhaps one of the draws for him. When we began to discuss Zen, his first comment was that "Zen is a path that is more suited to the educated people." He also recognized that Zen was becoming more interesting to men. He contrasted the Buddhism practiced at other pagodas as frequently being more concerned with money, but he believed that Zen was different, as it "mainly emphasizes education and sincerity [có tâm]." He therefore called it "more developed" than other Buddhist sects:

> Zen is a path that is more suited to the educated people. When you walk into the monastery, you release all of your issues and worries. When you meditate, it releases your stress, and you feel very unencumbered and peaceful. If you go to other pagodas, it is mostly women. Only in Sùng Phúc is it not just for women but also for the youth, including students and people who work. Men often like to do things that are more active and things that are strong and masculine, because they lack patience. When you go to the monastery, you have to have patience. But nowadays, they realize that Zen is very interesting. For example, you may be very busy with work, but when they go through the monastery gate, they leave that all behind.

Though he did not seem as deliberate about constructing that identity as Mr. Thiệu, Mr. Xuân nonetheless took measures to let me know that he considered himself to be a well-educated and cultured person (có văn hóa) and that he strived for self-cultivation:

> Not everyone has wisdom. I feel very lucky that I have had the opportunity to study in many places. I study very well. I have studied philosophy, then science, politics, and so many other subjects. So, I study well. I read something or listen to a lecture from the monks, and I understand them right away. Many of the monks teach at a high level and are very talented [and even so, I can follow what they teach].

The way he presented his practice and spoke of meditation came across as though he were engaged in a kind of battle with himself. The stakes were not just to appear cultivated but to see himself as rigorous, to not be one of the fidgeting "losers" but instead to be someone who is patient, motivated, intelligent, wise, and cultivated. In our discussion, he often brought up how Zen helps to develop wisdom (trí tuệ).

Mr. Xuân's view of Buddhism was more starkly secular than most, following interpretations that had been put forward by the reformers.

Regarding Sukhāvatī (Cực Lạc, Amitābha's Pure Land), for example, he insisted that there was no paradise separate from this world: "There is no [separate] world of Sukhāvatī, no paradise. Heaven is here and now. We are very happy to have the opportunity to meet. That is heaven already. You don't have to go anywhere to get to heaven!" He never described Buddhist practice as having any supernatural effect. Instead, he stressed the health benefits of meditation and how it helped train one to be a person with a better character, with more tolerance and patience. Unlike devotional Buddhists who pray for the buddhas' help in achieving harmony in the family, he felt that Buddhism's positive impact on his family life was entirely a result of his own self-cultivation and not of supernatural intervention. The humanistic views that he held of Buddhism meant that he also saw Buddhism as compatible with the ideas of Marx and Lenin. Above all, he saw Buddhism as being about the natural world, the here and now. His concluding remarks to me were that "Buddhism is very scientific, and also very cultured [*rất khoa học và rất văn hóa*]."

Mr. Thể, Road-Weary Truck Driver

I first noticed Mr. Thể helping manage the motorcycle parking in the Sùng Phúc courtyard on a busy Saturday. Probably in his late forties, his hair was a dark black, and his face had not lost the sternness gained from years of daily struggle. He had the features and unsmiling countenance of someone to avoid on the street, the hard look of a gangster. I later saw him helping out around the temple precinct—cleaning the main shrine, sweeping the balcony, or helping to cook food for the monks and daily visitors. I would also see him at the afternoon lectures, sitting behind the monks and taking notes. He always wore the gray Buddhist clothes commonly worn by lay Buddhists at Sùng Phúc. He was living at Sùng Phúc as a *cư sĩ*, a term denoting a lay resident who follows a semi-monastic life. The liminal status of being a *cư sĩ* living at Sùng Phúc was sometimes undertaken as a retreat, usually for a period of weeks or months, after which the *cư sĩ* would return to regular life. Sometimes, however, it was undertaken as a preliminary step to decide whether to take on a more religious life by pursuing monastic ordination.

Such was the case with Mr. Thể. By the time we finally had the opportunity to speak, he had been living at Sùng Phúc for a month and a half. Despite his fierce outward appearance, he was gentle and happy to talk with me. We sat on the balcony by the main shrine during a break from his chores, and he related to me a little of his experience living at Sùng Phúc. He had been a driver of a twenty-ton truck, but he did not like that life, and he longed to have the time and space to concentrate on exploring his inner self (*nội tâm*). He did not speak directly about why he objected to being a driver, but he did contrast the life inside the monastery with his perception of outside life:

> The main benefit of practicing here is that when something happens in your life, you are able to remain calm and detached. Before you start to meditate, you react right away to situations. For example, if you have a collision, you react right away by cursing or fighting. So now I am able to stay calm and think about it—about right and wrong—and I can control my temper. That is the practical benefit I have gained from meditation.

In 2004, he asked his mother to take him to their local pagoda in Lạng Sơn, north of Hanoi near the Chinese border. He eventually took refuge in the Buddha, dharma, and sangha (*quy y*) after long discussions with the local monk. As it was just a local pagoda, a devotional form of Pure Land Buddhism was practiced there. His practice at this time consisted of going to the pagoda on the first and fifteenth of the lunar month to make offerings and to pay homage to the Buddha. He began practicing more deeply, chanting sutras (*tụng kinh*) and reciting the name of Amitābha (niệm Phật), which led him to want to practice even deeper. It took several years for him to put his affairs in order so that he could live at Sùng Phúc Monastery.

Mr. Thể found that life at Sùng Phúc provided the peacefulness (*an lạc*) that he said he craved, but he also found it challenging: "You can stand the routine for a day or two—getting up really early, meditating for long hours, doing all the chores—but it is tiring, and it gets harder and harder. After a while I couldn't get up." Meditation was a trial for him. The daily meditation for monks from 3:30 to 5:00 a.m. was especially difficult. "I can't take it. After around forty-five to fifty minutes, I have to take a break for ten minutes or so before continuing. The monks are practiced at it and can sit for the entire time, but it's really not easy." Because of Zen's physical difficulty, he felt that the practice was particularly suitable for men. Contrasting Zen with the Pure Land devotional practices at regular pagodas, he said:

> Zen is hard on the body. So for women, it is easier to listen to dharma talks and to recite "*Nam mo A Di Đà Phật*" [niệm Phật, the practices at regular pagodas]. Listening to dharma talks is easy enough that even old people can do it. But here [at Sùng Phúc], you need to have a certain level of health to be able to meditate. For new people, even basic participation is not easy.

Mr. Thể's view of Buddhism was typical of most men I spoke with at Sùng Phúc in its emphasis on a modernist interpretation of Buddhism rooted in ideas of the Buddhist reformers. He felt that Pure Land Buddhism was a valid path, but he tended to interpret its central practices and tenets humanistically. For him, reciting Amitābha's name was useful not for bringing blessing or earning one's way into a paradise but because it calms one and brings peacefulness in this life. Just the act of going to a pagoda itself helps one to become a better, a gentler (*hiền lành*) person. He similarly interpreted the Pure Land along the lines of the humanistic Buddhist teachings of Taixu:

> Is there such a thing as Sukhāvatī? Yes, it exists, but it isn't a separate place somewhere out there. When someone goes to the pagoda and thinks about Sukhāvatī, they are already in the Pure Land. For example, the two of us being good to each other like this, that is the Pure Land already. We aren't fighting, we aren't arguing, we care for each other. That is the Pure Land already.

Mr. Thể was impressed by Sùng Phúc, its teachings, and the monks who lived there. He felt that society was in decline, with young people losing their culture and forgetting their debt to their ancestors and that consequently, people were very shallow. Zen provided balance in their lives. He gave the example of rich and well-educated people who have everything but lack balance in their lives, and he claimed that Zen can bring them that balance. This, for him, was the reason that so many people were attracted to practicing Zen. Under the guidance of the monks at Sùng Phúc, he felt that he had become a better person, and he said that this was the case for anyone who undertook this practice:

> When you come here and practice meditation for a few sessions, you start to change. Everything from the way you think to the way you act starts to change in important ways. It changes your nature [*bản tính*] and makes you calmer and makes your personality [*cá tính*] less aggressive.... When you meet people here, they aren't like people on the street; people here are nice. For example, when you need something . . . I'm not even talking about monks . . . when we see that someone needs help, even a stranger, we open our hearts and are willing to help to the extent of our ability. And the monks are even more compassionate [*từ bi*], because they have been practicing for a longer time.

The monks at Sùng Phúc, he felt, were a good example for all of the followers. In this, he contrasted Trúc Lâm Zen practiced at Sùng Phúc. While he did not criticize other pagodas or Pure Land Buddhism explicitly, he clearly implied that the exemplary nature of the practice at Sùng Phúc and of the monks who lived there distinguished it as uniquely suited to the problems of today:

> I have to say that the monks at Sùng Phúc are extremely compassionate and care about people a lot. I really respect the way that they are compassionate, and this is the reason I want to be a practitioner [đệ tử] at Sùng Phúc Monastery. I have been sick, and the monks helped me by giving me traditional massages [đánh gió, a kind of traditional medicinal practice] and helped me recover. Recently, I have had problems with my eyes. I didn't want to bother everyone, so I tried to take care of it using compresses made with leaves, but it didn't work. When one of the monks saw that I was having problems, he took me to the hospital for an examination and treatment. But when I left home [to live at Sùng Phúc], I didn't bring money with me, so the monk paid for my treatment. I felt very uncomfortable having the monk pay for my hospital bills. But I saw the compassion of the monk and that this was the way it was for these practitioners of Zen: people here are not greedy for fame or fortune. They lead simple lives, without interest in wealth, so I really admire the Zen monks. They said most of the Zen monks don't have money, cars, motorcycles, and other possessions. Every monk lives equally, simply, and compassionately. Whatever they eat, I eat the same thing. This is not like other places, where the higher monks have a different menu, the lower monks and lay people all eat different things. Here it's not like that; we eat from the same pot of rice.

Mr. Thể's story of his increasing involvement in Buddhism illustrates how Buddhism is commonly viewed as a refuge from the vagaries and difficulties of life. This view of monastic life is, of course, a common trope. Where the narrative departs from the trope is the way Trúc Lâm, and life at Trúc Lâm, is constructed as more authentic than Buddhism as practiced in regular pagodas. The attraction of a modernist form of Buddhism reverberates well with male ways of viewing religion so that the motivations for practice given by men are never oriented toward bringing material benefit to one's family, fortune, or career. Where this does not hold true is in the benefit that Zen meditation is believed to bring to one's health. However, at Sùng Phúc, this health benefit is uniformly described in natural terms as improving one's mental state and bringing physiological changes rather than being bestowed by supernatural means, either by the manipulation of supernatural forces, such as through feng shui, or by the interventions of divine beings.

One of the notable aspects of Trúc Lâm Zen as it is practiced at Sùng Phúc is that it is attracting a broader range of people than is typically seen at regular pagodas. It was clear from the men I spoke with that the reason for this is that Zen Buddhism as presented at Sùng Phúc fits more clearly into a masculine idea of acceptable religious practice. That is, Trúc Lâm was being constructed in ways that resonated with a secular view that stressed a humanistic individualism of self-reliance, contrasted with the reliance, which the men felt was misplaced, on the supernatural for assistance that is found at regular, devotional pagodas. Furthermore, the elite associations of Zen, especially when linked with the nationally important King Trần Nhân Tông, fits well with an ethos of self-cultivation that resonates with masculine constructs, particularly for older men.

CHAPTER SEVEN

||||||||

Zen for All Ages

While transient supplicants stream through pagodas in Hanoi on the first and fifteenth of every month, the core followers at the pagoda will usually hold the Penitence Rite at some point during the day. This core group of devout Buddhist practitioners, marked by the brown Buddhist robes they wear and by the ritual group chanting in which they participate, comprises almost exclusively people over the age of fifty. This leads to an overall perception that Buddhism is for old people. Generally speaking, the only time one sees young people is on the first and fifteenth of the lunar month, the days that Vietnamese understand as being supernaturally potent, when it is more likely that their offerings and supplications will bring good luck, health, and wealth. On these two days, the usual group of older women will be there chanting sutras, but young women will be there as well, and in recent years, young men have begun to enter the pagoda to make offerings and to ask the buddhas for help with passing exams, with health, or with relationships. While Buddhist pagodas are a frequent destination on the first and fifteenth, the same supplications can be made at any number of religious sites, not all of which are Buddhist. Most people, furthermore, are unable to distinguish the ideological difference between a Buddhist pagoda and a spirit shrine, other than knowing that the Buddhist pagodas are for worshiping buddhas, and the others are for worshiping spirits, gods, and goddesses. One youth at Sùng Phúc told me, "The purpose of the old women [for going to pagodas and chanting the name of Amitābha] is to make wishes [cầu an] and to bring luck to their families. They want luck getting money, and with improving karma."

There are several reasons why serious practitioners at most pagodas in Hanoi are older. The most obvious is that in their retirement, they have more free time. At regular pagodas, the ritual schedule follows the lunar calendar, so that most rituals end up taking place during the week, when younger people must go to work or school. Another important reason for participation among an older demographic is religious participation is a scripted response to the emotional and practical challenges and uncertainties of aging (McFadden 1999, 1097; Mjelde-Mossey, Chi, and Lou 2006). The change in roles and responsibilities, with children growing up and leaving home, creates anxiety and a diminished sense of self-worth. As a culturally prescribed activity, religious practice can also help alleviate the anxiety that comes with an increased sense of mortality (Pincharoen and Congdon 2003, 105–106).[1] Finally, there is a social expectation that frames religious practice as being particularly the concern of older people. The very predominance of old women defines these activities as being for old women only and therefore discourages younger women from joining.

Within the context of overall Buddhist participation in Hanoi, one of the most interesting developments at Sùng Phúc is the high level of youth participation. This youth involvement, and the younger age demographic more broadly, is driven partly by the concerted effort that Sùng Phúc makes to include young people through youth-specific programming. Indeed, much effort goes into framing Zen as suitable for young people and into designing programming for them. As the devotees at Sùng Phúc attest, there is a feeling that meditation is particularly suitable for young people. One woman in her early twenties at Sùng Phúc described it this way:

> Pure Land Buddhists chant sutras. Chanting sutras and niệm Phật [reciting the name of Amitābha] is for old people. Old people can't meditate because it is so painful. So, chanting and niệm Phật is more suitable for them. As for young people, they experience so much difficulty in society, so many tiring and stressful things. Meditation helps with stress, so meditation is very suitable for young people.

However, the reason why so many young people go to Sùng Phúc on a weekly basis goes beyond the youth-centered activities provided there. There is something fundamental about Zen and the modernist way in which Trúc Lâm presents it that makes it attractive to old and young alike. A young woman who is involved with the youth group and with the Sunday school for children told me:

Many people in Vietnam think that going to the pagoda is for old people but going to work and going out for fun is for young people. There is an expression: *"Trẻ vui nhà, già vui chùa"* [youths have fun at home, old people have fun at the pagoda]. But now I think that view is wrong, now it is different. Because society has eroded a lot, so [young people] just want to look for where there is a strong ethic so that they can find their own morality for themselves. So now, a lot of young people go to pagodas for this reason.

Trúc Lâm Zen's particularly modernist presentation resonates with contemporary notions of religiosity. In the past, religion was not differentiated or separated from other aspects of people's lives, but instead was thoroughly infused into family relationships and with economic enterprise, health, and so on. The buffering of selves (C. Taylor 2007, 37–38) is part of the larger creation of religion as a distinct function system. While the twentieth century has made a return to a "porous" reality difficult to achieve, the Buddhism practiced at regular pagodas largely reflects a former enchanted view that sees the supernatural as enmeshed with all aspects of life. However, this view does not always fit well with the orientation of youths who have been imbued with the modernist notion of differentiated religion. For those attracted to Trúc Lâm Zen, Buddhism is not about making wishes as part of a larger practice of fostering a web of social and supernatural relationships but about an individual quest for spirituality, moral righteousness, physical well-being, psychological equanimity, and perhaps eventual salvation.

This chapter will focus on the youths at Sùng Phúc, looking particularly at the way they approach Zen as a modernist world religion. It will first look at the structural elements that have been put in place at Sùng Phúc to create a space for young people's participation. It will then turn to a description of some of the activities for youths that took place at Sùng Phúc during my research. Finally, I will explore some of the reasons why Zen, Trúc Lâm, and Sùng Phúc more specifically are attractive to young people.

STRUCTURAL INCLUSION OF YOUNG PEOPLE AT SÙNG PHÚC

The inclusion of young people at Sùng Phúc involves more than adding a few activities. It emerges from an overall structural composition at Sùng Phúc that positions the institution as a space that tacitly includes young people in an equal way. The focus on youths has been a concern of Thích Thanh Từ's since early in his career. He wrote specifically about the importance of Buddhism for youths in an essay in perhaps his earliest published work, the 1959 book *Đạo Phật với Tuổi Trẻ* (Buddhism for young people).[2] The essay was later included, along with two other essays, in the book *Phật giáo với Dân tộc* (Buddhism with the people) (Thích Thanh Từ 1992).[3] It has also been one of the few books translated into English by the American Vietnamese devotee Tu Tam Hoang (Thích Thanh Từ 2002d).

At Sùng Phúc, youths are included in the activities and the programming and are incorporated into the spatial structure of the monastery. At major events, such as the ancestor day of Bodhidharma (described in chapter 2) and the festival day when they cast a bell for the new monastery in Tam Đảo, youths played prominent roles ushering dignitaries to their seats and entertaining the guests. While the general ritual and meditation day is held each Saturday and is open for everyone, Sunday at Sùng Phúc is entirely given over to programming for youths, including a Buddhist Sunday school for younger children and youth group activities (the youth group has its headquarters at the monastery). The youth programming is not unique to Sùng Phúc; as was explained to me by a monk, it was embedded in the administrative structure of the Trúc Lâm organization by Thích Thanh Từ's mandate that every Trúc Lâm temple have a youth program. The impact of this intentional structural inclusion can be seen in the overall feeling at Sùng Phúc that Zen is a kind of Buddhism that is meant for everyone, unlike the Buddhism practiced at regular pagodas, which is widely seen as being an activity for old people.

The Youth Group

The youth group was founded around 2007 by Thích Thái Phước, a monk who was prominent and active at Sùng Phúc during the main period of my research.[4] He was youthful, exuberant, charismatic, and engaged. He smiled constantly and drew young people to him because of his happy demeanor and approachability. As with all the monks at Sùng Phúc, Thích Thái Phước was from southern Vietnam and came north to reside at Sùng Phúc to help with what was, in effect, a missionary effort. Although he was active as a ritual expert and teacher (*giảng sư*), it was his involvement in the youth group at Sùng Phúc that made him stand out. He had founded the youth group at Sùng Phúc, with the support of the abbot, as the first organization for young Buddhists in Hanoi. The idea was quickly taken up by Quán Sứ Pagoda, and there are now groups at several pagodas in Hanoi, but the youth group at Sùng Phúc remains particularly vibrant and even central to the mission of the monastery. By his account, the youth group at Sùng Phúc was a priority for him, and as director of the youth group, he was always present during its activities on Sundays, unless he was out of town. He gave Dharma talks, presented awards, and acted as a judge during games. He was also a central figure in the youth jamboree that I attended over the course of a weekend in November 2011.

The structural importance of youths in Trúc Lâm and at Sùng Phúc can also be seen in the group's being named after Trần Thái Tông, the grandfather of the founder of Trúc Lâm and founder of the Trần dynasty. As such, it is on-brand as part of the Vietnamese Zen organization. Trúc Lâm's image as a Vietnamese Zen school was particularly important to Sùng Phúc's youth participants, who explained with pride that theirs was the first Buddhist youth group in Hanoi.[5] When I began my research in Hanoi in 1997, there were no real opportunities for young people to become involved in Buddhism. Now, according to Thích Thái Phước, there are fourteen groups in Hanoi, although they are all very new.[6] Notably, Quán Sứ Pagoda, the headquarters of the Vietnamese Buddhist Association, established a youth group around 2007, though it is apparently much smaller than the one at Sùng Phúc, and the programming is limited to providing opportunities for youths to chant sutras together. The youth group at Quán Sứ Pagoda is also described by youths at Sùng Phúc in sectarian terms, as belonging to the Pure Land school. This is significant, because my young informants used this as part of their explanation for why they were drawn to Sùng Phúc and were interested in Zen in particular, describing Pure Land Buddhism as a practice for old people, while Zen was congruous with their identities as contemporary youths. As one young woman said to me, "Pure Land Buddhism was suitable in the past, but Zen is much more suitable for today."

The importance of the youth group at Sùng Phúc is signaled by its having a physical presence at the temple. The committee has an office on the main floor near the bookstore that is marked with an official office plaque in the manner of offices in government buildings. This important position was recognized by the young people who managed the youth group under the leadership of Thích Thái Phước.

The community that the youth group provided was clearly an important motivation for young people to go to Sùng Phúc. The youth group provided members with the structure for meeting and spending time with other youths who shared their same desire for shelter from the turbulence and stress of their hectic everyday lives. In placing an importance on community, they were like the Korean youths in Kim and Choi's study who "recognize their life in adherence to the teachings of Buddhism and seek emotional stability by configuring communities of intimacy" (Kim and Choi 2016, 31).

Internet and Social Media

Another way that youth are placed in a prominent place at Sùng Phúc is by the attention given to them on the internet. They have a prominent place on the Sùng Phúc website, with one of the eight tabs on the home-page labeled "Thiền với Tuổi Trẻ" (Zen for young people) (Thích Minh Quang, Chánh Chí Bình, and Chánh Phúc Hiếu 2016).[7] The youth section of the website is divided into five sections: "Đoàn Thanh thiếu niên Phật tử Trần Thái Tông" (The Trần Thái Tông youth group), "Hoạt động Thanh niên" (Youth activities), "Con Hỏi Thầy Đáp" (You ask and the teacher answers), "Niềm Vui Nơi cửa Thiền" (Joy at the gate of Zen), and "Các Bài Viết cho Thanh niên" (Lessons written for youths). The youth section of the website reports about youth activities not only at Sùng Phúc but also at other Trúc Lâm temples. In doing so, they tie the youths at Sùng Phúc into a larger imagined community of young people dedicated to Zen Buddhism.

By contrast, Quán Sứ Pagoda has no website, and although they do have a Facebook page, the page is not youth oriented. Instead, most of the posts appear to be commentary pointing out social issues. Many of the posts are graphically violent—a young woman who has been severely beaten; two men sawing through an unexploded bomb to retrieve scrap metal; a severely injured young Buddhist who got in a traffic accident while doing an act of charity; or a drawing of a pregnant Chinese woman who, according to the accompanying story, was strung up and tortured after trying to defect from Falungong. Other posts bring attention to other social problems; one posted video, for example, shows a Vietnamese Buddhist nun with makeup and an ankle tattoo seated at a roadside cafe and smoking, with the accompanying inscription *Nam mô Bổn sư Đồng chí Thích Ca Mâu Ni Phật* (Nammo comrade Śākyamuni Buddha).

While the Facebook page for Sùng Phúc largely features sermons and schedule announcements, Sùng Phúc also has an Instagram account. When I looked at their Instagram feed, the first image I saw was of an attractive young woman around twenty years old with hair pulled back in a bun with a traditional hair pin and wearing a red lace *áo dài* (the Vietnamese split tunic dress worn over trousers), holding a red envelope given to young people at New Year's and standing in front of a large column of arranged roses.[8] With 1,136 likes, it was one of the most popular pictures, but its popularity did not come close to the image of a young woman in the gray robe of a Trúc Lâm follower, seated on the floor and holding a young (and distracted) child dressed in gray sweatpants and shoes, a gray puffy jacket, and a knit winter hat with two pompoms on either side. They are seated in the receiving area for the temple, with a statue of the Buddha depicting his first sermon to his five disciples under the bodhi tree. At 10,646 likes, it was by far the most popular image of the first one hundred I examined. The other two that received a substantial number of likes featured a toddler in monastic dark-brown clothes on his knees with hands folded in front of a bust of Thích Thanh Từ and a statue of the Buddha (9,098 likes), and a photo of the entrance staircase leading to the main shrine, elaborately decorated with flowers for New Year's (with 441 likes).

These images, while receiving far more likes than the other three hundred or so images I viewed, were largely representative of the major recurring themes. The images tended to show young people posing or having fun in different activities at Sùng Phúc (often in groups), cute photos of kids in Buddhist clothing (tailor-made robes for kids or kids in regular clothes but in appropriate Buddhist colors of gray or dark brown), scenery from the Sùng Phúc precinct (including statuary and a lot of garden images), and pictures of vegetarian dishes served at Sùng Phúc. There were also many photos that showed activities, particularly for young people, and a few of wedding ceremonies. The overall feel is of a place that is fun, attractive, and vibrant while aesthetically traditional. There is a tendency to show young people, seemingly making the point that Sùng Phúc is an appropriate place for youths. Middle-aged people are shown less frequently, and old people are largely absent in the Instagram posts. The images are also heavily weighted toward showing attractive young women.[9]

ACTIVITIES

One of the main ways that young people are attracted to Sùng Phúc is by activities organized specifically for youths. These are largely run by the young people of the youth group's committee, facilitated by monastics like Thích Thái Phước. There is a program held at Sùng Phúc every weekend, with Saturdays being for the regular adult program and Sundays being reserved for the youth program. The usual program goes all morning, but once a month there is a more extended program for youths that lasts all day, as there is for adults on Saturday. There are also special events that take place from time to time.

Sunday Youth Activities

The age of the young people who attend the events on Sundays range from teenagers to young adults in their twenties. The majority of participants are around twenty, with many studying in university. The regular youth event is not substantially different from the one for adults, and a few older people of retirement age also show up to meditate and listen to lectures with the youths. The event starts with a meditation session that lasts the same length of time as the adult session, after which is a lecture by one of the monks and a closing vegetarian lunch.

The extended monthly program also starts with meditation and then a lecture. The youth lectures are different from the Saturday adult lecture in that they are more interactive and the floor is usually open for questions following the lecture. After lunch and a rest period, there is usually an afternoon activity. Twice while I was there, the afternoon activity was a quiz game in which questions about the Buddha, Buddhist philosophy, and the history of the Trúc Lâm Zen school and its patriarchs were asked. The questions drew heavily from Trúc Lâm's core liturgy. For example, the following question from one of the quizzes stresses the secular nature of the Buddhism that is put forward and discourages the view commonly held by practitioners at regular pagodas:

What does the Penitence Rite accomplish?

a. The Virtuous Buddha will forgive your sins and grant happiness
b. Your soul will be peaceful, ending troubled feelings.
c. **Your conscience will stop being tormented and it will prevent sins from developing until you become cold and heartless. [Correct answer]**
d. All of the above

Participants held up numbered cards, and those who had answered incorrectly had to leave the floor; the last participant remaining was declared the winner. Thích Thái Phước and a nun who was also involved in the youth program sat at a table at the front, and after every two or three questions, they gave explanations or offered additional information. There were a few trial games, and then the winner of the final competition received a prize and was given the privilege of ringing the portable temple bell that is used in ritual processions. The prize for the winner of the first contest was a selection of books; the winner of the second contest was presented with a (supposed) relic of the Buddha that Thích Thái Phước had brought back from a recent trip to Myanmar. On one occasion, when no monks were available to give the lecture, a circle was formed by those present (there were fewer than usual), and older members spoke about Buddhism in their lives for the sake of newer attendees.

During the Sunday events, while youths are meeting in the ancestor hall, there is a Sunday school for children (called *ban thiếu nhi*) held in the lecture hall on the first floor, below the main shrine. The school for children began around 2009 and was unique in Hanoi at that time. It was set up partly as a way to occupy the small children when their young parents came to participate in the activities for adolescents and young adults. One of the teachers told me:

> If the kids come here, it is because their parents are involved in the youth activities. When they bring the kids here, we take the kids and form a separate kids' group to introduce them to the Buddha and to get closer to Buddhism, so they will behave better [sẽ ngoan hơn]. We don't teach them about philosophy, but we teach them about respecting parents, behaving properly toward them, and listening to them. Because they aren't able to understand the philosophy yet, the main purpose is just to bring the kids closer to the religion. . . . We only teach simple things like the life of the Buddha. In Hanoi, there is only a kids' class like this here [at Sùng Phúc], but other pagodas don't have that; they only have groups for teenagers.

Usually, the children spend about an hour being taught by one of the volunteers, who is a member of the youth group committee, while the older youths are meditating. The teachings focus on the basics of Buddhism (e.g., the Five Precepts and what they entail) and details of the life of the Buddha (e.g., memorizing the names of his mother, father, wife, and son). Following the lesson, they usually go out onto the balcony to sing songs in a circle and to play games. Sometimes they practice walking meditation, circling the lecture hall. One of the Sunday school teachers said, "Because they can't understand Dharma talks at the same level as adolescents, they have to be taught at a much lower level."

The young children also sometimes join the youths for the main activities in the ancestor hall. On one occasion, the children were called to listen to a nun who had helped found the youth group at Sùng Phúc and who had come to visit. She spoke about her life as a Buddhist, and then the vice abbot, Thích Tịnh Thiền, gave an emotional account of his own path to Buddhism and the regret he felt for the things he did before becoming a Buddhist. Some of the older and more involved children also took part in the afternoon quiz on the two occasions I was present.

Jamboree

In addition to the regular activities, there are special events organized for youths. The one that I witnessed was a large youth jamboree that took place over the course of a weekend. The event was called the Hội trại Thiền Vạn Hạnh (Vạn Hạnh Zen youth jamboree), which was on-brand for Trúc Lâm, as it evoked Vạn Hạnh (938–1018), one of the most eminent historic Vietnamese monks, who has been cast as a Zen master (e.g., Hân Mẫn and Thông Thiền 2010, 869; Lê Mạnh Thát 2002, 537).[10] I was told that they organized an event like this once or twice a year. Despite its apparent size—around a hundred participants ranging in age from seven-year-olds to adolescents and young adults in their twenties, including participants who had come from outside Hanoi and from other pagodas around Hanoi, including from Quán Sứ Pagoda—a monk who was helping with the activities told me that this one was a relatively modestly sized gathering because they hadn't had time to obtain the relevant government permissions.[11]

The youth jamboree started late in the afternoon on a Saturday. I had been sick for several days preceding the event, so unfortunately, I did not realize that it was taking place.[12] Arriving at 8:00 on a Sunday morning and expecting the regular youth program, I was surprised to find the parking lot that was usually filled with motorcycles and scooters was closed off, and in its place were erected three A-frame tents made of tarps draped and tied over bamboo poles. In each of the tents was a makeshift altar with a small statue of the Zen-branded Śākyamuni (holding up the lotus flower). The group had been divided into three teams (referred to as "families" [gia đình]). Each of the three teams designed and decorated the tent-shrines with Buddhist flags, foliage and flowers, stone, candles, cut paper, and balloons. In front of each tent was an offering arrangement. I arrived just as Thích Thái Phước and another monk were judging the shrine decoration competition.

The rest of the morning proceeded with more activities. They sang songs together and arranged themselves for a group photo, while the official photographer, a videographer, and a few of the senior organizers took pictures and filmed them, to be posted later on their website. After the singing, the teams continued to compete in races, quizzes, and a game akin to pin the tail on the donkey in which they had to draw faces on images of the fat Maitreya (Di Lạc) while blindfolded. Then there were physical activities such as piggyback races, walking on bricks while holding cups of water in their mouth, and so on.

Groups then competed to create a Buddhist poster on Bristol board, drawing on familiar themes. On one was a seated Buddha with a candle and lotus in his lap, with the expression Kính Phật, trọng Tăng (honor the Buddha, respect the sangha) written on either side as a couplet. In another, there was a lotus flower with "Pháp" (Dharma) written in the center petal and each component of the Noble Eightfold Path written on the other petals. On the lotus leaf below it was written:

Poster drawing competition at a youth jamboree, 2011

The Dharma incomparably profound and exquisite
Is rarely met with, even in hundreds of thousands of millions of kalpas;
We are now permitted to see it, to listen to it, to accept and hold it;
May we truly understand the meaning of the Tathagata's words![13]
(English translation from the *Manual of Zen Buddhism* by D. T. Suzuki
   [2005b, 2])

On either side of the lotus flower was written a couplet: "Open *bodhicitta* to bring harmony to the universe / Arrange thousands of ceremonies to bring enlightenment to sentient beings."[14] The final poster had a gate with a seated Buddha in the center and "Vạn Hạnh Zen" (Thiền Vạn Hạnh) written above it. In the center top of the poster was written "Immutable mind in the midst of life."[15]

Next came a speech contest in which a representative from each group was asked a question and then given two minutes to come up with an answer to present to the monastic judges. One sample question that was prepared by the committee was:

Seeing you often go to the pagoda, your parents start to worry that the pagoda is not a suitable place for young people but is only for elderly people who have retired or have free time. What will you do to make your parents understand and support you?[16]

Following each speech, there was an opportunity for the other team to offer an answer before moving on to ask the question to the next team. At times, the monastics interjected comments of their own. During the speeches, attentions waned, and most people not directly involved wandered off.

A vegetarian lunch for everyone was followed by a Dharma talk given by Sùng Phúc's abbot, Thích Tâm Thuần. It was the first time I had seen Thích Tâm Thuần give a Dharma talk at the temple, since he was usually too busy, possibly indicating that the youth event was particularly important for Sùng Phúc. The last event of the day was the quiz game sometimes held in the full-day programs, with the winners receiving a book, and everyone receiving a copy of Thích Thanh Từ's booklet *Tài sản không bao giờ mất* (Wealth you never lose) (2009d). The jamboree ended with a closing ceremony; prizes were given out, songs were sung, everyone held hands, and a final group photo was taken.

Open House for Children

A final example of youth programming at Sùng Phúc was also unique. I arrived at Sùng Phúc one weekday morning in November 2011 to find eight buses carrying over five hundred schoolchildren who were on a field trip to Sùng Phúc. They were from a public school located in the central part of Hanoi that had no particular association with Sùng Phúc. The visit was not requested or coordinated by a devotee who taught at the school. Instead, the school had heard that Sùng Phúc organized events such as these, so they contacted the monastery to ask if they could bring the children. I was told by several of the senior members of the youth group that there have been two or three such events in the past.

It took quite a while to get all the students seated. In their state of high excitement, it was left to the three youth group volunteers from Sùng Phúc, with a little help from the tour bus operators, to calm them down. Meanwhile, the teachers sat at a table off to the side and chatted, happy to have a break from their regular duties. After around ten minutes of the volunteers trying and failing to settle the young visitors, a young male teacher stepped in to settle the students. The program, once it started, began with meditation instruction. The children were taught how to get into the half-lotus position, how to fold their hands in their laps, and how to breathe and concentrate. When the instructions were completed, they were given a five-minute period to try it out. This was followed by massaging face and limbs and the stretching exercises that are a standard form in Trúc Lâm. The kids seemed to enjoy the singing that followed much more than the meditation, but both were preferred to the Dharma talk that was delivered by one of the visiting monks from the south. As the monk's talk proceeded, the kids became more and more unruly. The monk was clearly more used to lecturing adults, and while he started by engaging them directly, he quickly fell back into the standard lecture style that this monk employed when lecturing adults. He asked rhetorical questions that might have stimulated adult listeners but held little interest to the young students. Finally, practically mid-sentence, the monk's patience wore out and he abruptly got up and left. The event seemed to collapse after that, and the students were allowed to eat the lunches they had brought in the courtyard, despite its still being quite early, while the teachers ate a vegetarian meal provided by the monastery.

It was clear from the event that Sùng Phúc was very interested in attracting children and youths and were eager for the students to visit, but they had not quite worked out a formula for running an engaging program for so many young people. The content was only minimally religious, with only the meditation instruction given as an example of how to be Buddhist. The students were not given a tour of the monastery, so they never saw the shrine room or were given an explanation of the symbols and statues. Nor were they given a chance to see the Buddhist relics on the third floor (though it is hard to imagine how one could avoid engaging young children by showing them bits of dead people). The program introduced Buddhism as a meditation practice rather than as a religion. The event, despite being (in my view) a bit of a failure, was notable for simply having taking place.

The purpose for accommodating the school visit was mostly unstated, but there was a general sense that it was good for the children. One young person who was part of the youth group told me that it was probably organized by one of the Trúc Lâm followers at Sùng Phúc who worked either for the school or for the tourist company that had organized the trip. This person felt that it was likely that the motivation of the school was that introducing them to Buddhism would make them more submissive and well behaved (*ngoan hơn*). The teachers, though, seemed to take it as a way to hand over responsibility for the children and have the morning off.

ATTRACTIONS OF ZEN FOR THE YOUTHS

As with the men and women in the last chapter, the reasons why Zen is attractive to young people are diverse but coalesce around a range of themes related to finding a place and a practice that helps ease the stresses of their hectic worlds. None of the youths with whom I spoke mentioned being concerned with salvation, though many felt that in an era of perceived moral decline, they wanted to recover their sense of themselves as moral beings. Youth participants at Sùng Phúc also drew distinctions between Pure Land and Zen and between regular pagodas and Sùng Phúc.

The motivations and explanations given by the young people at Sùng Phúc show how Trúc Lâm Zen has been shaped by global discourses of Buddhism and is resurging in Vietnamese contemporary society. Little has been written about youth attraction to Buddhism in Asia. Kim and Choi, who present one of the few cases, attribute the increasing interest to the socioeconomic conditions in Korea. Contemporary Korean society places significant pressure on young people, and participation in Buddhist activities provides them with a way to face the future with optimism (Kim and Choi 2016, 33).

The young people at Sùng Phúc expressed similar levels of stress from the pressures of work and school. They, too, found that Buddhism—and particularly Trúc Lâm Zen—offered a way to reduce this stress and to achieve a better balance in their lives. However, the young people at Sùng Phúc were different in one significant aspect from the Korean youths in Kim and Choi's study, who, though drawn to Jungto Pure Land Buddhist practice as a way to ameliorate their stress, did not necessarily claim a Buddhist identity (Kim and Choi 2016, 20–23). The young people I spoke with at Sùng Phúc were generally quite committed to and emphatic about their Buddhist identity (*phật tử*) and did not disassociate their meditation from the religion as the Korean youth in Kim and Choi's study had. Nonetheless, the way that they spoke about their motivations drew a picture of Buddhism that was more secular than religious.

Stresses of Life

One of the most frequent reasons that young people gave me for their interest in Zen and their participation in activities at Sùng Phúc was the stress they felt in daily life as students or while starting out in their careers. When Vietnam moved away from a planned economy and toward a capitalist system in the late 1980s, although overall wealth increased (Fan et al. 2019, 150), disparities in income and access to social services were exacerbated (Pham and Mukhopadhaya 2018). The move has also resulted in a drastic increase in urbanization (Fan et al. 2019, 149). Diseases of poverty have decreased, while diseases associated with wealthy countries have become more prevalent. Mental-health issues are on the rise, with reports of depression, anxiety, stress, suicidal thoughts, and suicide attempts increasing among adolescents (Dat Tan Nguyen et al. 2013, 1). Despite a "high prevalence of poor mental health among Vietnamese adolescents," the health-care infrastructure is inadequate to deal with this issue (Dat Tan Nguyen et al. 2013, 2).

Within this context, the youths at Sùng Phúc have sought alternative ways to deal with this stress. In this, the situation is similar to that of the Korean youths described by Kim. They see Buddhist temples as offering "therapeutic spaces and discourses of self-improvement, alternative lifestyle, and spirituality to reach out and connect with others" (Kim 2016, 451). Participation helps ameliorate the stresses that contemporary youths in Korea are facing because of the highly competitive job market and stressful workplaces. As they strive to overcome attendant feelings of stress and anxiety, many are turning to the anti-materialist values of Buddhism. The parallels with young people I spoke with at Sùng Phúc were well articulated by a young woman named Thu, who was employed in the bookstore at Sùng Phúc after having quit a highly coveted government job to be more involved in Buddhism:

> I first found my way to Buddhism when I needed spiritual support. My life had met a roadblock [bế tắc]. At that time, I went to Quán Sứ Pagoda, when I was twenty-six. I was interested in Buddhism before that, as a student starting when I was twenty-two. When I was small, I would sometimes go to pagodas, but not often. I really started going when I came to Hanoi. I would take my bicycle to go to visit all kinds of different pagodas. As a student I had time to visit pagodas and still had time to study, but after I graduated, I had to work so hard and was always so tired. I felt my life was stuck. I always felt something spiritual was missing. . . . I lost my mom when I was three years old [so couldn't turn to her for help]. When I felt this lack of spiritual support, my situation made me cry; I felt so sad. I started to think more about the Buddha. I was working for the government at the time, and I was so busy and tired, but I started to go to Buddhist activities.

Miss Thu felt drawn to Buddhism for the therapeutic value that Buddhism represented in her life. While her account was intensely personal, it reflected what I heard from others. So, for example, Tuấn, a young man in his late twenties, was heavily involved in organizing events for the youth group. He had found his way to Sùng Phúc because of the pressure he was feeling at work: "My brain was fried, so I just wanted to find a way to balance. I was worried about everything and just felt completely exhausted. So, I asked Mr. Google if there was anything I could do to help find some equilibrium in my life." His web search led him to meditation as an answer to the stress he was feeling and from there to Sùng Phúc as a place he could learn how to meditate. A few years earlier, he had honeymooned in Đà Lạt, in southern Vietnam, where he visited Trúc Lâm Monastery, the headquarters of the Trúc Lâm organization and residence of Thích Thanh Từ. However, he had not realized that Trúc Lâm also had a center in Hanoi until he found it on the internet. He became increasingly involved and eventually found himself in a leadership position in the youth group, organizing many of the activities and speaking publicly about Buddhism and the benefits of meditation. Like many of the young people with whom I spoke, he mostly focused on meditation as a technique that calmed him and brought equilibrium to his life.

The therapeutic value of Zen meditation was also one of the views held by Thích Thái Phước:

> In their life, young people have to work with modern technology, and therefore they have to use their minds from morning to afternoon, so it is very stressful for their brains. The purpose [of meditation] is to stop and relax and balance your work with your life. When they have time to meditate, it means that they try to calm their minds and balance the way they work. After a week of hard work, they go to the Zen center in order to de-stress and try to be calm and balance their body and mind. When they apply Zen to their lives, they live in the present and don't let their minds [*tâm*] wander. The full name for Zen, *thiền na*, in Chinese is called *tinh lang* [the Sino-Vietnamese transliteration for 禪那]. It means you control your thoughts and don't let them wander. If young people can control their minds, it will help them return to calm and balance in their workweek. When you are able to quiet your mind, then your wisdom [*trí tuệ*] becomes clearer and brighter. For example, your mind is like a lake. When strong winds create waves, you cannot see through the water. But when there is no wind and the lake is calm and becomes clear, you can see everything through it. So, Zen is like the calm lake after a strong wind. And life is like a turbulent lake. People, like the lake, are very easily disturbed, like the waves, so if you keep going like that, you will get stressed. If you don't know how to de-stress and it builds up, you will get sick. . . . If you meditate, you will become calm and relaxed and feel more pleasant. After one week of work, they just need one day to balance it, and then they can continue on better for the following week. When you are calm in your mind, then your actions and thought processes are very precise. For example, if a young person knows how to meditate, they can become mindful of what they are doing at any given moment. When they are writing, they are aware that they are writing. Their mind doesn't wander around,

darting here and there. So when young people know Zen, they know how to live in the present and do their work well because their minds are not distracted. And furthermore, they can work more efficiently. . . . Zen is about coming back to the present moment, and young people see the value in this, and so they keep coming back. So we don't force them to come here; they come on their own.

A Search for Morality

Another common theme that emerged in discussions with young people at Sùng Phúc was their perception that there has been a moral decline in contemporary Vietnamese society. Perceptions like these, expressed to me by young Buddhists at Sùng Phúc, are typical of the explanations young people gave for why they are becoming interested in Buddhism in general and Zen in particular: "In society today, morality has decreased a lot. People like me are going to the pagoda as it helps to increase morality"; or "I feel like morality in society today, for many people, isn't like in the past. So that's why young people think about going to the pagoda for that reason." Buddhism was important for them as a solution to the problems of young people today being too selfish, being interested only in money and lacking respect for Vietnamese customs and for their ancestors. They saw the antidote to the contemporary condition as being a return to an imagined traditional time when people followed a purer form of Buddhism, free from superstitious beliefs and practices, one that involved self-cultivation through Zen meditation and a stronger sense of morality. For them, Zen and the practice of meditation had little to do with the next life and enlightenment and nothing to do with bringing benefit to their families.

The perception of immorality and materialism comes from several sources, but most notably, it is a discourse that was perpetuated by the state, reacting to the loosening of social restrictions and increased leisure activities, in its campaigns against "social evils" (*tệ nạn xã hội*) starting in the 1990s (Marr 1997; Rydstrøm 2006). This only increased the moral panic that centered on the new youth cultures that have emerged from the new economy and the focus on the newly created sites of commodified leisure (Cox 2012, 21). While the language of "social evils" has diminished in the 2000s, the sense that the rapid transformation of society in post-Renovation Vietnam has eroded traditional values and morality has continued to be felt. Today, the experience for youths in Hanoi has been transformed by consumer-driven society, with its trademark teen fashion, teen language, and youth culture. Features include individualism, worship of pop idols, and an emphasis on consumption. Shopping, Huong Nguyen points out, has replaced the ideals of previous decades: political maturation from 1975 to 1986 and social responsibility from 1986 to 1996 (H. Nguyen 2017, 1280).

The young people at Sùng Phúc typically contrasted present society with an idealized past when people were more concerned with their families and their communities. In this imagined past, youths were seen as having a superior orientation toward self-improvement through study and moral cultivation. Their present situation, on the other hand, was constructed as being selfish and materialist. A good example of this came in a conversation I had with Bình, a woman in her mid- to late twenties who volunteered as a teacher in the Sunday school for children:

> I think that morality is falling as society develops. Morality has decreased a lot in recent years. After we graduated from high school, the ones that came after us—the younger ones—are lazier in their studies and more interested in entertainment. They are more concerned about keeping up with trends [đua đòi] than they are with their studies, like we were. They seem only interested in entertaining themselves. They like to go out and have fun all over the place. They don't want to study anymore. We used to seek education, but it's not like that anymore. Keeping up with trends is all-consuming now. If the trend is to have a particular phone, or motorcycle, then they have to have them. That is called "đua đòi." Today they are almost all like that. There are only a small percentage of them that want to study and improve themselves. The majority just want to have fun. So the ones that are going to the pagoda are doing so to improve their morality.

The young people at Sùng Phúc saw the temple as a haven from the challenges imposed by the neoliberal competition and materialist focus of their daily circumstances, offering an opportunity to develop an alternate lifestyle in ways similar to the youths in Korea described by Kim (2016, 453). Utilizing meditation as an antidote for the stresses and problems of contemporary society is not uncommon among youths today. Even academics in the West have proposed that mindfulness training in the model of Thích Nhất Hạnh would help youths in Vietnam deal with social pressures and the youth problems that are on the rise, like risky sex, drug use, violence, and mental-health issues (Le and Trieu 2016).

An example of how Sùng Phúc is seen as a solution for the moral and character deficiencies of Vietnamese youths is evident in the story of Sơn. When I spoke with Sơn, he was eighteen years old and had been living at Sùng Phúc as a cư sĩ for a couple of weeks. He wore the standard gray tunic and trousers that all cư sĩ wear, but he stood out because he also wore a fat, square-cut diamond earring in his left ear and had the haircut of a lead singer in a V-Pop boy band. Though affable, he had the self-assured brashness of a rich kid. He told me that his father worked in the embassy in Korea. A few months before I met him, he had gone there to visit, and he was going to go there to study in the coming year.

However, by his own admission, he was a bit of a problem. He described himself as being lazy at home and overly enjoying going out with his friends. The principal reason why his parents had arranged for him to stay at Sùng Phúc was to cure him of his party-going habits; they viewed Sùng Phúc as a kind of Buddhist bootcamp. Sơn had been forced to go against his will, although I am not sure how hard he fought against his parents' decision. (He likely did not fight too much, as outright resistance against parents is not common among Vietnamese adolescents.) It did not cost anything for him to stay at Sùng Phúc as a *cư sĩ*, although he was required to contribute by his labor, and he claimed it was hard work and a challenging life. To attest to this claim, he lifted his sleeve to show me the scratches and bug bites. He found it particularly hard at the beginning, but by the time we met, he had begun to get used to it. The plan was for him to stay there for a month or two. Admittedly it was an unusual step, and his friends thought it strange:

Me: Are your friends Buddhist?

Sơn: Yes, ninety-nine percent. One percent follow Jesus.

Me: Of this ninety-nine percent, how many are practicing?

Sơn: Of my friends, none of them care about Buddhism.

Me: So, they are Buddhist but . . .

Sơn: . . . they don't go to the pagoda.

Me: . . . don't go to the pagoda, don't read anything about Buddhism?

Sơn: That's most youths.

Me: So when your parents said you had to come here for a month or two, what did your friends think?

Sơn: Crazy [*điên*]. Not really crazy, but silly [*hâm*]. Why not just stay home, go out and have fun [they thought]? Or they asked, what do you want to do, become a monk?

Me: What did you tell them?

Sơn: I had to come here to change, to study, and to learn to meditate.

Me: So to stop being lazy. . . . Because you said that you came here because you were too lazy at home.

Sơn: Yes, that's right. To learn how to be more hardworking [*học lao động*].

Sơn's family were practicing Buddhists and came frequently to Sùng Phúc. When I asked about their devotion, he told me that the Buddhist altar in their home was bigger than most people's. He had been to Sùng

Phúc on a number of occasions himself and considered himself to be a Buddhist, though he was not particularly knowledgeable about Buddhist philosophy or even the identity of different buddhas and bodhisattvas, with the exception of Guanyin and Śākyamuni. He said to me, "I enjoy going to the lectures, but they are hard for me to understand because my level of Buddhism, as a whole, is not very high." Regarding the goal of meditation, he told me that it was for health. When pressed, he said that it brought him equilibrium (he used the term *"tĩnh tâm,"* literally "calm the heart," but explained that what he meant was the mind, taking my notepad and writing "intelligence" on it in his limited English). He went on to explain the difference between Zen and Pure Land Buddhism by saying they were just two paths that lead to the Buddha (*hai đường đến Đức Phật*), but it was clear from his explanations that he was not entirely clear about the differences between the schools or their doctrines.

Sơn and other young people at Sùng Phúc believed that Trúc Lâm Zen was more useful for working on morality than at other pagodas, where practice was less rigorous and where there were many charlatan monks. The media is partly responsible for these impressions because of its propensity to publish reports about corrupt or greedy monks. For example, there was a story covered by Vietnamese media in 2014 of a monk who was facing punishment for posting on his Facebook page an unboxing video of an iPhone 6 just after it was released. The head of the Administrative Council for the Vietnamese Buddhist Association (trị sự Giáo hội Phật giáo Việt Nam) for Hải Dương Province, where the monk resided, said that the photos, along with other problematic photos also found on his Facebook page, "lowers the reputation of the [Sangha] Association" (*mất thanh danh giáo hội*).[17] Rumors of "business monks"—monks who are primarily concerned with getting donations from the laity—are commonly encountered in Hanoi and are a source of suspicion about the motives of many Buddhist monks. One man at Sùng Phúc described the difference between Sùng Phúc and regular pagodas this way:

> If you look at a Pure Land altar, you will see that there are places for offerings that are reclaimed as talismans [*lộc*] and also for money. . . .[18] There are some places that put up statues of spirits like Ông Hoàng and Bà Bảy [two spirits that are commonly manifested in spirit mediumship rituals (*lên đồng*)], so people go there, and they pray, and then put money on all of the different altars. At Sùng Phúc, we don't do that. There are no places for making offerings except at the altar in the main shrine, but not the rest.

There is therefore an impression that Sùng Phúc is more morally upright than many other regular temples. Mr. Thể, the truck driver in the previous chapter, implicitly contrasted the generosity of the monk who helped him by paying his hospital bill, which modeled the detachment to money that is the ideal of the sangha, with the deficiency in this regard of many Buddhist monks. The Buddhism practiced at Sùng Phúc, which is stripped of superstition, as explained in the account of Mr. Xuân, also contributes to this perception that Sùng Phúc is especially pure in its following of the Buddha Dharma (Phật Pháp), and that it is therefore an especially moral form of Buddhism.

As with the therapeutic motivation, the moral motivation for practicing Zen at Sùng Phúc reflected a secularized understanding of Buddhism. While the devotional Buddhism of regular pagodas was most often motivated by a desire to secure supernatural support from buddhas, bodhisattvas, and spirits, Zen Buddhism as presented by Trúc Lâm at Sùng Phúc engaged in discourses of self-improvement. The perception that Vietnamese society was in a moral decline made Sùng Phúc an especially attractive place for young people who were seeking a haven from the onslaught of consumerism and workplace competition.

Buddhism for the Individual

The interpretation of Buddhist practice as solely benefiting the individual practitioner has had particular currency in the West: "Drawing on, and indeed radicalizing, this discourse of freedom, individualism, and self-transformation, the American and European alternative spiritualities within which Buddhism was often interpreted tilted heavily toward this individualist model of spiritual fulfillment and liberation" (McMahan 2008, 196). It might have been possible in the 1970s to claim that this individualism is a Western, rather than an Asian, disposition. However, a mix of Asian Buddhist reformers, Western converts, and scholars have globalized the discourse of individualism, which is one of the key characteristics of the European Enlightenment.

The teachings given at Sùng Phúc through Dharma talks and in the writings of the founder emphasize self-cultivation. In his book *Đạo Phật và tuổi trẻ* (Buddhism and youth), Thích Thanh Từ writes:

Spiritually speaking, you should be aware that: "No one can liberate you but yourself." You should not entrust your soul to the spirits, buddhas or gods for them to give you salvation. The Buddha taught: "be a lamp unto yourself." You can't rely on your own body, much less entrust your delicate soul to divine beings. Praying to the gods for salvation is like climbing up a mountain holding a heavy rock, thinking that the great weight will help you get to the top. It's not that I want to deny you the blessings of the gods, but we are responsible for our own salvation. Their blessings won't help much. The Buddha often taught: "As a guide I can only show you the path, but it is up to you to follow it, and if you don't it is not the guide's fault." (Thích Thanh Từ 2009c, 96–97)[19]

The emphasis on meditation centered on the effect it had on the individual, whether it was on health, self-cultivation, or on the aspirations expressed by the young practitioners to find refuge from the stress of their daily lives or to become more moral beings.

Young people frequently cite *duyên* as the reason for their attraction to Zen and for practicing at Sùng Phúc. The concept of *duyên* is frequently used in Vietnam to give a name and explanation to the unknowable. Roughly equivalent to "fate," "natural bonds," or "predestination," *duyên* is a term with deep meaning and importance in both Vietnamese and Chinese religious thought. The term in Chinese is *yuan* (緣) or *yuan fen* (緣分), and in Chinese popular religion, the concept was likely taken from the Buddhist doctrine of karma but was de-sectarianized to denote a broader idea of fate or predestination (Yang and Ho 1998, 264–265). In a strictly Buddhist sense, *duyên* is the Vietnamese translation of the Sanskrit term *pratyaya*, or "cause," "condition," or "that on which something depends" (Keown 2004, 207). It is often used in China to remark on people being brought together by good luck or chance, as when two old friends bump into one another and exclaim that it was fate that brought them together. Much of the meaning of *duyên* in Vietnam maintains its Chinese roots. People will usually use the term to express a natural predilection for or a drawing toward something or someone. It is used, for example, to explain why lovers or friends are drawn toward one another. It is also used to express a person's charm or ability to draw people to them. In this, *duyên* stands apart from beauty. So people might remark that "she is not beautiful, but she has *duyên*." The idea is that there is an attractive quality to the person that draws you, though not necessarily because of strictures of normative physical beauty. So when people say they began to practice Zen because of *duyên*, they are expressing that their attraction is personal and inexplicable, that they were drawn to it naturally—in effect that they were compelled to begin. The implication of this natural draw is that there are inherent connections that are partly related to the experiences and formations from past lives.

Duyên is the most common reason people gave for why they began to follow Zen, why they ended up practicing at Sùng Phúc, and why they were interested in Zen rather than Pure Land Buddhism, and it was usually delivered in the single word, without elaboration. When I asked Tuấn, for example, why he became interested in Zen, he described himself as being "fated" (*duyên*) for Zen. He went on to elaborate: "Everyone has their own *duyên*, maybe *duyên* with Zen, or tantrism, or maybe Pure Land Buddhism. So each one should find the approach that is most suitable, and a teacher that is suitable for them, then they will go to that pagoda." One young woman who regularly participates in youth group activities put it this way: "I have been here for one year. I come from Hải Phòng, but I am a student here in Hanoi, and a friend introduced me. I had *duyên*." One final example comes from Bình, the Sunday school teacher: "I think that it is called divine predestination [*thiên duyên*]. In Buddhism, it is called being dependent on your fate [*tùy căn*]. So, for example some people have an affinity for Pure Land Buddhism and some for Zen. For example, for us [young people], we really like to meditate because it is immediate, making us feel more balanced in our lives. Life is hard. When we are too tired from working so hard, having to compete at work, we can meditate to recover."

While rooted in orthodox Buddhist ideas of karma, rebirth, and pre-conditioning, *duyên* in the context of Sùng Phúc seemed to be an individualistic explanation. It was used to explain why people were personally attracted to Zen and to Sùng Phúc. As such, in this context, a ubiquitous concept seemed to take on a new meaning or at the very least had new implications. *Duyên,* while tying into the idea of karma and rebirth, was not tied to a collective understanding of practice but functioned instead to cut off the practitioner from other social relationships in a uniquely modern way.

Secularity and Understanding

Young people who take up Zen practice at Sùng Phúc frame their explanations almost exclusively in secular terms. This orientation is a significant departure from the standard ways of being religious in Vietnam and comes about because of an acceleration of globalized structures and understandings of religion.

The restructuring of Buddhism into a religion, particularly by Buddhist reformers in the late nineteenth and early twentieth centuries, was filled with ambiguity. On the one hand, Buddhism was reshaped into a world religion, with Siddhārtha Gautama recast as the founder and with an effort made to find a unified core that could unite the various sects to form a single religion. On the other hand, at least from the time of the first World's Parliament of Religions in Chicago in 1889, there has been an attempt to claim that Buddhism is uniquely scientific and therefore more suited to modernity than other religions, particularly Christianity (Harding 2008, 123–124; Snodgrass 2003, 211–213). As McMahan writes,

"Buddhism has often been transformed and indeed strengthened through interface with secular discourses, not by resisting them but by incorporating them. Indeed, one of the major ways in which Buddhism around the world has modernized is through its rearticulation in the languages of science and secular thought" (McMahan 2020, 45).

This could especially be seen in the emphasis that people like Tuấn placed on understanding the meaning of sutras, contrasting the practice at Sùng Phúc with what they perceived was happening at regular pagodas:

> Tuấn: If I just sit and hit the wooden fish, chanting sutras in Sino-Vietnamese [as happens at regular pagodas], I don't understand the meaning. If I don't understand, then I can't believe, because I have no idea of the meaning. So here [at Sùng Phúc], all of the sutras are in [vernacular] Vietnamese, because when young people read, they want to understand.
>
> Me: So if you chant sutras in Sino-Vietnamese but don't understand anything, what is the point in them doing it then?
>
> Tuấn: It is just a bunch of old women who chant sutras to bring themselves peace [an lạc], but that's all. However, for young people, you have to explain, and they will search for the documents to understand the meaning of the Venerable Thích Thanh Từ and the abbot, using a variety of methods. If you read sutras, you need to understand them. That's why here [at Sùng Phúc] all of the sutras that we use are translated into [vernacular] Vietnamese. That is one of the main purposes of the [Trúc Lâm] association: to print all of the sutras into Vietnamese.
>
> Me: So Thích Thanh Từ's Trúc Lâm Zen is very suitable for young people, because it makes Buddhism intelligible?
>
> Tuấn: Because the Venerable [Thích Thanh Từ] said that Buddhism is a religion especially suited for young people. Only young people have the intellectual ability to remember and learn. How can the old people learn and remember everything?
>
> Me: So in your opinion, young people here believe in themselves more than old women, who only want to rely on Amitābha to help them. They just chant sutras and recite the name of Amitābha [niệm phật] to get Amitābha to help them with their lives.
>
> Tuấn: That's right.
>
> Me: And for young people, they don't believe that there are other beings that will help them, so they want to help themselves.
>
> Tuấn: Yes.
>
> Me: And so for this reason, Zen is more suitable for young people. Is my understanding correct?
>
> Tuấn: Zen can also be suitable for older people, but most importantly, you have to believe in yourself, rely on yourself, and have the Buddha mind [có tâm Phật], or it is pointless.

To establish an orthodoxy, the Buddhist Reform movement first stressed the importance of knowing the Buddha's teachings. Understanding the sutras, according to the reformers, places the onus for salvation on the individual and eliminates reliance on supernatural beings (i.e., buddhas and bodhisattvas). To achieve this goal, the reformers established monastic schools and held Dharma talks for the laity. In Hanoi, Dharma talks remain rare at most regular pagodas.

There was an ambiguity about the way that the young people at Sùng Phúc spoke about their Buddhist practice that reflected the way that Buddhist modernism has simultaneously constructed Buddhism as both a religious and a secular practice. In this, I would disagree with Frisk, who sees the loss of what she calls the "meaning and importance" of the difference between the religious and the secular as being a result of a "'postsecular' culture" (Frisk 2012, 59). The ambiguity of secularism and how Buddhism relates to it, or has been constructed by or in relation to it, seems to me to be a fundamental feature that has been present from the very beginning of the modernist reformulation of Buddhism. McMahan correctly asserts that expressions of secularism are tied to local and national formations (2020, 44) but also that the lines between the secular and the religious are "blurry, ambiguous, and negotiable" (2020, 51). He points out that Buddhist meditation is simultaneously being practiced in Buddhist temples and in more secular, clinical settings and that those who practice in either of these settings can hold varying ambiguous views about their practice, relating them to mental health but also seeing them as part of a larger spiritual life. The young people at Sùng Phúc evoke *duyên* as an individualistic interpretation of Buddhism—as everyone's being responsible only for themselves—but in doing so, they also touch on ideas of precondition and the impact that actions in past lives have on affinities in this life. The boundaries between the secular and the religious are porous.

The therapeutic understanding of meditation and of the temple space as a sanctuary from the stresses of everyday life are identified frequently by young people to explain their participation at Sùng Phúc. As Kim and Choi describe of Korea (2016, 460), young people access Buddhist practices to find a space away from the expectations of their families, the social pressures of friends, and the stress associated with studies and work. The explanations denote a definite secularist understanding that meditation is a tool of the mind that helps to bring personal equilibrium. This understanding of meditation as a therapeutic tool, the benefits of which can be scientifically measured through brain scans and EKGs, is prominent. At the same time, the young practitioners at Sùng Phúc still understood meditation to be a Buddhist practice, and the religious implications of this were not entirely lost. Thus, while meditation was a central focus of their practice, the young practitioners also revered the Buddha in a non-secular (i.e., religious) way.

The moral motivation is similarly ambiguous. Religion and magic became disassociated in the nineteenth century, with magic being cast as a failed science. At the same time, religion was restructured as a source of moral teaching. In doing so, religion was set up as being not in opposition to science but as an alternate source of authority. This in turn made the moral aspects of religions like Buddhism a central focus of attention, while the supernatural elements were dismissed as irrelevant, or at least as secondary (van der Veer 2014, 118). The young people at Sùng Phúc saw in Buddhism an important path for situating oneself as a moral being, especially in contrast to the perception of the moral decline that they attribute to the increasing pressures of laziness, consumerism, and self-interest endemic in Vietnamese society today. However, it would be a mistake to say that the moral refuge provided by Buddhism surpassed all else. Thus, every meditation session ended with a formal dedication to transfer the karmic merit accrued through meditation to all living beings, an act that is surely more religious than secular.

Until recently, Buddhism was portrayed as a religion for old women, and to a large extent it is still thought of this way. Young women continue to be engaged in Buddhist practice, but mainly through supplication for assistance with life problems, such as passing exams, advancing careers, finding a husband, or giving birth (preferably to a son).

The new Zen movement that I have been discussing here changes that discourse. It presents a form of Buddhism that complements the rational individualism that has dominated global discourses of modernity. Individual self-cultivation achieved through meditation is stressed, while devotion to, and supplication of, the supernatural is deemphasized or denied. In doing this, the goal of Buddhist practice is shifted. Devotional practice usually emphasized engaging in reciprocal relationships with the supernatural (whether spirits, gods, or buddhas) to bring about material benefit in the form of health and longevity, good luck, prosperity, and happiness. The modernist Zen practiced in the Trúc Lâm organization does not always explicitly deny that the supernatural can impact the world, but it denies the centrality of this sort of goal and instead refocuses on soteriological objectives. As such, at Sùng Phúc, offerings are not made, spirit money is not burned, and people do not pray to the buddhas for help with their lives (at least not out loud). This view was prominent in one young man's explanation:

The first reason [for why young people are attracted to Zen Buddhism at Sùng Phúc] is the necessity of the present time. Right now, people are living their lives only paying attention to their material needs. They are living fast and not caring about others [just themselves], bringing their lives into turmoil. Therefore, they want to return to a place where they can be balanced [an tâm]. The second reason is that [Trúc Lâm] is designed so that it is for everyone [not just old people and women]. Buddhism has existed for over two thousand years in Vietnam and it has always had the purpose of improving the national condition. So Trúc Lâm always tries to improve the lives of the Vietnamese. Also, there are so many lay Buddhists who understand and receive benefit from their practice, and they share with their children and grandchildren. Buddhism is a very modern and cultured religion, so there is no prayer, making wishes, or superstition.

Instead of the common practices of supplication and seeking supernatural aid, the young people at Sùng Phúc are attracted by seemingly secular goals. The first of these is a therapeutic benefit. Young people at Sùng Phúc feel set upon by the pressures of the external world and are seeking something to help reduce stress, and they find it in meditation. The second motivation is that many believe that there is a moral decline in Vietnamese society and regard their Buddhist engagement as a way to stand against the consumerism and selfishness that they see as endemic, particularly among young people. It is worth noting, however, that while young people couched their explanations in secularist rationalizations, they also thought of themselves as Buddhist and understood Buddhism to be a religion, not simply a secular therapeutic practice in the mold of Goenka's Vipassanā movement or Jon Kabat-Zinn's Mindfulness-Based Stress-Reduction program.

Apparently, the rationalist approach to Buddhism, which nonetheless maintains tropes of Buddhism as representative of Vietnamese moral virtue, fits well with the habitus of young people, as evidenced by Sùng Phúc's extreme success in attracting them. Of course, Sùng Phúc has also created the conditions for this attraction by structuring their activities in a way that makes a space for young people to participate. It is unlikely that they would be as successful, however, if the individual, rational discourses of modernity were not infused into their teachings and practices. So while there was also a youth group at Quán Sứ Pagoda, for example, I was told that it was small and not very successful, because "all they do is chant sutras together. That is not interesting for young people."

The motivations of the young people at Sùng Phúc, as with the older practitioners, were complex. The modernist discourse at Sùng Phúc created a break with standard devotional forms of Buddhist practice and belief that created the conditions for young people to practice. The motivations that they espoused for becoming involved in the youth group and for practicing Zen were expressed in very secular terms. The degree to which this was a rhetorical device to separate their modernist practices from the practices of old women at regular pagodas is an open question. While they certainly accentuated the therapeutic and moralistic aspects of their practice, they did not hedge in any way about their being Buddhists, as did the youths studied by Kim and Choi (Kim 2016; Kim and Choi 2016). They understood Buddhism as a religion and nonetheless situated Buddhism as an important part of their identity projects.

Conclusion

||||||||

On a busy morning on the first day of the lunar month in 2013, throngs of devotees were coming and going through the main gates of Quán Sứ Pagoda, the most politically important pagoda in Hanoi. Along one side of the main building, women were preparing trays of offerings to put on the altar of the buddhas and make wishes for family prosperity, success, and happiness. Smoke steadily rose from the furnace near the gate where people were burning fistfuls of spirit money, expecting that the essence of the money would help sway the buddhas' blessings in their favor. Later in the day, the main shrine would be filled with mostly old women who would chant from a liturgy that includes extracts of sutras associated with Pure Land Buddhism and a penitence rite called Sám Nguyện.

Across the Red River at Sùng Phúc Monastery, the compound was mostly empty. There were a few volunteer *cư sĩ* preparing the flowers for the altars. In each of the main rooms, a monk sat quietly and waited in case a lay Buddhist should come, wanting to pay respect to the Buddha or to speak with someone. The monk in the main shrine room rang the bowl gong whenever a lay Buddhist came and bowed before the Buddha's altar. Some of the monks and nuns did chores. All this was much like any other day, despite the popular belief that it was the most potent day of the lunar month, when the supernatural world was most responsive to requests from the living. And while all the other religious sites in Hanoi were busy, Sùng Phúc would remain quiet until the weekend.

Juxtaposing Quán Sứ Pagoda and Sùng Phúc reveals just how far removed Trúc Lâm Zen is from the way Buddhism is practiced and understood at other locations in northern Vietnam. Most Buddhists understand the buddhas as being part of an intricate, powerful, and responsive supernatural realm that can be petitioned, bribed, cajoled, or manipulated to assist people with their lives, often with the hired help of ritual specialists. Trúc Lâm, by contrast, teaches that the Buddha was a human example showing us a path of individual morality and personal effort through meditation. Every day—not just twice every lunar month—is a day for meditation. Activities are planned not around an understanding of supernatural responsiveness but around human convenience. Their message is rational, individualistic, and modern. It appeals not only to old women but also to young people and to men of all ages. Sùng Phúc is unique in Hanoi and has developed quickly, attracting large numbers of followers with its message.

The form of Buddhism practiced at Sùng Phúc is grounded in modernist interpretations of Buddhism that have been globalized in the last century. Unlike the Zen that Thích Nhất Hạnh has brought to the world, Trúc Lâm Buddhism remains more faithfully grounded in Vietnamese Buddhist modes and narratives. It evokes a long history of Zen Buddhism and claims affinity with the only school of Zen unique to Vietnam. While branding itself as teaching not just Zen but a uniquely Vietnamese Zen, Trúc Lâm is a form of Buddhism that is entirely modern.

THE INADEQUACIES OF WESTERNIZATION THEORY

It is not possible to explain the increased popularity of Zen, and particularly of Trúc Lâm Zen, in contemporary Vietnam by just attributing it to the Westernization of Buddhism. A more sophisticated, but still inadequate, theory might be to attribute it to a so-called pizza effect, whereby a Zen exported to the West and reconstituted to suit Western dispositions is now being imported back to the land of its origins and impacting the Buddhism practiced there. There are several problems with these theories. Foremost is the Western triumphalism that underlies them, with its implication that Asians had corrupted the Buddha's pristine teachings, which had to be saved by the West through its unique ability to expunge it of its superstitious, premodern ways. In terms of theoretical issues, the unilinear model, whereby a unitary tradition is transmitted, transformed, and returned, does not correspond to the historical record. When we look deeper, we see that while the first impetus for change may come out of the contact between Europe and Asia through European imperialism, the characteristics that mark Trúc Lâm Zen as distinct from the more usual forms of practice found in Vietnam are rooted in the Buddhist Reform movement that emerged in Vietnam in the 1920s and not from the Westernized Zen that emerged in the 1960s and 1970s.

The Reform movement in Vietnam was also not solely a direct result of French colonialism and the crisis of self-doubt that arose from Vietnam's evident inability to stand up against the military, organizational, and ideological onslaught. Nor was it strictly a result of the increased religious competition introduced by Catholic missionaries. These pressures were merely the local manifestations of a much larger process of change that globalization had unleashed throughout Asia. The encounter with European powers and ideas brought about reform movements in all Buddhist countries, though it was not in all cases a direct response to Western ideas and challenges. In China and Japan, for instance, the Buddhist reformers were responding not so much to direct Western challenges as to criticism and pressures emanating from within Chinese and Japanese societies (Chen Jidong 2009). Chinese monasteries were under threat of confiscation because they were seen as wasteful and not contributing to society. The Shin Bukkyō movement in Japan was similarly a response to threatening pressures from the Meiji Restoration.

These reform movements did not emerge in isolation but were connected in a web of communication that extended beyond Asia to Western sympathizers in North America and Europe and Western academics studying—and constructing—Buddhism as a religion. Anagārika Dharmapala traveled the world at the end of the nineteenth century trying to enlist support for reclaiming Bodhgaya for all Buddhists and turning it into the epicenter of the Buddhist world. Japanese Shin Buddhists were sending missions to China, feeling that Buddhism in China was stagnant (Chen Jidong 2009). As Tweed notes, "In the Meiji-Victorian Pacific World, a vast transoceanic cultural space, Modernity emerged from the crossing of cultural currents, including mass communication, transnational migration, and accelerated travel" (Tweed 2012, 41). In Vietnam, the links with China were particularly important, and the works of Taixu, the modernist monk and influential thinker, were regularly translated into Vietnamese and published in the various reform Buddhist journals published in the major centers of south, central, and northern Vietnam (DeVido 2007). Thus, Arjun Appadurai's understanding of global flows is a more apt description of how Buddhism was modernizing at a global level (1996). These flows were multidirectional (Tweed 2012, 42) and were quickly disseminating new ideas via new forms of mass communication and technologies that allowed for the increasingly rapid travel and migration that had such a uniquely transformative impact. It is notable that the colonial encounter had the effect of changing both colonizers and colonized. In fact, the very idea of religion as a universal social construct that can be compared across cultures was a result of the colonial encounter as well, and not arising in Europe apart from the exploration that took place during the early modern period (Beyer 2006, 73).

The forms of Buddhism that emerged from this rapid acceleration in the exchange of ideas and movements of people have, as Tweed notes, resulted in a plurality of hybridizations (Tweed 2012). These hybridizations were unique to the forms on which they were building and the historico-political circumstances to which they were reacting, to the dominant transnational interactions and influences, and to the local pressures and imperatives in which they were operating. The result was that even in Vietnam, there were multiple Buddhist responses, and the transformations took place in regionally specific ways. The case of Trúc Lâm Buddhism should therefore be understood as merely one possible recomposition of Buddhism in contemporary Vietnam. What this case illustrates is a prominent contemporary iteration of Buddhism in Vietnam that has manifested many of the modernist discourses that emerged in the Buddhist Reform movement. It shows how multiple flows have coalesced in a particular way to embody a hybrid construction of Buddhist orthodoxy that is resonating with a broader demographic range than was the case with the standard form of devotional Buddhism practiced in northern Vietnam. Before concluding this work, then, it is useful to summarize these multiple influences to understand how they have taken form in the context of contemporary Hanoi and how they are understood and lived by the lay Buddhists it has attracted.

At the beginning of this book, I introduced the idea of three interacting forces that bear on different manifestations in the contemporary globalized context. The first of these is a parochial force, perhaps better characterized as a disposition. It is inward looking, and it is perpetuated not so much through discourse as by embodied habituations and impulses to continue practicing in ways that are familiar. Often mischaracterized as "tradition," this parochialism is manifested in regular pagodas through habitual practice of devotional forms of Buddhism. The second force is globalization, which is often perpetuated through discourse and tends to be aligned with hegemonic political and economic forces such as neoliberalism. Since the start of the Buddhist reform movements in Asia and with the spread of Buddhism in the West, the dominant discourse of Buddhist globalism has been modernist and secularist, restructuring Buddhism into a differentiated religion with a unified core, distinct sects, shared symbols, and a founder. It should be noted, however, that while Buddhist modernism has been dominant, it is not the same as Buddhist globalism, and one can imagine that other discourses could be more dominant in the future. The final force is localism, by which I mean the force that compels Buddhism, whatever its form, to adapt to local conditions. This last force becomes particularly important when Buddhism moves around. So whether it is a Buddhism influenced by parochial dispositions, like Chùa Linh Thứu, a Vietnamese community pagoda in Berlin, or Thiền Viện Chánh Tâm, the Trúc Lâm center in Los Angeles, adaptations are made to adjust to those contexts. Notably, all these forces tend to express themselves in any one site, though in different ways and with varying levels of influence. Thus, while a regular devotional pagoda in Hanoi, for example, is naturally localized and tends to be most influenced by parochial dispositions, it is also inevitably influenced by the powerful discourses of globalism. While members of the community continue to worship an array of spirits alongside the Buddhist pantheon and practice with the expectation of worldly benefit, they might also attend major events, like the new celebrations of Wesak (Phật Đản), or go on pilgrimages to international sites like Bodhgaya.

As for Sùng Phúc, parochial dispositions are not prominent, but the globalist modernist discourses are prevalent. Its international outlook, reliance on national sentiments and symbolic references, secularist statements, and discouragement of standard propitiative practices all exhibit the extent to which the modernist discourse of Buddhist globalism informs the way Buddhism takes form and is lived there. As for its localization, we see that while Trúc Lâm is a re-creation of Zen that emerged in the south and while the monks there are all from the south, the organization must take into account the dynamics that bear on its establishment in the northern context of Hanoi, including operating in a climate where state actors may not be as accustomed to the scale of the organization and may hold it in suspicion, or where not all locals will accept that their local pagoda has been transformed.

A MODERNIST GLOBAL VIETNAMESE ZEN

Zen Buddhism has had a long historical presence in the imagination of Vietnamese Buddhists. Trần Văn Giáp's discovery of a transmission-of-the-lamp style text usefully provided a framework for describing Vietnamese Buddhist history through a Zen lens. His publications of this history during the Buddhist Reform movement of the 1920s asserted a Vietnamese Zen identity at a time when Vietnamese intellectuals such as he, who was a scholar but also involved in the Reform movement in northern Vietnam, were trying to conceptualize Vietnam's place in the contemporary world. The resulting affirmation that Zen was at the core of Vietnamese Buddhism was quickly taken up by academics and practitioners alike. While a survey of materials in English or Vietnamese might convince a reader of the primacy of Zen in Vietnam, Zen remains mostly an imagined tradition there and in the Vietnamese diaspora. Most Vietnamese Buddhists around the world still practice a devotional Buddhism that tends to be focused on smoothing the conditions of this life and caring for the dead. Despite the overwhelming predominance of devotional Buddhist practices, the centrality of Zen in the imagining of Vietnamese Buddhism was reaffirmed in southern Vietnam in the 1960s, when translations of D. T. Suzuki in the package of a Japanese cultural tradition were having a huge impact in Vietnam. Vietnamese monks like Thích Nhất Hạnh and Thích Thiên Ân were going abroad to study, the former at Princeton and Columbia Universities in the United States and the latter at Toyo and Waseda Universities in Japan. Both styled themselves as Zen masters only after resettling in the West in the late 1960s, when they were compelled to teach a non-Vietnamese, convert following.

At the same time, Thích Thanh Từ became interested in reclaiming what he believed to be a lost Vietnamese Zen tradition, and he set about organizing meditation classes for lay Buddhists in southern Vietnam. During the 1960s and early 1970s, he was not particularly prominent, and there are few mentions of him in the Vietnamese Buddhist publications of the time. In 1964, he published a short article about a poem in the magazine founded by Thích Nhất Hạnh, *Hải triều âm* (The sound of the tide), titled "Hai đội binh Hồng Thập Tự" (Two troops from the Red Cross), though there was nothing related to Zen in it. By 1974, he had published a couple of articles (that I know of) on Zen and Buddhist practice (1974a; 1974b), and notifications appear in five issues of *Từ Quang* magazine announcing teaching and meditation instruction at Tu viện Chơn Không, the center he had set up in Vũng Tàu.[1] After that, it is difficult to say what he was doing until he began publishing articles again in Buddhist magazines in the late 1990s. After the Renovation brought loosened restrictions on religious practice in the late 1980s, he began to expand his network of Zen centers throughout southern Vietnam.

In the north, Buddhist reform had more or less gone into hibernation in 1954, when the Communists formed the government and promoted atheistic humanism. By the late 1990s, government restrictions had relaxed sufficiently enough to allow Thích Thanh Từ to create a foothold in the north with Sùng Phúc in Hanoi. In 2002, he also reestablished Trúc Lâm Yên Tử Monastery, at the site of the birthplace of Trúc Lâm Zen in the fourteenth century, by taking over a small village pagoda on the slopes of

Mount Yên Tử and building a large complex. The Zen Buddhism that is being established in Hanoi and other points in northern Vietnam is in a way a missionary movement—a Zen conquest of the North. The Buddhists who continued to reform in the south after the end of French colonialism in 1954 are now colonizing Buddhism in northern Vietnam. All the senior monks at Sùng Phúc, and a majority overall, are from southern or central Vietnam. They are introducing a modernist form of Buddhism that, through the period of war and state pressure against religion, had not persevered in the north. While it has not displaced the older form of Buddhist practice that maintains a porous boundary between a Buddhist orthodoxy and other beliefs and practices, this new form of Buddhism has been attractive to demographics, especially youths and men, that found devotional forms antithetical to their identity projects.

As we have seen, the teachings of Trúc Lâm as reenvisioned by Thích Thanh Từ are based on a modernist interpretation of Buddhism that emerged in the early twentieth century. Several features of this have been discussed in this book. The first is an interpretation of Buddhism that is influenced by global Buddhist forces that push for the orthodoxification of Buddhism. This process has involved creating external distinctions that define Buddhism as a world religion vis-à-vis other religions. It has also involved creating internal distinctions between ideas and practices that could be considered "true" Buddhism and those that are mere cultural accretions. Of these, some are seen as benign and worthy of maintenance, while others are considered to be a threat to the purity of Buddhism; these latter ideas and practices are then marginalized as superstition. While this discourse is present throughout Buddhism in Vietnam and is particularly prominent in the presentation of Buddhism by the Buddhist institution, at most pagodas, it is not a major influence. At the local level, it is often men who hold to this orthodoxy for the symbolic capital it brings within the Buddhist field (Soucy 2009; 2012, chapter 9)

The process of turning Buddhism into a religion also involved isolating and accentuating key unifying aspects while downplaying those aspects that are more specific to regional forms or Buddhist schools. The core of Buddhism came to be encoded in the Four Noble Truths and the Noble Eightfold Path, upon which Buddhists from all sects and schools can agree. Perhaps more important, however, is the elevation of the historical Buddha as the founder and symbolic center of the religion. It is for this reason that Anagārika Dharmapala worked so hard to establish Bodhgaya as Buddhism's symbolic center. The importance of this in prominent global Buddhist discourses can be seen in how individual countries have set up their own national pagodas at Bodhgaya. Vietnamese

Buddhists have participated in this by constructing three pagodas, two by overseas Vietnamese Buddhists and one by Buddhists from Vietnam. The elevation of the historical Buddha to the symbolic center of the religion can also be seen by the way Wesak has been made the central holiday for all Buddhists and is now celebrated globally on a rotating basis (with Vietnam being the host twice so far).

At Sùng Phúc, we have seen how the space has been constructed to give the historical Buddha the preeminent position. The main shrine is dedicated entirely to the historical Buddha, with a large statue of the Buddha in the Flower Sermon pose dominating the altar. A bas-relief frieze on the upper walls of the shrine room encapsulates the key moments of the Buddha's life. The rest of the center reiterates the importance of the historical Buddha both through the inclusion of imagery related to the Buddha and by exclusion of iconography depicting other members of the Buddhist Mahāyāna pantheon, with some exceptions (Mañjuśrī [Văn Thù Sư Lợi] and Samantabhadra [Phổ Hiền] flank the Buddha on the main altar and statues of Maitreya (Di Lạc) are displayed in the dining room and meditation hall).

The central practices of Zen, and particularly Trúc Lâm, also fit well with a modernist understanding of Buddhism that accentuates the importance of individual endeavor and diminishes the importance of supernatural assistance. At Sùng Phúc, there are three main forms of activities. The first is the Penitence Rite (Sám Hối). However, while this ritual is common in all Vietnamese Buddhist pagodas in Vietnam and in the diaspora, in Trúc Lâm it has been altered. The first alteration is that it is translated from Sino-Vietnamese to vernacular Vietnamese so people can understand its meaning. Unlike at other places, where followers spoke of the purpose of the Penitence Rite as obtaining the pardon (tha thứ) of the Buddha to diminish the consequence of one's sins, at Sùng Phúc, people spoke of the Penitence Rite in strictly humanistic moral terms, as providing the opportunity to reflect on one's faults, adding that it means nothing if one does not actually correct those faults after the ritual.

The practice that defines Zen is, of course, meditation. This, too, is expressed in humanistic terms, as not primarily generating karma or merit but as a technique that allows people to become more aware of their psychology, to reduce stress, or for general health benefits. People at Sùng Phúc also contrasted meditation with Pure Land Buddhism and its central practice of chanting sutras, which is seen by many at other pagodas as having a magical capacity to boost merit and bring good luck to oneself and one's family. The final core practice at Sùng Phúc was listening to Dharma talks. These talks are central features of all weekend programs and are also given at special events. In fact, Dharma talks are given at every possible occasion, including weddings and memorial services held for families at Sùng Phúc and even when schoolchildren come to visit. At Sùng Phúc, unlike at most other pagodas around Hanoi, understanding the Dharma is considered fundamentally important, and studying diligently is promoted. Thus, several times a week, classes are given in the afternoons as part of a program of courses offered to the laity that leads to the awarding of a certificate upon completion. The reason for this emphasis on understanding is that the modernist ideology behind Trúc Lâm places the onus on the individual to make progress, and understanding the Dharma is fundamentally important for this.

Each of these practices—the Penitence Rite, meditation, and Dharma talks—are notable for the rational and secular approach they take to Buddhism, stripping away any expectation of supernatural assistance or interference. The buddhas do not grant wishes, nor do they pardon sins. Instead, people are responsible for their own salvation, which comes through understanding the Dharma, practicing meditation, and acting morally. The individualistic nature of this approach is radically different from the way many Buddhists conceive of Buddhist practice at regular pagodas, where women regularly expressed to me that they went to the pagoda, made offerings, and chanted sutras with the expectation that their religious actions would bring benefit not only to themselves but also their families. In this conception, the faith or actions of those family members was independent from the perceived efficacy of their Buddhist actions. Thus, for mothers, it made no difference if their children did not practice Buddhism, did not believe in Buddhism, or mocked their mother's Buddhist devotion. Similarly, mortuary rituals were performed by Buddhists with the expectation that it would help expiate the sins of the dead, ease their passage through the underworld, and aid in their rebirth. In this conceptualization of death, therefore, it was not solely the individual's actions in life that affected their karmic path but the actions of the community. This possibility for community action, and the ritual efficacy that is decoupled from individual faith and effort, is denied at Sùng Phúc. Instead, the message given by the authority there, which is mostly upheld by its followers, is that individual effort is required and that such efforts do not significantly impact others. For that reason, one of the central features of memorial rituals at Sùng Phúc is a Dharma talk given by the monk conducting the ritual and aimed at the family of the deceased. Similarly, the occasion of weddings conducted at Sùng Phúc—itself an innovation for Buddhism in Vietnam and one conducted only at modernist pagodas—is also an opportunity for sermons that exhort the newlyweds to build a Buddhist family and for their extended families to support them.

A LIVING ZEN TRADITION

I have tried to show in this book how Buddhism is presented at Sùng Phúc through its space, its liturgy, and its practices and to show that despite the highly consistent message disseminated through its Dharma talks, literature, recordings, videos, and website, its practitioners absorb and express its core values in diverse and often idiosyncratic ways. The motivations for participating in the activities of Sùng Phúc and making Trúc Lâm Zen a part of their identity projects can vary from person to person. These may include desires to distinguish oneself from others in an attempt to build cultural capital through association with an elite tradition. It may involve personal dissatisfaction with the contemporary situation in Vietnam—with its accelerated economic growth, widening wealth disparity, pollution, and loss of culture and morality as the price of economic development—or a belief that meditation will improve health, among myriad other possible reasons.

Trúc Lâm Zen systematically presents itself in a way that is intended to attract a wide demographic. One of the most notable marketing strategies is the way that it draws on the Vietnamese national narrative. A major feature of Vietnamese national identity revolves around Vietnam's success in resisting foreign invaders who were far stronger. Trần Nhân Tông's triumph over the Yuan invaders and subsequent founding of Vietnam's Zen school—and the assertion by some that he is nothing less than the Vietnamese Buddha—is compelling. The fact that this narrative is primarily a modern creation does not detract from its resonance with the presentation of Trúc Lâm as the Vietnamese Zen. While Thích Thanh Từ was likely unaware that this nationalist narrative is relatively new, it seems clear that he chose to associate his teachings with Trúc Lâm because of the way that it expressed a nationalist discourse that would be attractive to contemporary Vietnamese. It was a successful strategy. Trúc Lâm continues to build new monasteries and to spread through northern Vietnam and abroad, introducing people to a modern form of Buddhist practice packaged as an authentic Vietnamese Zen tradition.

Notes

||||||||

Introduction

1. References to these mummies periodically appear in magazine articles, such as "The Restoration of the Tu bổ nhục thân hai Thiền sư Vũ Khắc Minh, Vũ Khắc Trường" (Flesh Bodies of Two Zen Masters Vũ Khắc Minh, Vũ Khắc Trường) (Nguyễn Mỹ 2002), reprinted in the Buddhist magazine *Giác ngộ* from the newspaper *Thể thao và văn hóa*.

2. For example, Rick Fields documents this movement, ending his book by stating that "American Buddhism is hammering out its own shape" (1981, 379). More recently, Storhoff and Whalen Bridge state that "American Buddhists have developed a kind of reciprocity with their faith: As Buddhism changes them, they have changed the faith itself. Historically Buddhism has evolved wherever it has spread" (2010, 3). Jeff Ouvran, in a book seemingly intended for a Buddhist rather than an academic audience and titled *The Star Spangled Buddhist*, makes a similar statement (2013, 155). While not explicit, this assumption seems also to underlie Ellen Pearlman's work on the influence of Buddhism on avant-garde Americans (2012, vii).

3. I use "reform movements" rather than the often-used "revival movements" because the latter implies that Buddhism had declined. The discourse of decline is rooted in the reformist construction of Buddhism, which, in its establishment of a Buddhist orthodoxy, felt that Buddhism had been corrupted over time from the original teachings of the Buddha. If the health of Buddhism is measured not by corruption of a "true doctrine" but by participation or financial support, it becomes difficult to argue that there was a decline and hence a revival.

4. This division between white/convert and ethnic/traditional Buddhism has been part of the scholarship of Buddhism in the West since the beginning, with Prebish's introduction of the elite/convert vs. ethnic Buddhist categories in his book *American Buddhism* (1979). There have been critiques of the division ever since, mostly trying to refine it to take into account greater nuances (e.g., Nattier's tripartite division of import, export, and baggage Buddhisms [1998]; Tweed's addition of the third category of "nightstand Buddhists" [2002]; and Baumann's "traditionalist vs. modernist" Buddhists [2002]). Han (2021) has more recently exposed how this division exists as racist undercurrents in Buddhist practice

communities in the United States and illustrates the on-the-ground complexity of such divisions as seen through the eyes of Asian American Buddhists. I am suggesting here that the cataloguing of types of Buddhism is ultimately unhelpful and deceptive.

5. In Vietnam, the state-recognized organization is the Vietnamese Buddhist Association, or Giáo hội Phật giáo Việt Nam. The only competing organization is the Unified Buddhist Church of Vietnam (Giáo hội Phật giáo Việt Nam Thống nhất), which is outlawed by the Vietnamese government. Internationally, there are several autonomous associations formed at the national level in various countries, like the European Unified Buddhist Church of Vietnam, German Branch (Giáo hội Phật giáo Việt Nam Thống nhất Âu Châu—Chi bộ Đức Quốc), headquartered at Viên Giác Pagoda in Hanover; and the Unified Buddhist Church of Vietnam in Canada (Hội Phật giáo Việt Nam Thống nhất tại Canada), headquartered at Tam Bảo Pagoda in Montreal. There are other international associations formed around particular leaders, like Thích Huyền Vi's World Linh Son Buddhist Congregation (Hội Phật giáo Linh Sơn Thế giới) and Thích Nhất Hạnh's Tiếp Hiện–Order of Interbeing. By and large, however, individual temples are autonomous, and the associations have limited influence.

6. I use the term "Buddhisms" in a way that is analogous to the pervasive use of "modernities" (as a shorthand for "multiple modernities"), first introduced by Eisenstadt (2000) to underline the role that the local plays in the experiences and manifestations of modernity. The plural usage here underlines that the Zen Buddhist "tradition" discussed in this book is no less Vietnamese than the more usual devotional approach. Nor is it like Thích Nhất Hạnh's popular reinterpretation of the tradition, which is often not included in discussions of "Vietnamese Buddhism." This is not because Thích Nhất Hạnh is removed from his tradition but that the categorization of a distinct and monolithic "Vietnamese Buddhism" is fallacious.

7. The Vietnamese term for "superstition," *mê tín*, comes from the Chinese word *mixin* (迷信). It has a classical precursor in a Buddhist phrase, but it was not until 1889 that the Japanese used the term "*mei-shin*" to denote superstition in the sense used today (Nedostup 2009, 304n20).

8. See Humphreys (1968) for an insider account of early efforts to establish the Buddhist Society in the first half of the twentieth century.

9. Anna Sun notes that Buddhism was included in the original list of world religions by the inventor of the term, Cornelis Petrus Tiele, the others being Christianity and Islam. Max Müller's list was broader, also including Hinduism, Zoroastrianism, Confucianism, and Daoism (Sun 2013, 60–61).

10. Dharmapala wrote in *The Buddhist* in 1892 that "from Gaya [the Buddha] started as a preacher of that religion which was destined to become at one time the faith of one half of the population of the globe, and after twenty-four centuries still has a large[r] number of adherents than any other *world religion*" (Guruge 1965, 646; italics mine).

11. Early Europeans only very gradually realized that the disparate religious phenomena they encountered in different places in Buddhist Asia were related, and then constructed them as "Buddhism" (Almond 1988, 8).

12. The extent to which the narrative of the Buddha's life has been created and globalized only in the modern period can be seen in the account of Śākyamuni's life as recorded by the Italian missionary Adriano di St. Thecla, who described religion in Tonkin (northern Vietnam) in 1750. The story of the Buddha's life as briefly recorded in his account differs widely from the now standardized narrative, missing such key elements as Queen Maya's dream, his birth in Lumbini, his protected and opulent upbringing, the Four Encounters, his escape, his religious search, his enlightenment under the bodhi tree, and his death (see Dror 2002, 182–185).

13. For example, an article on the Three Refuges and the Five Precepts appeared in the first issue of *Viên âm* (The voice of exposition), the most important reform journal in central Vietnam, taken from a speech given at Từ Quang Pagoda in 1933 (Thích-Mật-Thể 1933).

14. For example, in 1940, the journal published by the Tonkin Buddhist Association, called *Đuốc tuệ* (The torch of wisdom), published a series of articles written by Bernard L. Broughton, the head of the English Maha Bodhi Society, titled "Vì sao tôi tin Phật giáo" (Why I believe in Buddhism) (Broughton 1940).

15. My current research project is examining this issue, but my starting hypothesis is that re-enchantment is not merely a resumption or perseverance of previous religiosities.

16. By "Buddhist institution," I am referring to an abstract authority. This Buddhist authority is represented in Vietnam today by the organization sponsored by the state, the Vietnamese Buddhist Association (Giáo hội Phật giáo Việt Nam). The organization is a member of the Vietnamese Fatherland Front (Mặt trận Tổ quốc Việt Nam), which is the state-aligned umbrella organization that represents and exerts control over "mass movements" in Vietnam. However, the Buddhist institution in a more abstract sense can also be seen as being represented by other organizations—overseas, notably the Unified Buddhist Church of Vietnam (Giáo hội Phật giáo Việt Nam Thống nhất)—or in more diffused forms.

Chapter One: The Rise of Zen in Twentieth-Century Vietnam

1. Thích Thiên Ân wrote several books in Vietnamese that were not really about Zen. His most notable contribution on Zen is *Buddhism and Zen in Vietnam in Relation to the Development of Buddhism in Asia* (1975a), published only in English. Thích Nhất Hạnh outlined some of the Zen connection in *Vietnam: Lotus in a Sea of Fire* (1968), but his most important outline of Vietnamese Buddhist history and its connection to Thiền was written by him under the pseudonym Nguyễn Lang ([1973] 2000) after he was exiled from Vietnam (Soucy, forthcoming).

2. The *Thiền uyển tập anh* is also known as the *Đại nam thiền uyển truyền đăng tập lục*. See Cuong Tu Nguyen (1995, 81n1) for an explanation of the differences between the two.

3. For example, in an article called "Vì sao phải học Phật" (Why study the Buddha), the author briefly mentions the Zen doctrine of the mind seal (Mật-Nguyện 1934, 19).

4. There is some discrepancy about the date of Trần Văn Giáp's birth. Nguyễn Quang Ân points out that on his résumé before 1960, Trần Văn Giáp states that his date of birth is January 13, 1902, but on his staff profile from November 12, 1960, and in all documents since that time, he has recorded his birth date as November 26, 1898. Nguyễn Quang Ân speculates that he changed his age to be eligible to enter the Trường Pháp Việt Yên Phụ school (Nguyễn Quang Ân 1996, 9n1). The biographical information sheet from the Hanoi office of L'École française d'Extrême-Orient office states his date of birth as 1896.

5. There is little information available on Trần Văn Giáp, despite the important role he played in constructing the historical understanding of Vietnamese Buddhism. Biographical information in this section comes from a one-page handout available from the library of the École française d'Extrême-Orient's Hanoi office, and from Nguyễn Quang Ân (1996).

6. For example, on April 15, 1938, at the celebration of the Buddha's birthday, he gave a public lecture that was printed shortly after in *Đuốc tuệ* (Trần Văn Giáp 1938), in which he explains the meanings of Buddhist terms like *phật* (buddha) and *giác* (awaken).

7. These include Maurice Durand (1959), Mai Thọ Truyền (1959), Thích Nhất Hạnh (1968), Thích Thiên-Ân (1975a), Heinz Bechert and Vu Duy Tu (1976), Nguyễn Tài Thư (1992), and Minh Chi et al. (1999). Cuong Tu Nguyen (1995, 82n5) gives a concise appraisal of all available works dealing with Vietnamese history up to that time. Since Cuong Tu Nguyen completed his important work, descriptions by Western academics have adopted Nguyen's assessment (e.g., McHale 2004).

8. The search for books on Zen at the National Library in Hanoi returns a result of 299 books. Of those, 67 have no date, 4 are from 1927 to the 1980s, 29 are from the 1990s, and 199 were published after 2000. Of those, 18 of the 67 with no dates, 5 of the 29 from the 1990s, and 47 of the 199 from 2000–2009 have non-Vietnamese authors. I am not sure which of the rest might be translations. Leaving aside the large number of records without dates, this admittedly cursory search indicates the increased interest in Zen in the first decade of the twenty-first century, and it is backed up by the increasing number of books on Zen that can be found in bookstores in Hanoi and Ho Chi Minh City.

9. It is not entirely clear when Suzuki's works were first translated into Vietnamese. A search of the Worldcat catalogue shows the earliest translation in that system is *Cốt tủy của Đạo Phật* (The essence of Buddhism), which was first published in 1949 but not published in Vietnamese translation until 1968. *Thiền và phân tâm học* (Zen and psychoanalysis) was not published until 1973, thirteen years after publication of the original English version (Suzuki, Fromm, and de Martino 1973). It was not until 1974 that *Huyền học Đạo phật và Thiên chúa* (Mysticism: Christian and Buddhist) was published in Saigon (Suzuki 1974). There is also a vague reference to *Thiền luận* (Essays in Zen Buddhism) being published perhaps in 1976, but no publisher or place of publication is mentioned. All other translations have been published either in California after the end of the war or in Vietnam after 1992. A search of the catalog of the National Library in Hanoi was less successful, showing only a scattering of translations, all published after 1992. A full list of translations, aside from the ones mentioned above, include *Trực chỉ chơn tâm* (The awakening of Zen) (1983), *Nghiên cứu Kinh Lăng già* (Studies of the Lankavatara Sutra) (1999), *Lăng già Đại Thừa Kinh* (The Lankavatara Sutra: A Mahāyāna text) (2005a; likely the same book), *Thiền* (Zen) (2000), and *Thiền và bát nhã* (Zen and the pursuit of wisdom) (2007).

10. I have been unable to find proof for this assumption, so tantalizing because it neatly ties Thích Thiên Ân to a major center of Buddhist reform in Japan that had a global impact on the trajectory of Buddhist development.

11. His earliest book, written in 1963, documents cultural relations between Vietnam and Japan (Thích Thiên Ân 1963a). His time in Japan, however, must have sparked an interest in Zen philosophy, for he went on to publish a book on Zen philosophy: *Triết-học Zen tư-tưởng Nhật-bản và các nước Á-châu* (Zen philosophy: Japanese thought and Asian nations) (Thích Thiên Ân 1963b). His next three books are all published in 1965; two of them are about Japanese thought and the education system (1965a; 1965b) and the third marks an interest in Vietnam, with the publishing of *Phật-giáo Việt-nam: xưa & nay* (Vietnamese Buddhism: In the past and present) (1965c). He continued to pursue his interest in literature and philosophy with a book on Nguyễn Du (who wrote the Vietnamese masterpiece *The Tale of Kiều*), published in 1966, the same year that he moved to the United States to take up a teaching position at UCLA. From then until his death in 1980, he published exclusively in English, and all of his books dealt with Zen Buddhism (Thích Thiên-Ân 1970, 1971, 1975a). Two of these books, *Zen Buddhism: Awareness in Action* (1973) and *Zen Philosophy, Zen Practice* (1975b), deal with Zen in a general way, without much reference to Vietnam. *Zen Buddhism: Awareness in Action* uses an illustration from an unspecified "Zen master" in the section on "Meditation: Key to Self-Realization," along with examples from the Christian Bible and the *Avataṃsaka Sutra* [Thích Thiên-Ân 1973, 22]). It was during this time that he wrote his major work on Vietnamese Buddhist history, *Buddhism and Zen in Vietnam in Relation to the Development of Buddhism in Asia*, which for many years was the only major source in English on Vietnamese Buddhism. As Cuong Tu Nguyen describes, it is based uncritically on the *Thiền uyển tập anh* work of Trần Văn Giáp (C. T. Nguyen 1997, 343n54) and "reads like fiction, since it does not coincide at all with any Vietnamese Buddhist reality" (Nguyen and Barber 1998, 309n7). In the prologue, Thích Thiên Ân writes that this book is an expansion on an

earlier booklet that he wrote while teaching in Vietnam but does not specify which (1975a, 12). Presumably it is *Phật-giáo Việt-Nam: Xưa & nay* (Vietnamese Buddhism: In the past and present) (Thích Thiên Ân 1965c) or *Triết-học Zen tư-tưởng Nhật-bản và các nước Á-châu* (Zen Philosophy: Buddhist thought of Japan and Asian Nations) (Thích Thiên Ân 1963b).

12. These observations were published in Vietnamese in 1966 as *Nẻo về của ý* and were eventually translated into English and published as *Fragrant Palm Leaves: Journals 1962–1966* in 1998 (Thích Nhất Hạnh 1998a, 96–97). This is my translation of the Vietnamese original. While it is frequently the case that the English translations of Thích Nhất Hạnh's works introduce elements not in the original, in this case the translation is fairly accurate to the spirit of the original.

13. There are few biographical accounts of Thích Thanh Từ. I rely mainly on the account by Trần Huệ Hiền (2006). This account is repeated virtually word for word on the websites associated with his organization, such as http://www.thuong-chieu.org/uni /HanhTrang/TieuSu.htm and http://www.thientongvietnam.net/thichthanhtu/index .html. The latter lists its source as "Thích Tâm Hạnh—Thiền Viện Trúc Lâm." Another account I have found is from Hân Mẫn and Thông Thiền's *Từ điển Thiền tông Hán Việt* (Sino-Vietnamese dictionary of the Zen sect) (2010, 634). This account, which again adds little, follows the same pattern and often repeats whole sections. It appears to be a condensed version with some alteration of wording but is otherwise the same. The only other account I have found is on Tu Tam Hoang's website, which introduces Trúc Lâm Thiền in English (Hoang 2006). The account by Tu Tam Hoang, a disciple of Thích Thanh Từ living in California, appears to be independent from the others and is not merely a translation. It is not a scholarly account of Thích Thanh Từ but was instead written with the intention of introducing him to potential followers in the West. As such, all my sources must be understood as being basically hagiographical accounts put forward by the Trúc Lâm organization and should be approached critically.

14. According to the website associated with his organization: http://www.thuong -chieu.org/uni/CacThienVien/CacThienVien.htm.

15. The original Vietnamese poem is:

> Non đảnh là nơi thú lắm ai,
> Đó cảnh nhàn du của khách tài.
> Tiếng mõ công phu người tính giấc,
> Chuông hồi văng vẳng quá bi ai!

16. There are a few pagodas by this name in southern Vietnam, one in Ho Chi Minh City, one in Vũng Tàu, and one in Rạch Giá. The latter pagoda is the most likely, as it is closer to his home.

17. The Buddhist Studies School of Southern Vietnam was founded in 1946 by Thích Thiện Hoa, a prominent Buddhist reformer in southern Vietnam (Thích Thắng Hoan n.d.).

18. Vietnam: In Bà Rịa-Vũng Tàu there are Thiền viện Chân (Chơn) Không (for monks), Thiền viện Huệ Chiếu (nuns), Thiền viện Phổ Chiếu (nuns), and Thiền viện Tịch Chiếu (nuns). In Đồng Nai Province, there are Thiền viện Đạo Huệ (monks), Thiền viện Hương Hải (nuns), Thiền viện Hiện Quang (monks), Thiền viện Liễu Đức (nuns), Thiền viện Linh Chiếu (nuns), Thiền viện Thường Chiếu (monks), Thiền viện Tuệ Thông (nuns), and Thiền viện Viên Chiếu (nuns). In Ho Chi Minh City, there is one monastery, Thiền viện Tuệ Quang. The headquarters where Thích Thanh Từ resides is in Đà Lạt and is called Thiền viện Trúc Lâm Phụng Hoàng. In central Vietnam, there is one monastery in Huế called Thiền Viện Trúc Lâm Bạch Mã. In the north, there are four monasteries: Thiền viện Sùng Phúc (monks and nuns) in Hà Nội, Thiền viện Trúc Lâm Yên Tử (monks) at the ancestral

birthplace of Trúc Lâm Zen at Mount Yên Tử, and the newest in Tam Đảo, called Thiền viện Trúc Lâm Tây Thiên (monks), and Thiền viện Trúc Lâm Đại Giác, the most recent in the north, currently being established in Sa Pa.

United States: Thiền Viện Bảo Chơn (New Hampshire), Thiền viện Bồ-Đề (Massachusetts), Thiền Viện Chánh Pháp (Oklahoma), Thiền Viện Chân Tâm (Oklahoma), Thiền tự Chân Nguyên (California), Thiền viện Diệu Nhân (California), Thiền viện Đại Đăng (California), Thiền tự Ngọc Chiếu (California), Thiền tự Vô Ưu (California), Thiền tự Minh Chánh—Vietnamese Buddhist Meditation Congregation (Washington), and Thiền viện Quang Chiếu (Texas).

Canada: Thiền tự Đạo Viên (Québec), Hương Hải Zen Forest (Ontario), and Thiền Tự Tuệ Viên (Ontario).

France: Thiền tự Thường Lạc (Vitry/Seine, France).

Australia: Thiền tự Hỉ Xã—Upeksa Meditation Village (South Australia), Thiền tự Hiện Quang (Victoria), Thiền tự Pháp Loa (Victoria), Thiền tự Tiêu Dao (Victoria), Thiền tự Tuệ Căn (Western Australia), and Thiền Đường Vô Ưu (New South Wales).

19. Although he identified with Trúc Lâm Zen, he did not really know much about Thích Thanh Từ, nor was he particularly interested in the Vietnamese cultural roots of the Zen that he was practicing. For him, the main draw was the teaching of the master at the center and the practice of meditation.

20. In the English translation (*Fragrant Palm Leaves*), Thích Thanh Từ is referred to as "Zen Master" (Thích Nhất Hạnh 19989, 17); however, in the original Vietnamese version, *Nẻo về của ý*, Thích Nhất Hạnh simply refers to him as "Thầy" (Thích Nhất Hạnh [1966] 2006, 16), an honorific commonly used for a senior monk, most correctly translated as "teacher."

21. The date comes from a list of all his travels from the website of Thường Chiếu (Thường Chiếu n.d.).

22. While Trần Nhân Tông was king at the time, the defeat of the Mongols was under the military leadership of Trần Hưng Đạo. The narrative as evoked by the Trúc Lâm organization and Thích Thanh Từ accentuates Trần Nhân Tông's role, but Trần Hưng Đạo is more popularly given credit for defeating the invaders, and Trần Hưng Đạo is consequently memorialized throughout Vietnam to a much greater extent than Trần Nhân Tông, deified as a national hero and saint (*thần*) and even incarnated in possession rituals (Phạm Quỳnh Phương 2009).

23. For Tu Tam Hoang's translation, see Thích Thanh Từ (2000b, 49–50).

24. The Japanese delegates at the World's Parliament of Religions packaged Japanese Buddhism, and particularly Zen, as both uniquely Japanese but also modern and universal, and Suzuki carried on this argument (Snodgrass 2009a, 65).

Chapter Two: The Sùng Phúc Zen Monastery

1. As Kirsten Endres explains, this designation as a "religion" is actually a recent label constructed by Vietnamese folklorists (Endres 2011, 12–13).

2. The principal resemblance is the fact that there is a meditation hall at all. However, the configuration on the inside differs from the meditation halls described by Welch (1973, 47–88) or the meditation hall at Foguangshan in Taiwan (described by Chandler 2004, 15–16), where practitioners face the center of the room rather than the front, as at Sùng Phúc Monastery.

3. The historical information on Sùng Phúc comes from Hân Mẫn and Thông Thiền (2010, 586–587), which is the only published account I have come across, along with a description of its history on Sùng Phúc's website (Thiền viện Sùng Phúc 2008) and an

interview with the current abbot, Thích Tâm Thuần (conducted in December 2011), who has been resident there since 1999.

4. See Malarney (2002) for a description of the easing of restrictions in the post-Renovation period and the effect it has had on religious renewal in a village in northern Vietnam.

5. The process by which this agreement came about is unclear. The official Trúc Lâm version is that they were welcomed there. Rumors from some locals is that the takeover by the Trúc Lâm organization was not universally accepted. One man of around forty whom I have known for several years and whose home village is beside Xuân Đỗ Thượng cannot speak about Sùng Phúc without seething with anger. He claims that the villagers were tricked into giving over their local pagoda to an organization that does not, now, serve their ritual needs. He also charged that the antique statuary of the old pagoda had been sold off. I was not in a position to explore the truth of these charges, so they remain just hearsay. However, they do indicate that the transition from local pagoda to Zen monastery whose focus is regional, national, and international (but not local) has not been entirely smooth and unanimously accepted.

6. The name Sùng Phúc (崇福) can be translated as "lofty fortune," "noble luck," or "sublime blessings." However, as the name is in Sino-Vietnamese, no lay follower was able to explain its meaning to me. I did not ask the abbot, and so I am unsure why they chose this name. However, it may be that it was named after a temple elsewhere. Possibilities include Chongfu Temple in Shanxi Province, China; Chongfu Temple in Jiangxi Province, China, an important temple of the Caodong Chan sect; Chongfu Temple in Zhejiang Province, China; Chongfu Temple in Fujian Province, China (Hân Mẫn and Thông Thiền 2010, 587–588); or Sōfukuji Temple in Nagasaki, Japan, associated with the Ōbaku Zen sect. However, as far as I was able to determine, there is no connection with any of these temples.

The translations of the terms "tự" and "viện" as temple and monastery, respectively, are rough, as they can be used to convey a range of meanings. In Chinese, sì (寺; tự) can be used to designate a kind of government office in imperial China as well as a Buddhist monastery or temple. Yuan (院; viện) similarly can be an institution or public building or a courtyard. I was told by one monk at Sùng Phúc that the change in designation was given in recognition of its expanded size, a conclusion that is supported by Hân Mẫn and Thông Thiền (2010, 587).

7. In Vietnamese, they read "Sùng Phúc hoằng khai vô nhất vật, Trúc Lâm quảng giáo bất nhị môn"; and "Thưởng chiếu vô ngôn ngôn bất tuyệt / Chân không bất biến biến hằng sa." Thưởng Chiếu and Chân Không were Vietnamese Zen masters; they are also the names of two of the first monasteries that Thích Thanh Từ founded. Many thanks to Phạm Thị Hường and my old friend Choi Byung Wook (최병욱) for their help translating this.

8. His biography (in Vietnamese) can be found at Giác ngộ Online (2009).

9. The images and the book (Tinh Vân [Hsing Yun] 2011) originate with Fo Guang Shan, an important international modernist organization based in Taiwan (see Chandler 2004).

10. I haven't found any information about a Zen Master Minh Chánh in the books I usually use to identify Vietnamese Buddhist figures. The only reference I found online is from the website of the Thường Chiếu Monastery, a prominent Trúc Lâm monastery in southern Vietnam (nguyen 2008).

11. Ở đời vui đạo hãy tùy duyên
Đói đến thì ăn mệt ngủ liền
Trong Nhà có báu thôi tìm kiếm
Đối cảnh không tâm chớ hỏi thiền
Translation by Nguyen Giac (2010, 54)

12. One may question the authenticity of these relics. For our purposes, the claim itself, rather than its veracity, is the only significant point of interest.

13. *Nhân dân* newspaper wrote that work began on the new monastery on May 10, 2015 (*Báo nhân dân* 2015). It is not clear to me whether it was built with the intention of serving/converting the large ethnic minority community that lives in the region (the growing ethnic Kinh [Vietnamese] settlers who have moved there) or was intended as a pilgrimage center for followers from all over Vietnam and abroad. I suspect that funding imperatives mean that it is mostly the latter, though their motivation may actually be toward bringing Zen to the locals.

14. The liturgy is found in two books sold in the bookstore at Sùng Phúc (see Thích Thanh Từ 2009a; and Thích Tỉnh Thiền 2010, 7–27). It is standard for all Zen centers and monasteries in the Trúc Lâm organization and can be found on many sites online, for example the website of Thường Chiếu Thiền Monastery (in Đồng Nai Province) at <http://thuongchieu.net/index.php?option=com_content&view=article&id=22&Itemid=320>). It is also translated by one of Thích Thanh Từ's followers in the United States and appears on the English language website dedicated to Trúc Lâm at http://www.truclamvietzen.net/Rites.htm and in a self-published book called *The Practicing Method of Vietnamese Zen* (Thích Thanh Từ 2002b, 47–61).

15. Thích Khế Định is a charismatic young monk who seems to be often traveling away from his home monastery, Thiền viện Thường Chiếu in Đồng Nai Province (near Ho Chi Minh City). He has been to Australia, the United States, and Canada, and during the time I was at Sùng Phúc, he went to India. The bookstore has CDs and DVDs of him giving Dharma talks, and several of his lectures can be found on YouTube. During the time that I was at Sùng Phúc he gave the majority of these lectures.

16. As with the Penitence Rite, the meditation rites can be found in *Các nghi lễ trong Thiền viện* (Monastery rites) (Thích Tỉnh Thiền 2010, 138–145), the English translation being *The Practicing Method of Vietnamese Zen* (Thích Thanh Từ 2002b).

17. I never saw it being used harder than a tap, whereas in Rinzai temples in Japan, they strike quite hard with it.

18. The verse goes, "*Nguyện đem công đức này, hướng về khắp tất cả, đệ tử và chúng sanh, đều trọn thành Phật đạo*" (Thích Tỉnh Thiền 2010b, 145).

19. *Áo dài* are considered the Vietnamese national dress and are principally worn by women. They consist of a long, tight-fitting tunic with a split down the sides worn over loose-fitting silk trousers.

20. For more on heightened emotion in festivals, see Chau (2006, chapter 8).

21. I witnessed five weddings during the three months I was there.

22. The term "engaged Buddhism" was coined by Thích Nhất Hạnh, though he credits the founder of Trúc Lâm, King Trần Nhân Tông, with being the original practitioner of engaged Buddhism (Hunt-Perry and Fine 2000, 36–37).

23. For example, *Tư tưởng*, published at Văn Hạnh University (the reformist university for monastics in Saigon), continued at least until May 1974, eleven months before the fall of Saigon; *Từ quang*, published at Xá Lợi Pagoda (a center of Buddhist political activism), published at least until March 1975; *Hoằng pháp*, published by the Unified Buddhist Church of Vietnam (the main activist Buddhist organization in the south), had at least three special issues in 1974.

24. Mô is a shortened form of Nam Mô, the first part of the *nianfo*, "Nam Mô Phật Bổn Sư Thích Ca Mâu Ni," and roughly means "hail to the Buddha."

25. By "identity projects," I am borrowing from R. W. Connell, who uses the term "gender projects" to underline the ongoing nature of identity construction (1987).

26. For Tu Tam Hoang's translation, see Thích Thanh Từ (2000b, 33).

27. She is referring to the practice of reading a petition (*sớ*) to the gods or buddhas for their blessings, which includes the name of participants who have made donations.

28. This interaction also seems to indicate that a level of competition may exist between Buddhist masters.

29. For Tu Tam Hoang's translation, see Thích Thanh Từ (2000b, 32–33).

Chapter Three: Secular Buddhism

1. He seems to be referring to a passage in the *Ugga Sutta* of the Aṅguttara Nikāya (V. Tăng Chi Bộ Kinh) that lists these five dangers to one's wealth in order to underline the impermanence of wealth in comparison to the six "treasures":

> That is treasure, Ugga. I don't say that it's not. And that treasure is open to fire, floods, kings, thieves, & hateful heirs. But these seven treasures are not open to fire, flood, kings, thieves, or hateful heirs. Which seven? The treasure of conviction, the treasure of virtue, the treasure of conscience, the treasure of concern, the treasure of listening, the treasure of generosity, the treasure of discernment. These, Ugga, are the seven treasures that are not open to fire, flood, kings, thieves, or hateful heirs. (AN 7.7—Thanissaro Bhikkhu 2000)

2. I have written about this extensively in *The Buddha Side* (2012, chapter 4).

3. In my experience, it is usually a volunteer lay woman, though I have seen nuns do it. I have never seen a monk or lay man fulfill this role.

4. This results, for example, in the Vietnamese distinction between belief (*tín ngưỡng*) and religion (*tôn giáo*), a distinction that has legal implications. While the law recognizes religion, belief holds a more ambiguous position, while superstition (*mê tín*), the label given to the deceptive effervescence, is viewed negatively and has been subject to periodic crackdowns.

5. I should note that this does not mean that all those who become involved in Trúc Lâm turn their backs on devotional forms of Buddhism; nor are they expected to do so. Some older women, particularly, continue to chant sutras and take part in rituals at other pagodas while simultaneously taking up meditation and other activities at Sùng Phúc. Nonetheless, at Sùng Phúc, there is a constant pressure to move away from views of Buddhism that see the world as enchanted.

6. For another translation, see Thích Thanh Từ (2000b, 39).

7. As academics, we do significant symbolic violence against many who are already marginalized if we champion the assertions of the powerful against the weak without assuming a more objective understanding of what constitutes Buddhism (Soucy 2009). Another important reason to not dismiss these supplicants is that it is largely their donations that have supported Buddhist institutions, and consequently, they are responsible for the continued existence of Buddhism in Vietnam (and likely everywhere). It therefore seems misguided to dismiss them as being anything other than central.

8. A number of the expressions here are unusual, but this translation is a fair approximation.

9. The statues of the earth god (Ông Địa) were common in the south but only started to gain popularity in Hanoi in the last twenty years or so.

10. "*Tâm*" is a multivalent term that can mean heart, feelings, mind, or soul (Bùi Phụng 1995, 1448).

11. I discuss the interpretations of the Penitence Rite at regular pagodas at length elsewhere (Soucy 2012, 165–176).

12. *Chúng con nguyện suốt đời quy y Phật, quy y Pháp, quy y Tăng.*

- *Quy y Phật là: Chúng con trọn đời tôn thờ kính trọng, tu theo đức Phật Thích Ca Mâu Ni, là bậc thầy giác ngộ sáng suốt của chúng con.*
- *Quy y Pháp là: Chúng con trọn đời tôn thờ kính trọng, tu theo chánh pháp từ kim khẩu đức Phật nói ra.*

- *Quy y Tăng là: Chúng con trọn đời tôn thờ kính trọng, tu theo những Tăng sĩ tu hành đúng chánh pháp của Như Lai.*
  * *Quy y Phật rồi, chúng con không kính trọng tu theo Trời, thần, quỷ, vật.*
  * *Quy y Pháp rồi, chúng con không kính trọng tu theo ngoại đạo, tà giáo.*
  * *Quy y Tăng rồi, chúng con không kính trọng, làm thân với bạn dữ, nhóm ác.*

13.
- *Tự quy-y Phật, xin nguyện chúng sanh, thể—theo đạo cả lòng vô thượng.*
- *Tự quy y Pháp, xin nguyện chúng sanh thấu rõ kinh tạng, * trí huệ như biển.*
- *Tự quy y Tăng, xin nguyện chúng sanh, quản lý đại chúng, Hết thảy không ngại.*

14. See Thích Thanh Từ (2002e, 33) for another translation.

Chapter Four: Nationalism and Internationalism

1. See Nguyễn Đại Đồng's (2008) description of the journals that were published by the reformist associations in Vietnam. The publication of this material in *quốc ngữ* should be seen in the context of the broader literacy movement (Marr 1981; McHale 2004).

2. Malcolm Browne won the World Press Photo of the Year in 1963 for his image of Thích Quảng Đức seated serenely on the street engulfed by flames. The image has become an iconic image of the Vietnam War.

3. Many of the most prominent monks in the diaspora were also products of these schools (Soucy 2014, 49). Miller (2014) argues that the clash between the Buddhists and the Diệm regime was rooted in differing visions of Vietnam's future, with the Buddhist view having been formulated during the reform period in the first half of the twentieth century.

4. Thích Nhất Hạnh wrote frequently about this in the 1950s as editor of the magazine *Phật giáo Việt Nam* (Vietnamese Buddhism).

5. The Buddhist uprising in 1966 was put down by Prime Minister Nguyễn Cao Kỳ, effectively ending Buddhist unrest in South Vietnam for the duration of the war

6. In this, he is referring to entering "Zen gates" (*Thiền môn*) as a euphemism for following a path, so the sentence is essentially saying that one can be confident of the consistency of any particular sect to be true to its doctrine.

7. Thích Minh Châu is the rector of the Vietnam Buddhist Research Institute in Ho Chi Minh City (http://www.saigon.com/~anson/ebud/personality/person-00.htm).

8. For Tu Tam Hoang's translation, see Thích Thanh Từ (2000b, 50–51).

9. For an alternate translation, see Thích Thanh Từ (2002e, 50).

10. Translated by Tu Tam Hoang under the title *Truc Lam Founder: Two Stages of Life*, Thích Thanh Từ (2005).

11. The process by which this monastery was established is illustrative of the local, national, and global tensions present in the organization. While the lay Buddhists and monastics expressed pride in the monastery at Yên Tử, it appears that there was some tension at the local level. The unconfirmed story that I was told was that a few years ago, the local council at Yên Tử decided that they wanted to renovate their local pagoda. They initially approached a wealthy woman from Hanoi who had been a generous donor. The woman expressed a willingness to donate statues for the interior but was unwilling to be involved in financing building itself, as she wanted to avoid the complex process of obtaining government permissions. Without a patron, the local council turned to the Trúc Lâm organization, which had previously expressed interest in the pagoda. The organization brought in an army of construction workers from southern Vietnam to quickly build the monumental new structures. For the first weeks, there were attempts to include locals in the meditation sessions. Not long after, however, the locals realized that their pagoda had been taken over by an organization from the south that had no intention of fulfilling some of the expected

ritual roles of local pagodas. The new Trúc Lâm Monastery refused to conduct funerals, for example, though they would chant sutras for the dead at the temple. This left the people in the area bitter that their local pagoda was no longer theirs and that the new monastery was unresponsive to their needs. I have not had occasion to corroborate the story, but it nevertheless illustrates some of the tensions between local practices and new forms of Buddhism that are not always responsive to local needs. Thanks to Đào Thế Đức for sharing this story from his research on pilgrims at Yên Tử.

12. The title of the poem is "Vịnh chùa Yên-tử":

Chênh vênh
Yên-tử đứng mà trông,
Lãm thắng phen này thỏa ước mong.
Nước trắng lưng đèo treo suối Giá,
Mây xanh đỉnh núi ngất chùa Đồng.
Bia phong tỏ tích ba rừng trúc,
Bóng rợp thuyền-môn mấy rặng thông.
Lặn suối chèo non quên khó nhọc,
Tìm tòi muốn biết cảnh hư không.

13. For Tu Tam Hoang's translation see Thích Thanh Từ (2000b, 59–60)

14. For Tu Tam Hoang's translation, see Thích Thanh Từ (2000b, 45).

15. An overseas Vietnamese informant from Australia told me in 2011 that many overseas Vietnamese are suspicious of Thích Thanh Từ. His prominent position in the state-controlled Vietnamese Buddhist sangha and his seeming ability to travel overseas at will suggest a level of complicity with the Communist Party that does not sit well with the diasporic community.

16. This information comes from a website associated with his organization: http://www.thuong-chieu.org/uni/HanhTrang/TieuSu.htm.

Chapter Five: Zen Women

1. This description comes close to the way C. T. Nguyen (1997, 94) and McHale (2004, 146–150) describe Vietnamese Buddhist practice in both medieval Vietnam and in the twentieth century, respectively.

2. I am using "props" in the sense used by Erving Goffman (1956), as an object used to support a person's social role.

3. I do not intend this analysis to be pejorative in any way. Indeed, I see this performativity as very human and normal. I could just as easily write about this book's being part of my academic performativity in much the same way.

4. See Nedostup (2009, 8–11) for a discussion on the way older categories of orthodoxy and heterodoxy were folded into modernist distinctions between religion and superstition.

5. This can be seen in the media, for example by the frequent attention given to the Zen "tradition" at Mount Yên Tử, the government's recognition of it as a Special National Relic (Ministry of Culture, Sports and Tourism 2013), and subsequent application to UNESCO for world heritage status in 2014. In the application, Trúc Lâm is described as "a pure Vietnamese Zen Buddhism which focuses on inner feelings but at the same time enters into life with a forgiveness approach. Trúc Lâm aims to connect religion to life in a positive way and builds a close link to true patriotism" (UNESCO 2014).

6. These texts were transcriptions of messages from the spirit of Hồ Chí Minh obtained through spirit channeling done by the founder of the sect.

Chapter Six: Zen Men

1. This was, and to some extent still is, true of other forms of religious expression. Of particular note is the close association between homosexuality and spirit mediumship (Blanc 2005, 665).

2. Philip Taylor notes that in the Renovation period, many of the religiosities that were excluded as superstition were rebranded as folk beliefs, and "ignorant" practices became "culture" to serve a nationalist agenda of claiming distinction (2003, 389–390).

3. This view has been around for a while, at least since the early part of the twentieth century (Marr 1981, 345).

4. The meaning of "*có tâm*" is difficult to translate. According to Bùi Phụng's Vietnamese English dictionary (1995, 1449), "*tâm*" can mean heart, feelings, mind, soul, or center. However, in the Buddhist context, people often talk about having heart with the Buddha (*có tâm với Phật*), meaning a heartfelt or sincere belief in the Buddha or an affinity with his teachings that implied a karmic destiny.

Chapter Seven: Zen for All Ages

1. For a review of research done on aging and spirituality, see Dalby (2006).

2. According to the global catalogue WorldCat, *Đạo Phật với tuổi trẻ* is the earliest recorded publication from Thích Thanh Từ.

3. The two other essays are *Vài nét chính luân lý Phật giáo* (Some aspects of Buddhist morality), first published as a book in 1967, and *Phật giáo trong mạch sống dân tộc* (Buddhism in the pulse of the people), published in Saigon in 1966 by Lá Bối, the press established by Thích Nhất Hạnh. Both dates are according to WorldCat.

4. He is now the abbot of a new Trúc Lâm monastery being built in Sa Pa, called Thiền viện Trúc Lâm Đại Giác.

5. There is a much stronger pattern of youth involvement in Buddhism in southern Vietnam. Particularly through the war period, in the 1960s and early 1970s, young people were very involved in Buddhist protests and relief work (Nguyen-Marshall 2015). It is not clear from existing research the extent to which their involvement in Buddhist-led political and social activism was closely tied to a sense of religious purpose. The Buddhist Scouts were founded in the 1960s and were very active during the war period. They have remained active in the diaspora as well, with many branches at pagodas in North America. However, until very recently, there was no comparable movement in northern Vietnam.

6. Some of these are at Đình Quán Pagoda, Quán Sứ Pagoda, Lý Quốc Sư Pagoda, and Bằng Pagoda, among others.

7. The tabs on the Sùng Phúc website are Home (*Trang chủ*), Introduction (*Giới thiệu*), Study Schedule (*Lịch tu học*), News (*Tin tức*); the Zen Sect (*Thiền tông*), Buddhist Studies (*Tu học*); Zen for Young People (*Thiền với tuổi trẻ*); and Buddhism in Everyday Life (*Đạo Phật với đời Sống*) (Thích Minh Quang, Chánh Chí Bình, and Chánh Phúc Hiếu 2016).

8. Viewed November 3, 2019. Their account is titled "Thiền Viện Trúc Lâm Sùng Phúc."

9. Of the first one hundred images, there are twelve photos of children and thirty-eight of youths (late teens to early twenties), while there are only sixteen images of middle-aged people. Thirty-one of the images are of females, while only eight are of males. The remainder of the images are of scenery of the Sùng Phúc precinct (twenty-eight), weddings (four), food (three), quirky images (four), and unrelated images with aphorisms (two).

10. Vạn Hạnh helped Lý Thái Tổ (974–1028) ascend the throne to start the Lý dynasty. Vạn Hạnh was known as having uncanny powers of precognition but was recast in the *Thiền uyển tập anh* as being a Zen master (C. T. Nguyen 1997, 78).

11. A monk told me that the youth jamboree, because of its modest size, needed only district permission, but if they had organized a larger event, they would have had to get permission from the Hanoi municipal government.

12. I am not sure what the activities had been the previous afternoon and evening. However, I was told that they had all awakened at 3:30 a.m. to meditate for an hour and a half.

13. *Pháp Phật sâu mầu chẳng gì hơn,*
Trăm ngàn muôn kiếp khó được gặp.
Nay con nghe thấy vâng gìn giữ,
Nguyện hiểu nghĩa chơn Đức Thế Tôn.
This verse is part of the regular Penitence Rite (Nghi thức Sám hối và Tụng giới) performed at Sùng Phúc and at other Trúc Lâm temples (Thích Thanh Từ 2009a, 10).

14. In Vietnamese it was *"Mở tâm bồ đề để hòa thông vạn vật, Bày muôn ngàn phép để giác ngộ chúng sinh."*

15. *"Tâm bất biến giữa dòng đời vạn biến."*

16. *"Thấy bạn hay đi chùa, cha mẹ bạn bắt đầu lo lắng và cho rằng chùa chiền không phải là nơi phù hợp với tuổi trẻ mà chỉ phù hợp với những người lớn tuổi đã về hưu hoặc có thời gian rảnh rỗi. Bạn sẽ làm như thế nào để cha mẹ bạn hiểu và ủng hộ bạn?"*

17. The story was carried widely, for example, in *Người lao động* [Workers] (Trọng Đức 2014) and in the English online version of *Tuoi tre News* (2014).

18. For a deeper description of lộc, see Soucy (2012, chapter 4).

19. For an alternate English translation, see Thích Thanh Từ (2002d, 87).

Conclusion

1. For the announcements, see issues 252–254, 256, and 258 of *Tạp chí Phật học từ quang* (Merciful light Buddhist magazine) (1974).

Bibliography

||||||||

Almond, Philip C. 1988. *The British Discovery of Buddhism.* Cambridge: Cambridge University Press.

Anderson, Benedict. 1983. *Imagined Communities: Reflections on the Origin and Spread of Nationalism.* London: Verso.

Appadurai, Arjun. 1996. *Modernity at Large: Cultural Dimensions of Globalization.* Minneapolis: University of Minnesota Press.

Báo nhân dân [The people's newspaper]. 2015. "Work Starts on Trúc Lâm Dai Giac Zen Monastery in Sapa." May 11. http://en.nhandan.com.vn/society/item/3335702-work-starts-on-truc-lam-dai-giac-zen-monastery-in-sapa.html.

Baumann, Martin. 2002. "Protective Amulets and Awareness Techniques: How to Make Sense of Buddhism in the West." In *Westward Dharma: Buddhism Beyond Asia,* edited by Charles S. Prebish and Martin Baumann, 51–65. Berkeley: University of California Press.

Bechert, Heinz. 1994. "Buddhistic Modernism: Present Situation and Current Trends." In *Buddhism in the Year 2000: International Conference Proceedings,* 251–260. Bangkok: Dhamakaya Foundation.

Bechert, Heinz, and Vu Duy-Tu. 1976. "Buddhism in Vietnam." In *The Cultural, Political, and Religious Significance of Buddhism in the Modern World,* edited by Henry Dumoulin, 186–193. New York: Collier Books.

Beyer, Peter. 2006. *Religions in Global Society.* Abingdon: Routledge.

Bích Liên. 1932a. "Thiền-tông" [The Zen school]. *Từ bi âm* [The voice of compassion] 18 (September 15): 16–21.

———. 1932b. "Thiền-tông" [The Zen school]. *Từ bi âm* [The voice of compassion] 19 (October 1): 12–18.

Birnbaum, Raoul. 2003. "Buddhist China at the Century's Turn." *China Quarterly* 174 (June): 428–450.

Blanc, Marie Eve. 2005. "Social Construction of Male Homosexualities in Vietnam. Some Keys to Understanding Discrimination and Implications for HIV Prevention Strategy." *International Social Science Journal* 57 (186): 661–673.

Broughton, Bernard L. 1940. "Vì sao tôi tin Phật-giáo" [Why I believe in Buddhism]. *Đuốc tuệ* [The torch of wisdom] 142–143 (October 15–November 1): 3–22.

Bùi Đức Triệu. 1935a. "Truyện Trúc Lâm Tam Tổ" [The story of the first three patriarchs of Trúc Lâm]. *Đuốc tuệ* [The torch of wisdom] 3 (December 24): 7–16.

———. 1935b. "Truyện Trúc Lâm Tam Tổ" [The story of the first three patriarchs of Trúc Lâm]. *Đuốc tuệ* [The torch of wisdom] 3 (December 31): 7–12.

Bùi Phụng. 1995. *Từ điển Việt-Anh* [Vietnamese-English dictionary]. Hanoi: Nhà xuất bản Giáo dục; Công ty Phát hành Sách Hà Nội.

Chandler, Stuart. 2004. *Establishing a Pure Land on Earth: The Foguang Buddhist Perspective on Modernization and Globalization.* Honolulu: University of Hawai'i Press.

Chatterjee, Partha. 1993. *Nationalist Thought and the Colonial World: A Derivative Discourse.* London: Zed Books.

Chau, Adam Yuet. 2006. *Miraculous Response: Doing Popular Religion in Contemporary China.* Stanford: Stanford University Press.

Chen Jidong. 2009. "The Transmission of the Jōdo Shinshū Doctrine to China: The Discovery of the 'Nanjingyu Shuojiao' and its Significance." *Eastern Buddhist* 40 (1–2): 139–150.

Ch'en, Kenneth. 1972. *Buddhism in China: A Historical Survey.* Princeton, NJ: Princeton University Press.

Choi, Horim. 2007. "Ritual Revitalization and Nativist Ideology in Hanoi." In *Modernity and Re-enchantment: Religion in Post-revolutionary Vietnam,* edited by Philip Taylor, 1–56. Singapore: Institute of Southeast Asian Studies.

CHUNG. 1935. "Truyện Ma-Đăng-Già" [The story of Matanga]. *Đuốc tuệ* [The torch of wisdom] 2 (December 17): 18–22.

Cleary, J. C. 1991. "Buddhism and Popular Religion in Medieval Vietnam." *Journal of the American Academy of Religion* 59 (1): 93–118.

Coleman, James William. 2001. *The New Buddhism: The Western Transformation of an Ancient Tradition.* New York: Oxford University Press.

Connell, Robert. 1987. *Gender and Power: Society, the Person and Sexual Politics.* Stanford: Stanford University Press.

Cox, Pamela. 2012. "History and Global Criminology: (Re)Inventing Delinquency in Vietnam." *British Journal of Criminology* 52:17–31.

Đ. N. T. 1936–1939. "Việt-Nam Thiền tông thế hệ (Theo sách *Thiền-uyển tập anh ngữ lục*)" [The Vietnamese Zen Lineage (According to the Text *Thiền-uyển tập anh ngữ lục*)]. *Đuốc tuệ* [The torch of wisdom], serialized: no. 49 (November 17, 1936): 18–22; no. 52 (December 22, 1936): 24–28; no. 58 (April 1, 1937): 7–10; no. 60 (May 1, 1937): 5–11; no. 61 (May 15, 1937): 8–13; no. 62 (June 1, 1937): 7–11; no. 63 (June 15, 1937): 14–18; no. 64 (July 1, 1937): 20–23; no. 65 (July 15, 1937): 7–11; no. 66 (August 1, 1937): 18–21; no. 67 (August 15, 1937): 12–16; no. 68 (September 1, 1937): 9–14; no. 69 (September 15, 1937): 21–25; no. 70 (October 1, 1937): 12–16; no. 71 (October 15, 1937): 14–17; no. 74 (December 1, 1937): 25–18; no. 75 (December 15, 1937): 36–37; no. 76 (January 1, 1938): 18–23; no. 77 (January 15, 1938): 11–14 ; no. 78 (February 1, 1938): 22–24; no. 79 (February 15, 1938): 11–15; no. 81 (March 15, 1938): 24–26; no. 82 (April 1, 1938): 8–11; no. 83 (March 15, 1938): 15–18; no. 84 (May 1, 1938): 35–36; no. 87 (July 15, 1938): 31–34; no. 90 (August 1, 1938): 22–25; no. 91 (August 15, 1938): 35–39; no. 93 (September 15, 1938): 21–26; no. 94 (October 1, 1938): 18–20; no. 95 (October 15, 1938): 18–21; no. 97 (November 15, 1938): 8–10; no. 101 (January 15, 1939): 16–18; no. 105 (April 1, 1939): 8–12; no. 106 (April 15, 1939): 22–24; no. 111 (July 15, 1939): 17–18; no. 114

(August 15, 1939): 10–11; no. 116 (September 15, 1939): 21–23; no. 118 (October 15, 1939): 5–8; no. 119 (November 1, 1939): 5–8; no. 120 (November 15, 1939): 13–15.

Dalby, Padmaprabha. 2006. "Is There a Process of Spiritual Change or Development Associated with Ageing? A Critical Review of Research." *Aging & Mental Health* 10 (1): 4–12.

Đạo Phật ngày nay [Buddhism today]. 2012. "Đại Đức Thích Giác Nghĩa và việc lớn đầu tiên ở Trường Sa" [Reverend Thích Giác Nghĩa and the first great work at Trường Sa]. May 16. http://www.daophatngaynay.com/vn/phatgiao-vn/con-nguoi-vn/10992-Dai-duc-Thich-Giac-Nghia-va-viec-lon-dau-tien-o-Truong-Sa.html.

DeVido, Elise. 2007. "Buddhism for This World: The Buddhist Revival in Vietnam, 1920–51 and its Legacy." In *Modernity and Re-enchantment: Religion in Post-revolutionary Vietnam*, edited by Philip Taylor, 250–296. Singapore: Institute of Southeast Asian Studies.

———. 2009. "The Influence of Chinese Master Taixu on Buddhism in Vietnam." *Journal of Global Buddhism* 10:413–458. http://www.globalbuddhism.org/jgb/index.php/jgb/article/view/95/108.

Do, Hien Duc. 2006. "Reproducing Vietnam in America: San Jose's Perfect Harmony Temple." In *A Nation of Religions: The Politics of Pluralism in Multireligious America*, edited by Stephen Prothero, 79–93. Chapel Hill: University of North Carolina Press.

Do, Thien. 2003. *Vietnamese Supernaturalism: Views from the Southern Area*. London: RoutledgeCurzon.

Dorais, L. 2006. "Buddhism in Quebec." In *Buddhism in Canada*, edited by B. Matthews, 120–141. New York: Routledge.

Dror, Olga, trans. 2002. *Opusculum de Sectis apund Sinenses et Tunkinenses—A Small Treatise on the Sects among the Chinese and Tonkinese*. Ithaca, NY: Cornell University Press.

Đuốc tuệ [The torch of wisdom]. 1935. "Công việc tiến hành của Hội Phật-giáo" [Work carried out by the Buddhist Association]. *Đuốc tuệ* [The torch of wisdom] 4 (December 31): 31.

Dương Quốc An. 2004. *Phật giáo và sức khỏe* [Buddhism and health]. Hồ Chí Minh City: Nhà xuất bản Tổng hợp Thành phố Hồ Chí Minh.

Durand, Maurice. 1959. "Introduction du bouddhisme au Viêt-Nam." *France-Asie* (February–June: 797–800.

Dutton, George E., Jayne S. Werner, and John K. Whitmore, eds. 2012. *Sources of Vietnamese Tradition*. New York: Columbia University Press.

Eisenstadt, S. N. 2000. "Multiple Modernities." *Daedalus* 129 (1): 1–29.

Endres, Kirsten W. 2011. *Performing the Divine: Mediums, Markets and Modernity in Urban Vietnam*. Copenhagen: NIAS Press.

Fan, Peilei, Zutao Ouyang, Dinh Duong Nguyen, Thi Thuy Hang Nguyen, Hogeun Park, and Jiquan Chen. 2019. "Urbanization, Economic Development, Environmental and Social Changes in Transitional Economies: Vietnam after Doi Moi." *Landscape and Urban Planning* 187:145–155.

Fields, Rick. 1981. *How the Swans Came to the Lake: A Narrative History of Buddhism in America*. Boston: Shambhala.

Frisk, Liselotte. 2012. "The Practice of Mindfulness: From Buddhism to Secular Mainstream in a Post-secular Society." *Scripta Instituti Donneriani Aboensis* 24:48–61.

Geertz, Clifford. 1966. "Religion as a Cultural System." In *Anthropological Approaches to the Study of Religion*, edited by M. Banton, 1–46. London: Tavistock.

Giác ngộ Online [Enlightenment online]. 2009. "Tiểu sử Cố Hòa Thượng Thích Thiện Hoa (1918–1973)" [Biography of the most venerable Thích Thiện Hoa (1918–1973)]. January 18. http://www.giacngo.vn/lichsu/2009/01/18/5BC411/.

Gildow, Douglas Matthew. 2005. "Flesh Bodies, Stiff Corpses, and Gathered Gold: Mummy Worship, Corpse Processing, and Mortuary Ritual in Contemporary Taiwan." *Journal of Chinese Religions* 33:1–37.

Gildow, Douglas, and Marcus Bingenheimer. 2002. "Buddhist Mummification in Taiwan: Two Case Studies." *Asia Major*, 3rd series, 15 (2): 87–127.

Gimello, Robert M. 2004. "Icon and Incantation: The Goddess Zhunti and the Role of Images in the Occult Buddhism of China." In *Images in Asian Religions: Texts and Contexts*, edited by Phyllis Granoff and Koichi Shinohara, 225–255. Vancouver: University of British Columbia Press.

Goffman, Erving. 1956. *The Presentation of Self in Everyday Life*. Edinburgh: University of Edinburgh, Social Sciences Research Centre.

Guruge, Ananda, ed. 1965. *Return to Righteousness: A Collection of Speeches, Essays and Letters of the Anagarika Dharmapala*. Columbo: The Anagarika Dharmapala Birth Centenary Committee and the Ministry of Education and Cultural Affairs.

Hallisey, Charles. 1995. "Roads Taken and Not Taken in the Study of Theravāda Buddhism." In *Curators of the Buddha: The Study of Buddhism under Colonialism*, edited by Donald S. Lopez Jr., 31–61. Chicago: University of Chicago Press.

Han, Chenxing. 2021. *Be the Refuge: Raising the Voices of Asian American Buddhists*. Berkeley, CA: North Atlantic Books.

Hân Mẫn and Thông Thiền. 2010. *Từ điển Thiền Tông Hán Việt* [Sino-Vietnamese dictionary of the Zen sect]. Ho Chi Minh City: Nhà xuất bản Văn hóa Sài Gòn.

Hansen, Valerie. 1990. *Changing Gods in Medieval China, 1127–1276*. Princeton, NJ: Princeton University Press.

Harding, John S. 2008. *Mahāyāna Phoenix: Japan's Buddhists at the 1893 World's Parliament of Religions*. New York: Peter Lang.

Harding, John S., Victor Sōgen Hori, and Alexander Soucy, eds. 2020. *Buddhism in the Global Eye: Beyond East and West*. London: Bloomsbury Academic.

Hickey, Gerald Cannon. 1987. "The Vietnamese Village through Time and War." *Vietnam Forum* 10:1–25.

Higgins, Winton. 2012. "The Coming of Secular Buddhism: A Synoptic View." *Journal of Global Buddhism* 13:109–126.

Hoang, Tu Tam. 2000. "To the Readers." In *My Whole Life*, by Thich Thanh Tu, translated by Tu Tam Hoang, 9–10. Westminster, CA: Tu Tam Hoang.

———. 2006. "Zen Master Thích Thanh Từ." *Vietnamese Zen by Zen Master Thích Thanh Từ.* http://www.truclamvietzen.net/MasterTTT.htm.

Humphreys, Christmas. 1968. *Sixty Years of Buddhism in England (1907–1967): A History and a Survey*. London: Buddhist Society.

Hunt-Perry, Patricia, and Lyn Fine. 2000. "All Buddhism Is Engaged: Thich Nhat Hanh and the Order of Interbeing." In *Engaged Buddhism in the West*, edited by Christopher S. Queen, 35–66. Boston: Wisdom Publications.

Huynh, Thuan. 2000. "Centre for Vietnamese Buddhism: Recreating Home." In *Religion and the New Immigrants: Continuities and Adaptations in Immigrant Congregations,* edited by Helen R. Ebaugh and Janet S. Chafetz, 163–179. Walnut Creek, CA: Altamira.

Jamieson, Neil L. 1986. "The Traditional Village of Vietnam." *Vietnam Forum* 7:88–126.

———. 1993. *Understanding Vietnam.* Berkeley: University of California Press.

Jones, Charles B. 2003. "Transitions in the Practice and Defense of Chinese Pure Land Buddhism." In *Buddhism in the Modern World: Adaptations of an Ancient Tradition,* edited by Steven Heiene and Charles S. Prebish, 125–142. New York: Oxford University Press.

Josephson-Storm, Jason Ā. 2017. *The Myth of Disenchantment: Magic, Modernity, and the Birth of the Human Sciences.* Chicago: University of Chicago Press.

Keith, Charles. 2012. *Catholic Vietnam: A Church from Empire to Nation.* Berkeley: University of California Press.

Kelley, Liam C. 2015. "From Moral Exemplar to National Hero: The Transformations of Trần Hưng Đạo and the Emergence of Vietnamese Nationalism." *Modern Asian Studies* 49 (6): 1963–1993.

Keown, Damien. 2004. *A Dictionary of Buddhism.* Oxford: Oxford University Press.

Kim, Hyun Mee. 2016. "Becoming a City Buddhist among the Young Generation in Seoul." *International Sociology* 31 (4): 450–466.

Kim, Hyun Mee, and Si Hyun Choi. 2016. "Engaged Buddhism for the Curative Self among Young Jungto Buddhist Practitioners in South Korea." *Journal of Korean Religions* 7 (2): 11–36.

King, Sallie B. 1996. "Thích Nhất Hạnh and the Unified Buddhist Church of Vietnam: Nondualism in Action." In *Engaged Buddhism: Buddhist Liberation Movements in Asia,* edited by Christopher S. Queen and Sally B. King, 321–363. Albany: State University of New York Press.

Kleinen, John. 1999. *Facing the Future, Reviving the Past: A Study of Social Change in a Northern Vietnamese Village.* Singapore: Institute of Southeast Asian Studies.

Knott, Kim. 2008. "Spatial Theory and the Study of Religion." *Religion Compass* 2 (6): 1102–1116.

Larsson, Viveca, and Kirsten W. Endres. 2006. "'Children of the Spirits, Followers of a Master': Spirit Mediums in Post-renovation Vietnam." In *Possessed by the Spirits: Mediumship in Contemporary Vietnamese Communities,* edited by Karen Fjelstad and Nguyen Thi Hien, 143–160. Ithaca, NY: Cornell Southeast Asia Program.

Lauser, Andrea. 2015. "Traveling to Yên Tử (North Vietnam): Religious Resurgence, Cultural Nationalism and Touristic Heritage in the Shaping of a Pilgrimage Landscape." *DORISEA Working Paper* 20. https://www.academia.edu/17509262/Traveling_to_Y%C3%AAn_T%E1%BB%AD_North_Vietnam_._Religious_Resurgence_Cultural_Nationalism_and_Touristic_Heritage_in_the_Shaping_of_a_Pilgrimage_Landscape.

Law, Judith. 1991. "The Religious Beliefs and Practices of the Vietnamese Community in Britain." *Community Religions Project Research Paper* (New Series). Leeds: University of Leeds, Department of Theology and Religious Studies.

Lê Cung. 2008. *Phong trào Phật giáo miền Nam Việt Nam năm 1963* [The Buddhist movement in southern Vietnam in 1963]. Huế: Nhà xuất bản Thuận Hóa.

Lê Mạnh Thát. 2002. *Lịch sử Phật giáo Việt Nam, Tập 2: Từ Lý Nam Đế (544) đến Lý Thái Tông (1054)* [The history of Vietnamese Buddhism, Volume 2: From Lý Nam Đế (544) to Lý Thái Tông (1054)]. Ho Chi Minh City: Nhà xuất bản Thành phố Hồ Chí Minh.

Le, Thao N., and Don T. Trieu. 2016. "Feasibility of a Mindfulness-Based Intervention to Address Youth Issues in Vietnam." *Health Promotion International* 31 (2): 470–479.

Lefebvre, Henri. 1991. *The Production of Space*. Malden, MA: Blackwell.

Levering, Miriam L. 1992. "Lin-chi (Rinzai) Chan and Gender: The Rhetoric of Equality and the Rhetoric of Heroism." In *Buddhism, Sexuality and Gender*, edited by J. I. Cabezon, 137–156. Albany: State University of New York Press.

Lopez, Donald S. 2002. "Introduction to *A Modern Buddhist Bible: Essential Readings from East and West*, edited by Donald S. Lopez, vii–xli. Boston: Beacon.

———. 2008. *Buddhism and Science: A Guide for the Perplexed*. Chicago: University of Chicago Press.

Luong, Hy V. 1993. "Economic Reform and the Intensification of Rituals in Two North Vietnamese Villages, 1980–90." In *The Challenge of Reform in Indochina*, edited by B. Ljunggren, 259–291. Cambridge, MA: Harvard Institute for International Development, Harvard University.

———. 2010. *Tradition, Revolution, and Market Economy in a North Vietnamese Village, 1925–2006*. Honolulu: University of Hawai'i Press.

Luu Tuong Quang. 2011. "Changes and Challenges to Vietnamese Buddhism in Australia." In *Buddhism in Australia: Traditions in Change*, edited by Cristina Rocha and Michelle Barker, 134–139. Abingdon: Routledge.

Mai Thọ Truyền. 1959. "Le bouddhisme au Viêt-Nam." *France-Asie* (February–June): 801–810.

Main, Jessica L., and Rongdao Lai. 2013. "Introduction: Reformulating 'Socially Engaged Buddhism' as an Analytical Category." *Eastern Buddhist* 44 (2): 1–34.

Malarney, Shaun Kingsley. 1993. "Ritual and Revolution in Vietnam." PhD diss., University of Michigan, Ann Arbor.

———. 1996. "The Limits of 'State Functionalism' and the Reconstruction of Funerary Ritual in Contemporary Northern Vietnam." *American Ethnologist* 23 (3): 540–560.

———. 1999. "Buddhist Practices in Rural Northern Viêt Nam." In *Liber Amicorum: Mélanges offerts au Professeur Phan Huy Lê*, edited by P. Papin and J. Kleinen, 183–200. Hanoi: Nhà xuất bản Thanh niên.

———. 2002. *Culture, Ritual and Revolution in Vietnam*. Honolulu: University of Hawai'i Press.

Malinowski, Bronislaw. 1948. *Magic, Science and Religion and other Essays*. Boston: Beacon Press.

Marr, David G. 1971. *Vietnamese Anticolonialism: 1885–1925*. Berkeley: University of California Press.

———. 1981. *Vietnamese Tradition on Trial, 1920–1945*. Berkeley: University of California Press.

———. 1997. "Vietnamese Youth in the 1990s." *Vietnam Review* 2:288–354.

Mật-Nguyện, Trúc Lâm. 1934. "Vì sao phải học Phật" [Why study the Buddha]. *Viên âm* [The voice of exposition] 9 (September 1, 1934): 16–24.

Matthews, Bruce. 1992. "The Place of Religion in Vietnam Today." *Buddhist-Christian Studies* 12:65–74.

Mcfadden, Susan H. 1999. "Religion, Personality, and Aging: A Life Span Perspective." *Journal of Personality* 67 (6): 1081–1104.

McHale, Shawn Frederick. 2004. *Print and Power: Confucianism, Communism, and Buddhism in the Making of Modern Vietnam*. Honolulu: University of Hawai'i Press.

McMahan, David L. 2008. *The Making of Buddhist Modernism*. New York: Oxford University Press.

———. 2020. "Buddhism and Global Secularisms." In *Buddhism in the Global Eye: Beyond East and West*, edited by John S. Harding, Victor Sōgen Hori, and Alexander Soucy, 42–55. London: Bloomsbury Academic.

Miller, Edward. 2014. "Religious Revival and the Politics of Nation Building: Reinterpreting the 1963 'Buddhist Crisis' in South Vietnam." *Modern Asian Studies* (August): 1–60.

Minh Chi, Hà Văn Tấn, and Nguyễn Tài Thư. 1999. *Buddhism in Vietnam, from its Origins to the 19th Century*. Hanoi: Thế Giới Publishers.

Ministry of Culture, Sports and Tourism, Viet Nam National Administration of Tourism. 2013. "World Heritage Title Eyed for Yên Tử Buddhism Relic." March 19. http://www.vietnamtourism.com/en/index.php/news/items/6534.

Mjelde-Mossey, L. A., Iris Chi, and Vivian W. Q. Lou. 2006. "Relationship between Adherence to Tradition and Depression in Chinese Elders in China." *Aging & Mental Health* 10 (1): 19–26.

Nattier, Jan. 1998. "Who Is a Buddhist? Charting the Landscape of Buddhist America." In *The Faces of Buddhism in America*, edited by Charles S. Prebish and Kenneth K. Tanaka, 183–195. Berkeley: University of California Press.

Nedostup, Rebecca. 2009. *Superstitious Regimes: Religion and the Politics of Chinese Modernity*. Cambridge, MA: Harvard University Asia Center.

Nghi-thức tụng-niệm của gia-đình Phật-tử [The rite of prayer for the Vietnamese family of Buddhists]. 1960. Saigon?: Nhà in Sen-vàng.

nguyen. 2008. "Thiền sư Thanh Đàm hiệu Minh Chánh" [Zen Master Thanh Đàm, also called Minh Chán]. *Thiền Viện Thường Chiếu*. http://thuongchieu.net/index.php/chuyende/thiensuvn/879-thin-s-thanh-am-hiu-minh-chanh.

Nguyen, Coung Tu. 1995. "Rethinking Vietnamese Buddhist History: Is the *Thiền Uyển Tập Anh* a 'Transmission of the Lamp' Text?" In *Essays into Vietnamese Pasts*, edited by K. W. Taylor and John K. Whitmore, 81–115. Ithaca, NY: Southeast Asia Program, Cornell University.

Nguyen, Cuong Tu, and A. W. Barber. 1998. "Vietnamese Buddhism in North America: Tradition and Acculturation." In *The Faces of Buddhism in America*, edited by Charles S. Prebish and Kenneth K. Tanaka, 183–195. Berkeley: University of California Press.

———. 1997. *Zen in Medieval Vietnam: A Study and Translation of the* Thiền Uyển Tập Anh. Honolulu: University of Hawai'i Press.

Nguyễn Đại Đồng. 2006. *Chùa Quán Sứ* [Quán Sứ Pagoda]. Hanoi: Nhà xuất bản Tôn giáo.

———. 2008. *Lược khảo báo chí Phật giáo Việt Nam (1929–2008)* [Survey of Vietnamese Buddhist periodicals (1929–2008)]. Hanoi: Nhà xuất bản Tôn giáo.

Nguyễn Đăng Thục. 1967. *Thiền học Việt Nam* [Vietnamese Zen studies]. Saigon: Lá Bối.

Nguyen, Dat Tan, Christine Dedding, Tam Thi Pham, and Joske Bunders. 2013. "Perspectives of Pupils, Parents, and Teachers on Mental Health Problems among Vietnamese Secondary School Pupils." *Medical Humanities BMC Public Health* 13 (1): 1–10.

Nguyen Giac. *Tran Nhan Tong: The King Who Founded a Zen School*. California: Thien Tri Thuc Publications.

Nguyen, Huong. 2017. "From Vanguards of Revolution to Vanguards of Consumption: Changing Conceptualizations of Adolescence in Contemporary Vietnam and Implications for Adolescent/Youth Services." *International Social Work* 60 (5): 1268–1285.

Nguyễn-Khoa-Tân. 1934. "Supplément en Française: Traduction française du discourse S. E. Nguyễn-Khoa-Tân [French supplement: French translation of the speech given by Nguyễn-Khoa-Tân]. *Viên âm* [The voice of exposition] 12 (November and December): 60–64.

Nguyễn Lân Cường. 2009. *Bí mật phía sau nhục thân của các vị Thiền Sư* [Mysteries behind the flesh bodies of Zen masters]. Hanoi: Nhà xuất bản Thế giới.

Nguyễn Lang [Thích Nhất Hạnh]. (1973) 2000. *Việt Nam Phật giáo sử luận* [History of Buddhism in Vietnam], vols. 1–3. Hanoi: Nhà xuất bản Văn học.

Nguyễn Mỹ. 2002. "Tu bổ nhục thân hai Thiền sư Vũ Khắc Minh, Vũ Khắc Trường" [The restoration of the flesh bodies of two Zen Masters, Vũ Khắc Minh, Vũ Khắc Trường]. *Tuần báo giác ngộ* [Enlightenment weekly magazine] 117 (April 24): 17.

Nguyễn Quang Ân. 1996. "Tóm tắt tiểu sử Trần Văn Giáp" [Biographical summary of Trần Văn Giáp]. In *Nhà sử học Trần Văn Giáp* [Literature of Trần Văn Giáp]. Hanoi: Nhà xuất bản Khoa học Xã hội.

Nguyen Tai Thu, ed. 1992. *History of Buddhism in Vietnam*. Hanoi: Social Sciences Publishing House.

Nguyễn Thanh Xuân. 2012. *Religions in Việt Nam*. Hanoi: Thế Giới Publishers.

Nguyễn Thiện Chính. 1936. "Vịnh Chùa Yên-tử" [A tribute to Yên Tử Pagoda]. *Đuốc tuệ* [The torch of wisdom] 18:21.

Nguyen-Marshall, Van. 2015. "Student Activism in Time of War: Youth in the Republic of Vietnam, 1960s–1970s." *Journal of Vietnamese Studies* 10 (2): 43–81.

Olcott, Henry S. 1886. *A Buddhist Catechism*. Madras: Self-published.

Ouvran, Jeff. 2013. *The Star Spangled Buddhist: Zen, Tibetan and Soka Gakkai Buddhism and the Quest for Enlightenment in America*. New York: Skyhorse.

Pearlman, Ellen. 2012. *Nothing and Everything: The Influence of Buddhism on the American Avant-Garde*. Berkeley, CA: Evolver Editions.

Pham, Anh, and Pundarik Mukhopadhaya. 2018. "Measurement of Poverty in Multiple Dimensions: The Case of Vietnam." *Social Indicators Research* 138 (3): 953–990.

Phạm Quỳnh Phương. 2006. "Trần Hưng Đạo and the Mother Goddess Religion." In *Possessed by the Spirits: Mediumship in Contemporary Vietnamese Communities*, edited by Karen Fjelstad and Nguyen Thi Hien, 31–54. Ithaca, NY: Cornell Southeast Asia Program.

———. 2007. "Empowerment and Innovation among Saint Trần's Female Mediums." In *Modernity and Re-enchantment: Religion in Post-revolutionary Vietnam*, edited by Philip Taylor, 221–249. Singapore: Institute of Southeast Asian Studies.

———. 2009. *Hero and Deity: Trần Hưng Đạo and the Resurgence of Popular Religion in Vietnam*. Chiang Mai: Mekong Press.

Phạm Văn Minh. 2002. *Vietnamese Engaged Buddhism: The Struggle Movement of 1963–1966*. Westminster, CA: Van Nghe.

Picard, Michel. 2017. "Introduction: Local Traditions and World Religions. Encountering 'Religion' in Southeast Asia and Melanesia." In *The Appropriation of Religion in Southeast Asia and Beyond*, edited by Michel Picard, 1–38. Cham: Palgrave Macmillan.

Pincharoen, Sumon, and Joann G. Congdon. 2003. "Spirituality and Health in Older Thai Persons in the United States." *Western Journal of Nursing Research* 25 (1): 93–108.

Pittman, Don A. 2001. *Toward a Modern Chinese Buddhism: Taixu's Reforms*. Honolulu: University of Hawai'i Press.

Prebish, Charles S. 1979. *American Buddhism*. North Scituate: Duxbury.

Rahula, Walpola. 1959. *What the Buddha Taught*. New York: Grove.

Robertson, Roland. 1995. "Glocalization: Time-Space and Homogeneity-Heterogeneity." In *Global Modernities,* edited by Mike Fetaherstons, Scott Lash, and Roland Robertson, 25–44. London: Sage.

Rutledge, Paul. 1985. *The Role of Religion in Ethnic Self-Identity: A Vietnamese Community.* Lanham, MD: University Press of America.

Rydstrøm, Helle. 2006. "Sexual Desires and 'Social Evils': Young Women in Rural Vietnam." *Gender, Place & Culture* 13 (3): 283–301.

Sangharakshita, Bhikkhu. (1952) 2008. *Anagarika Dharmapala: A Biographical Sketch and Other Maha Bodhi Writings.* Kandy: Buddhist Publication Society. http://www.bps.lk/olib/wh/wh070-p.html#PilgrimageinIndia.

Schecter, Jerrold. 1967. *The New Face of the Buddha: Buddhism and Political Power in Southeast Asia.* London: Victor Gollancz.

Schwenkel, Christina, and Ann Marie Leshkowich. 2012. "How Is Neoliberalism Good to Think Vietnam? How Is Vietnam Good to Think Neoliberalism?" *Positions* 20 (2): 379–401.

Sharf, Robert H. 1992 "The Idolization of Enlightenment: On the Mummification of Chan Masters in Medieval China." *History of Religions* 32 (1): 1–31.

———. 1993. "The Zen of Japanese Nationalism." *History of Religions* 33 (1): 1–43.

Snodgrass, Judith. 2003. *Presenting Japanese Buddhism to the West: Orientalism, Occidentalism and the Columbian Exposition.* Chapel Hill: University of North Carolina Press.

———. 2007. "Defining Modern Buddhism: Mr. and Mrs. Rhys Davids and the Pāli Text Society." *Comparative Studies of South Asia, Africa and the Middle East* 27 (1): 186–202.

———. 2009a. "Publishing Eastern Buddhism: D. T. Suzuki's Journey to the West." In *Casting Faiths: Imperialism and the Transformation of Religion in East and Southeast Asia,* edited by Thomas David Dubois, 46–72. Basingstoke: Palgrave Macmillan.

———. 2009b. "Discourse, Authority, Demand: The Politics of Early English Publications on Buddhism." In *TransBuddhism: Transmission, Translation, Transformation,* edited by Nalini Bhushan, Jay L. Garfield, and Abraham Zablocki, 21–41. Amherst: University of Massachusetts Press.

Soucy, Alexander. 1996. "The Dynamics of Change in an Exiled Temple: Vietnamese Buddhism in Montréal." *Canberra Anthropology* 19 (2): 29–45.

———. 2007. "Nationalism, Globalism and the Re-establishment of the Trúc Lâm Thiền Buddhist Sect in Northern Vietnam." In *Modernity and Re-enchantment: Religion in Post-revolutionary Vietnam,* edited by Philip Taylor, 342–370. Singapore: Institute of Southeast Asian Studies.

———. 2009. "Language, Orthodoxy and Performances of Authority in Vietnamese Buddhism." *Journal of the American Academy of Religion* 77 (2): 348–371.

———. 2010. "Asian Reformers, Global Organizations: An Exploration of the Possibility of a 'Canadian Buddhism.'" In *Wild Geese: Buddhism in Canada,* edited by John Harding, Victor Sōgen Hori, and Alexander Soucy, 39–60. Montreal: McGill-Queens University Press.

———. 2012. *The Buddha Side: Gender, Power, and Buddhist Practice in Vietnam.* Honolulu: University of Hawai'i Press.

———. 2014. "Buddhist Globalism and the Search for Canadian Buddhism." In *Flowers on the Rock: Global and Local Buddhisms in Canada,* edited by John Harding, Victor Sōgen Hori, and Alexander Soucy, 25–52. Montreal: McGill-Queen's University Press.

———. 2016. "Constructing Modern Zen Spaces in Vietnam." *Religion, Place and Modernity: Spatial Articulations in Southeast and East Asia,* edited by Michael Dickhardt and Andrea Lauser, 125–145. Leiden: Brill.

———. 2017a. "Global Flows of Vietnamese Zen." In *Eastspirit: Transnational Spirituality and Religious Circulation in East and West,* edited by Jørn Borup and Marianne Q. Fibiger, 149–171. Leiden: Brill.

———. 2017b. "A Reappraisal of Vietnamese Buddhism's Status as 'Ethnic.'" *Journal of Vietnamese Studies* 12 (2): 20–48.

———. Forthcoming. "Thích Nhất Hạnh in the Context of the Modern Developments of Vietnamese Buddhism." *Oxford Encyclopedia of Buddhism,* edited by Richard Payne and Georgios Halkias. New York and Oxford: Oxford University Press. doi: 10.1093/acrefore/9780199340378.013.944.

Storhoff, Gary, and John Whalen-Bridge. 2010. *American Buddhism as a Way of Life.* Albany: State University of New York Press.

Sun, Anna. 2013. *Confucianism as a World Religion.* Princeton, NJ: Princeton University Press.

Suzuki, Daisetz Teitaro. 1968. *Cốt tủy của Đạo Phật* [The essence of Buddhism]. Translated by Trúc Thiên. Saigon: An-tiêm.

———. 1974. *Huyền học Đạo phật và Thiên chúa* [Mysticism: Christian and Buddhist]. Translated by Như Hạnh. Saigon: Kinh Thi.

———. 1976. *Thiền luận* [Essays in Zen Buddhism]. n.p.

———. 1983. *Trực chỉ chơn tâm* [The awakening of Zen]. Translated by Thích Trường Lạc. Sepulveda, CA: Phật Học Viện Quốc Tế.

———. 1999. *Nghiên cứu Kinh Lăng Già* [Studies of the Lankavatara Sutra]. Translated by Thích Chơn Thiện and Tuấn Mẫn Trần. Huế: Nhà xuất bản Thuận Hóa.

———. 2000. *Thiền* [Zen]. Translated by Thuần Bạch. Ho Chi Minh City: Nhà xuất bản Thành phố Hồ Chí Minh.

———. 2005a. *Lăng già đại thừa kinh* [The Lankavatara Sutra: A Mahāyāna text]. Translated by Thích Chơn Thiện and Tuấn Mẫn Trần. Hanoi: Nhà xuất bản Tôn giáo.

———. (1935) 2005b. *Manual of Zen Buddhism.* Bagdad: M. G. Sheet. buddhanet.net /pdf_file/manual_zen.pdf.

———. 2007. *Thiền và bát nhã* [Zen and the pursuit of wisdom]. Translated by Tuệ Sỹ. Cà Mau: Nhà xuất bản Phương Đông.

Suzuki, Daisetz Teitaro, Erich Fromm, and Richard de Martino. 1973. *Thiền và phân tâm học* [Zen Buddhism and psychoanalysis]. California [no city given]: Xuân Thu.

Tao Jiang. 2002. "A Buddhist Scheme for Engaging Modern Science: The Case of Taixu." *Journal of Chinese Philosophy* 29 (4): 533–552.

Taylor, Charles. 1989. *Sources of the Self: The Making of the Modern Identity.* Cambridge, MA: Harvard University Press.

———. 2007. *A Secular Age.* Cambridge, MA: Harvard University Press.

———. 2011. "Western Secularity." In *Rethinking Secularism,* edited by Craig Calhoun, Mark Juergensmeyer, and Jonathan VanAntwerpen, 31–53. New York: Oxford University Press.

Taylor, Keith W. 1990. "Authority and Legitimacy in 11th Century Vietnam." In *Southeast Asia in the 9th to 14th Centuries,* edited by David G. Marr and S. C. Milner, 139–176. Singapore: Institute of Southeast Asian Studies.

Taylor, Philip K. 2003. "The Goddess, the Ethnologist, the Folklorist and the Cadre: Situating Exegesis of Vietnam's Folk Religion in Time and Place." *Australian Journal of Anthropology* 14 (3): 383–401.

————. 2007. "Modernity and Re-enchantment in Post-revolutionary Vietnam." In *Modernity and Re-enchantment: Religion in Post-revolutionary Vietnam*, 1–56. Singapore: Institute of Southeast Asian Studies.

Temprano, Victor Gerrard. 2012. "The Scholar and the Sage: Sallie B. King, David Loy, and Thích Nhất Hạnh." Master's thesis, McGill University.

Thanissaro Bhikkhu, trans. 2000. *Ugga Sutta: To Ugga*. AN 7.7 PTS: A iv 6. https://www.accesstoinsight.org/tipitaka/an/an07/an07.007.than.html.

Thích Đồng Bổn. 2002. "Hòa Thượng Thích Thiên Ân (1925–1980)" [The most venerable Thích Thiên Ân (1925–1980)]. In *Tiểu sử danh tăng Việt Nam thế kỷ XX—tập II* [Biography of famous Vietnamese monks of the twentieth century, volume 2]. Hanoi: Nhà xuất bản Tôn giáo. http://www.quangduc.com/Danhnhanvn/htthich thienan.html.

Thích Mãn Giác. 1984a. *Cố Hòa Thượng Thích Thiên Ân* [The late most venerable Thích Thiên Ân]. Los Angeles: Trung tâm Văn hóa Phật giáo Việt Nam.

————. 1984b. *In Memory of Ven. Dr. Thích Thiên Ân*. Los Angeles: Vietnamese Buddhist Cultural Institute.

Thích-Mật-Thể. 1933. "Tam-qui tam và ngũ giới" [The three refuges and four virtues]. *Viên âm* [The voice of exposition] 1:14–23.

————. 1960. *Việt Nam Phật giáo sử lược* [A brief history of Vietnamese Buddhism]. Saigon: Minh Đức.

Thích Minh Châu. 1994. "A Brief History of Vietnamese Buddhism." http://www.bud dhismtoday.com/english/vietnam/country/003-buddhism%20in%20VN .htm.ssZS.

Thích Minh Quang, Chánh Chí Bình, and Chánh Phúc Hiếu, eds. 2016. "Thiền viện Trúc Lâm Sùng Phúc" [Trúc Lâm Sùng Phúc Monastery]. http://www.tvsungphuc.net.

Thích Nhất Hạnh. (1966) 2006. *Nẻo về của ý* [The return of an idea]. Ho Chi Minh City: Nhà xuất bản Văn hóa Sài Gòn.

————. 1968. *Vietnam: Lotus in a Sea of Fire*. New York: Hill and Wang.

————. 1982. *Am mây ngủ* [Hermitage among the clouds]. Paris: Lá Bối.

————. 1998a. *Fragrant Palm Leaves: Journals 1962–1966*. New York: Riverhead.

————. 1998b. *Hermitage among the Clouds: An Historical Novel of Fourteenth Century Vietnam*. Berkeley: Parallax.

Thích Thắng Hoan. 2016. "Tiểu sử Hòa Thượng Thích Thiện Hoa (1918–1973)" [Biography of the most venerable Thích Thiện Hoa (1918–1973)]. https://thuvienhoasen.org /a26257/tieu-su-hoa-thuong-thich-thien-hoa-1918–1973-.

Thích Thanh Từ. 1957–1958. "Phật-giáo Trung-hoa: quá ba mươi năm cách-mạng" [Chinese Buddhism: Over thirty years of revolution]. Translation of an article by Taixu. *Phật giáo Việt Nam* [Vietnamese Buddhism] serialized as follows: 17–18 (December 15): 51–55; 20–21 (special issue): 76–79; 22 (June 15): 42–46.

————. 1959. *Đạo phật với tuổi trẻ* [Buddhism for young people]. Saigon: Hương-Đạo.

————. 1964. "Hai đội binh Hồng Thập Tự" [Two troops from the Red Cross]. *Hải triều âm* [The sound of the tide] 11 (July 2): 9.

————. 1966. *Phật giáo trong mạch sống dân tộc* [Buddhism in the pulse of the people]. Saigon: Lá Bối.

————. 1967. *Vài nét chính luân lý Phật giáo* [Some aspects of Buddhist morality]. Saigon: Hoa Đàm.

————. 1974a. "Then chốt của luân hồi và giải thoát" [The key to rebirth and liberation]. *Tạp chí Phật học từ quang* [Merciful light Buddhist magazine] 11, no. 256 (July 15): 3–7.

———. 1974b. "Xuân trong cửa Thiền" [Spring in the Zen gate]. *Hoằng pháp—Dharmaduta* [Propagation of the Dharma] 6:16–20.

———. 1992. *Phật giáo với dân tộc* [Buddhism for the people]. Ho Chi Minh City: Thành hội Phật giáo TP. Hồ Chí Minh.

———. 1996. *Khóa hư lục giảng giải* [Instructions on emptiness]. Ho Chi Minh City: Thiền viện Thường Chiếu.

———. 1997. *Ba vấn đề trọng đại trong đời tu của tôi* [Three significant issues in my life as a renunciate]. Hanoi: Nhà xuất bản Hà Nội.

———. 2000a. *Trọn một đời tôi* [My whole life]. https://thientruclam.info/ht-thich-thanh-tu/tron-mot-doi-toi-2000.

———. 2000b. *My Whole Life*. Translated by Tu Tam Hoang. Westminster, CA: Self-published.

———. 2001. *Thiền tông Việt Nam cuối thế kỷ 20* [Vietnamese Zen in the late twentieth century]. Los Angeles: Kim Ấn Quán.

———. 2002a. *Hai quãng đời của sơ tổ Trúc Lâm* [Two stages of life of the founder of Trúc Lâm]. Hanoi: Nhà xuất bản Tôn giáo.

———. 2002b. *The Practicing Method of Vietnamese Zen*. Translated by Tu Tam Hoang. Westminster, CA: Self-published.

———. 2002c. *Hoa vô ưu, tập IV* [Carefree flowers, vol. 4]. Hanoi: Nhà xuất bản Tôn giáo.

———. 2002d. *Buddhism and the Youths*. Translated by Tu Tam Hoang. Westminster, CA: Self-published.

———. 2002e. *Vietnamese Zen in the Late 20th Century*. Translated by Toàn Kiên, Lan Lê, Quí Hoàng, and Thanh Hoàng. Camino Del Rey: Dai Dang Monastery.

———. 2005. *Truc Lam Founder: Two Stages of Life*. Translated by Tu Tam Hoang. Westminster, CA: Self-published.

———. 2009a. *Nghi thức sám hối va tụng giới (của Phật tử)* [The Rite of contrition and the precepts (for Buddhists)] Hanoi: Nhà xuất bản Lao động.

———. 2009b. *Nguồn an lạc* [The source of peace]. Hanoi: Nhà xuất bản Tôn giáo.

———. 2009c. *Đạo Phật và tuổi trẻ* [Buddhism and youths]. Hanoi: Nhà xuất bản Tôn giáo.

———. 2009d. *Tài sản không bao giờ mất* [Wealth you never lose]. Hanoi: Nhà xuất bản Tôn giáo.

———. 2010a. *Phương pháp tọa thiền* [The meditation method]. Hanoi: Nhà xuất bản Tôn giáo.

———. 2010b. *Cành lá vô ưu* [Careless leaves]. Hanoi: Nhà xuất bản Tôn giáo

———. 2011. *Nghi thức sám hối và tụng giới (của Phật tử)* [The Penitence Rite and precepts (for Buddhists)]. Hanoi: Thiền viện Sùng Phúc.

———. n.d. *Phương pháp tu Tịnh độ tông và Thiền tông* [The methods of the Pure Land and Zen schools]. Hanoi: Thiền viện Sùng Phúc.

Thích Thiên Ân. 1963a. *Trao-đổi văn-hóa Việt-Nhật* [Cultural relations between Vietnam and Japan.] Saigon: Nhà xuất-bản Đông-phương.

———. 1963b. *Triết-học Zen tư-tưởng Nhật-ban và các nước Á-châu* [Zen philosophy: Japanese thought and other Asian nations]. Saigon: Nhà xuất-bản Đông-phương.

———. 1965a. *Lịch-sử tư-tưởng Nhật-bản* [History of Japanese thought]. Saigon: Nhà xuất-bản Đông-phương.

———. 1965b. *Giáo-dục Nhật-bản hiện-đại* [Education in modern Japan]. Saigon: Bộ Văn-hóa Giáo-dục.

———. 1965c. *Phật-giáo Việt-nam: xưa & nay* [Vietnamese Buddhism: In the past and present]. Saigon: Nhà xuất-bản Đông-phương.

———. 1966, *Giá-trị triết-học tôn giáo trong Truyện Kiều (kỷ-niệm 200 năm thi hào Nguyễn Du)* [The value of religious philosophy in *The Story of Kiều* (200 Year Anniversary of Nguyễn Du)]. Saigon: Nhà xuất bản Đông Phương.

———. 1970. *Zen Buddhism and Nationalism in Vietnam*. Los Angeles: International Buddhist Meditation Center.

———. 1971. *The Zen-Pure Land Union and Modern Vietnamese Buddhism*. Los Angeles: International Buddhist Meditation Center.

———. 1973. *Zen Buddhism: Awareness in Action*. Los Angeles: College of Oriental Studies, Graduate School.

———. 1975a. *Buddhism and Zen in Vietnam in Relation to the Development of Buddhism in Asia*. Los Angeles: C. E. Tuttle.

———. 1975b. *Zen Philosophy, Zen Practice*. Emeryville, CA: Dharma Publications, College of Oriental Studies.

Thích Thông Phương. 2003. *Thiền phái Trúc Lâm Yên Tử* [The Zen school]. Hanoi: Nhà xuất bản Tôn giáo.

———. 2008. *Trần Nhân Tông với Thiền phái Trúc Lâm* [Trần Nhân Tông with the Trúc Lâm Sect]. Hanoi: Nhà xuất bản Tôn giáo.

Thích Tịnh Thiền, ed. 2010. *Các nghi lễ trong thiền viện* [Ceremonies of the Zen monastery]. Hanoi: Thiền viện Sùng Phúc.

Thiện Tòng. 2008. "Nên chấn hung Phật giáo nước nhà" [The need to reform Buddhism in our country]. In *Phong trào chấn hung Phật giáo: Tư liệu báo chí Việt Nam từ 1927–1938* [The Buddhist reform movement: Through Vietnamese journals from 1927–1938], edited by Nguyễn Đại Đồng, 26–29. Hanoi: Nhà xuất bản Tôn giáo.

Thiền viện Sùng Phúc. 2008. "Giới thiệu Thiền viện Sùng Phúc" [Introducing Thiền viện Sùng Phúc]. http://tvsungphuc.net/index.php?option=com_content&task=view&id=1&Itemid=14.

Thường Chiếu, n.d. "Tóm lược hành trạng Hòa thượng Zen sư Thích Thanh Từ" [A short summary of the activities of the most venerable Zen Master Thích Thanh Từ]. http://www.thuong-chieu.org/uni/HanhTrang/TieuSu.htm.

"Tin tức Phật giáo." 1974. *Tạp chí Phật học từ quang* [Merciful light Buddhist magazine] 7, no. 252 (March 15): 57–58.

———. 1974. "Tin tức Phật giáo." *Tạp chí Phật học từ quang* [Merciful light Buddhist magazine] 8, no. 253 (April 15): 63.

———. 1974. "Tin tức Phật giáo." *Tạp chí Phật học từ quang* [Merciful light Buddhist magazine] 9, no. 254 (May 15): 63.

———. 1974. "Tin tức Phật giáo." *Tạp chí Phật học từ quang* [Merciful light Buddhist magazine] 11, no. 256 (July 15): 60.

———. 1974. "Tin tức Phật giáo." *Tạp chí Phật học từ quang* [Merciful light Buddhist magazine] 1, no. 258 (September 15): 60.

Tin tức phật giáo. 1953. "Thong-nhât Phat-lich [*sic*]" [Unified Buddhist calender]. 1 (October 1): 5.

Tịnh Lạc Am. n.d. "Zen Master Thích Thanh Từ." https://sites.google.com/site/tinhlacam/tai-lieu-tong-hop/ve-ht-thich-thanh-tu—english.

Tinh Vân, Hòa thượng [Hsing Yun]. 2011. *Tranh minh họa giai thoại Thiền* [Illustrations of Zen anecdotes]. Vietnamese translation by Thích Tuệ Thông. Hanoi: Nhà xuất bản Tôn giáo.

Topmiller, Robert. 2002. *The Lotus Unleashed: The Buddhist Peace Movement in South Vietnam, 1964–1966*. Lexington: University Press of Kentucky.

Trần Huệ Hiền. 2006. "Hòa Thượng Thích Thanh Từ: Khôi phục Thiền tông Việt Nam, tiếp nối ngọn nhiên đăng, làm rạng rỡ Thiền phái Trúc Lâm Yên Tử" [The most venerable Thích Thanh Từ: Recovering the Vietnamese Zen sect, continuing the light, celebrating the Trúc Lâm Zen Sect]. In *Danh nhân văn hóa Phật giáo Việt Nam đương đại: Chân dung & đối thoại* [Notable figures in contemporary Vietnamese Buddhist culture: Portraits and conversations], edited by Minh Mẫn, 10–61. Ho Chi Minh City: Nhà xuất bản Lao động.

Trần-Nguyên-Chấn. 1940. "Mỗi người Phật-giáo-đồ nên rõ biết lịch-sử của Đức Thích-Ca" [Every Buddhist should know the history of Śākyamuni]. *Từ-bi âm* [The voice of compassion] 175 (July): 35–36.

Trần Văn Giáp. 1932. "Le Bouddhisme en Annam des origins au XIIIe siècle." *Bulletin de l'École français d'Extrême Orient* 32:191–286.

———. 1934a. "Esquisse d'une histoire de bouddhise au Tonkin" [A Sketch of the history of Buddhism in Tonkin]. *Viên âm* [The voice of exposition], no. 6 (June 1): 57–64.

———. 1934b. "Esquisse d'une histoire de bouddhise au Tonkin (Suite et fin)" [A sketch of the history of Buddhism in Tonkin (Continuation and end)]. *Viên âm* [The voice of exposition], no. 7 (July 1): 51–66.

———. 1938. "Nghĩa chữ Phật" [The meaning of Buddhist characters]. *Đuốc tuệ* [The torch of wisdom], no. 86 (June): 16–29.

Trí-Hải. 1937a. "Bàn về sự đốt mã" [A discussion on the burning of spirit money], part 1. *Đuốc tuệ* [The torch of wisdom], no. 75: 31–34.

———. 1937b. "Bàn về sự đốt mã" [A Discussion on the burning of spirit money], part 2. *Đuốc tuệ* [The torch of wisdom], no. 76: 8–13.

Trọng Đức. 2014. "Sư thầy 'đập hộp iPhone 6'" Trần tình việc mặc áo rằn ri chụp ảnh" [Monk does "iPhone 6 unboxing" and revealed wearing a camouflage shirt]. *Người lao động* [Laborer]. October 3. https://nld.com.vn/thoi-su-trong-nuoc/su-thay-dap-hop-iphone-6-tran-tinh-viec-mac-ao-ran-ri-chup-anh-20141003110424918.htm.

Từ bi âm [The voice of compassion]. 1932–1933. "Lược truyện Phật Thích-Ca-Mâu-Ni (Sakya Muni)" [Biographical Sketches of Shakyamuni Buddha]. *Từ-bi âm* [The voice of compassion] 2–29 (serialized).

Tuoi Tre News. 2014. "Vietnam Monk Faces Penalty for Unboxing iPhone 6, Posting Lavish Lifestyle Photos on Facebook." October 1. https://tuoitrenews.vn/lifestyle/22872/vietnam-monk-faces-penalty-for-unboxing-iphone-6-posting-lavish-lifestyle-photos-on-facebook.

Tweed, Thomas A. 2002. "Who Is a Buddhist? Night-Stand Buddhists and Other Creatures." In *Westward Dharma: Buddhism Beyond Asia,* edited by Charles S. Prebish and Martin Baumann, 17–33. Berkeley: University of California Press.

———. 2008. *Crossing and Dwelling: A Theory of Religion.* Cambridge, MA: Harvard University Press

———. 2012. "Tracing Modernity's Flows: Buddhist Currents in the Pacific World." *Eastern Buddhist* 43 (1–2): 35–56.

Tworkov, Helen. 1991. "Many Is More." *Tricycle: The Buddhist Review* 1 (2): 4.

UNESCO. 2014. "The Complex of Yên Tử Monuments and Landscape." Ref. 5940. http://whc.unesco.org/en/tentativelists/5940.

van der Veer, Peter. 2014. *The Modern Spirit of Asia: The Spiritual and the Secular in China and India.* Princeton, NJ: Princeton University Press.

Wallace, B. Alan, ed. 2003a. *Buddhism and Science: Breaking New Ground.* New York: Columbia University Press.

Watson, James L. 1985. "Standardizing the Gods: The Empress of Heaven (Tianhou) along the South China Coast, 960–1960." In *Popular Culture in Late Imperial China,* edited by David Johnson, Andrew J. Nathan, Evelyn S. Rawski, Judith A. Berling, and American Council of Learned Societies. Berkeley: University of California Press.

Welch, Holmes. 1973. *The Practice of Chinese Buddhism: 1900–1950.* Cambridge, MA: Harvard University Press.

Weller, Robert P. 1987. *Unities and Diversities in Chinese Religion.* Seattle: University of Washington Press.

———. 1996. "Matricidal Magistrates and Gambling Gods: Weak States and Strong Spirits in China." In *Unruly Gods: Divinity and Society in Chin,* edited by Meir Shahar and Robert P. Weller, 250–268. Honolulu: University of Hawai'i Press.

Welter, Albert. 2000. "Mahākāśyapa's Smile Silent Transmission and the Kung-an (Koan) Tradition." In *The Koan: Texts and Contexts in Zen Buddhism,* edited by Steven Heine and Dale S. Wright, 75–109. New York: Oxford University Press.

Woodside, Alexander B. 1971. *Vietnam and the Chinese Model: A Comparative Study of Vietnamese and Chinese Government in the First Half of the Nineteenth Century.* Cambridge, MA: Council on East Asian Studies Harvard University; distributed by Harvard University Press.

———. 1976. *Community and Revolution in Modern Vietnam.* Boston: Houghton Mifflin.

Yang, K. S., and David Y. F. Ho. 1988. "The Role of Yuan in Chinese Social Life: A Conceptual and Empirical Analysis." *Asian Contributions to Psychology,* edited by Anand C. Paranjpe, David Y. F. Ho, and Robert W. Rieber, 263–281. New York: Praeger.

Index

||||||||

Page references to illustrations set bold

About the Author

Alexander Soucy is professor and chair of the Department for the Study of Religion at Saint Mary's University (Halifax). He is the author of *The Buddha Side: Gender, Power, and Buddhist Practice in Vietnam* (2012). He co-edited *Wild Geese: Studies of Buddhism in Canada* (2010), *Flowers on the Rock: Global and Local Buddhisms in Canada* (2014), and *Buddhism in the Global Eye: Beyond East and West* (2020). His research focuses on Vietnamese Buddhism, Buddhism and globalization, and gender and religious practice.